Criterial Features in L2 English

Specifying the Reference Levels of the Common European Framework

Also in this series:

Language Functions Revisited
Anthony Green

Criterial Features in L2 English

Specifying the Reference Levels of the Common European Framework

John A Hawkins
University of Cambridge and University of California Davis

and

Luna Filipović
University of Cambridge

with input from

Paula Buttery

Annette Capel

Roger Hawkey

Angeliki Salamoura

Nick Saville

John L M Trim

CAMBRIDGE UNIVERSITY PRESS
Cambridge, New York, Melbourne, Madrid, Cape Town,
Singapore, São Paulo, Delhi, Mexico City

Cambridge University Press
The Edinburgh Building, Cambridge CB2 8RU, UK

www.cambridge.org
Information on this title: www.cambridge.org/9780521

First published 2012

Printed in the United Kingdom at the University Press, Cambridge

A catalogue record for this publication is available from the British Library

Library of Congress Cataloging-in-Publication data

Hawkins, John A.
  Criterial features in L2 English : specifying the reference levels of the Common
European Framework / John A. Hawkins and Luna Filipovic with input from
Paula Buttery, Annette Capel, Roger Hawkey, Angeliki Salamoura, Nick Saville,
John L.M. Trim.
     pages cm
  Includes bibliographical references and index.
  ISBN 978-0-521-18477-9 (pbk.)
  1. English language--Study and teaching--Foreign speakers. 2. English language-
-Ability testing. 3. Second language acquisition--Ability testing. 4. Language and
languages--Ability testing. I. Filipovic, Luna. II. Title.

  PE1128.A2H377 2012
  428.0076--dc23
  2011052357

ISBN 978-0-521-18477-9

Contents

Acknowledgements

The authors are indebted to **Michael Milanovic** and **Nick Saville** for initiating the English Profile Programme and for co-ordinating the research carried out within the University of Cambridge. The work reported here was conducted within that programme and the preparation of this volume was commissioned and funded by University of Cambridge ESOL Examinations (Cambridge ESOL). We are also grateful for the support and input provided by members of the English Profile research team in Cambridge (Cambridge ESOL, Cambridge University Press (CUP), the Research Centre for English and Applied Linguistics (RCEAL), the Cambridge Computer Laboratory) and elsewhere and whose contributions we acknowledge below.

We would like to acknowledge in particular the contributions of the following people who are listed on the title page:

Paula Buttery of RCEAL Cambridge for tagging and parsing the Cambridge Learner Corpus using RASP, for conducting a number of searches, and for help with the quantification of the error counts.

Annette Capel of CUP for sharing data from her Wordlist searches and for invaluable comments and feedback.

John Trim for information on the role of the Council of Europe in setting up the Common European Framework, for important discussions on the 'Threshold' series of books that he co-authored with Jan van Ek, and for feedback on material presented here.

Roger Hawkey and **Angeliki Salamoura** of Cambridge ESOL for detailed comments and extensive feedback throughout the writing of this book.

In addition we would like to acknowledge the following:

Ted Briscoe of the Cambridge Computer Laboratory and his colleagues for use and implementation of the RASP parser.

Caroline Williams of RCEAL Cambridge for verb subcategorisation searches in the CLC and the British National Corpus.

Fiona Barker and **Szilvia Papp** of Cambridge ESOL for information about learner corpora and for assistance in preparing a manual subcorpus of the Cambridge Learner Corpus (CLC).

Andrew Caines of RCEAL Cambridge for conducting numerous searches in the CLC.

Evelina Galaczi of Cambridge ESOL for information and references about Cambridge ESOL's research on training examiners.

Kristen Kennedy of the University of California, Davis for assistance with Mean Length of Utterance calculations.

Stephen Spencer of RCEAL Cambridge for help with double embedding searches involving two genitives in the CLC.

CUP's computational linguists, who prepared *The Compleat|Complete Learner Corpus Document* 2006, which formed the basis of error codes used extensively in CUP research.

Series Editors' note

We are pleased to introduce the English Profile Studies series, dedicated to reporting different aspects of research and development related to the English Profile Programme (EPP).

A major objective of the EP Programme is to analyse language produced by learners of English in order to throw light on what they *can* and *can't* do with the language at each of the Common European Framework of Reference (CEFR levels), for example, in using the grammar and lexis at their disposal.

Criterial Features in L2 English by Professor Hawkins and Dr Filipović is the first volume in the series which is being published in 2012 at the same time as a second volume by Dr Anthony Green, entitled *Language Functions Revisited.*.

Together these volumes report on two important areas of investigation which have been central to the English Profile research programme since its inception, namely *lexico-grammatical* features of English and *functional progression* across the proficiency range.

The CEFR itself appeared in its published form in 2001, ten years after the Rüschlikon Conference of 1991 which concluded that a "common framework of reference" of this kind would be useful as a planning tool to promote "transparency and coherence" in language education. In the decade since its publication this ambition has been achieved to a large extent and the document itself has been translated into 37 languages. It has been disseminated very widely in Europe, and also in parts of Asia and Latin America (see Little 2006 for an overview). It is important to remember, however, that the CEFR in that format was intended to be "a work in progress" rather than the finished article.

The six reference levels have been particularly influential and have generated a great deal of discussion in the fields of curriculum development, language teaching, and especially in assessment, (see Coste 2007). The levels are described through the six-level *Global Scale* (A1 to C2) and the *Illustrative Descriptors* that can be applied to the learning and teaching of *any* language. However, to ensure that the framework is used appropriately and can be adapted to local contexts and purposes, the Council of Europe has encouraged the production of instruments and support materials to complement the CEFR. These instruments (sometimes known as the CEFR toolkit) include *Reference Level Descriptions (RLDs) for national and regional languages.*

The RLDs represent a new generation of descriptions which identify the specific forms of any given language (words, grammar, etc.) at each of the six reference levels which can be set as objectives for learning or used to establish whether a user has attained the level of proficiency in question.

To assist the teams in developing RLDs for their own languages, the Language Policy Division of the Council of Europe produced a general *Guide for the production of RLDs.* which was discussed at a seminar held in Strasbourg in December 2005. The participants were able to discuss how to set up projects and in some case progress already being made was reported for various languages (for details see the Council of Europe website <http://www.coe.int>). At that time the RLDs for German, *Profile deutsch* (covering A1, A2, B1, B2,) had already been published as a result of an international collaborative project, and were presented in detail at this seminar. In total, projects representing seventeen languages were presented, including a proposal for English put forward by the University of Cambridge (represented at the meeting by Cambridge ESOL). This proposal subsequently became known as the English Profile Programme.

The founder members of the EPP first met in Cambridge in 2005 to discuss the possibility of setting up an RLD project for English. Participating in those discussion were several departments of the University of Cambridge led by Cambridge ESOL (the others being Cambridge University Press, the Research Centre for English and Applied Linguistics and the Computer Laboratory), together with representatives from the British Council, English UK, and the University of Bedfordshire (Centre for Research in English Language Learning and Assessment – CRELLA).

As a result of those meetings, an initial three-year project funded largely by Cambridge ESOL and Cambridge University Press, with a contribution from the British Council, was set up with project coordination based in Cambridge. The English Profile was formally established as an officially recognised RLD project for the English language when the British Ambassador to the Council of Europe proposed the EP project in Strasbourg. Since then regular progress reports have been submitted to the Language Policy Division through John Trim, who has acted as an observer on the Council of Europe's behalf, as well as playing an important advisory role within the Cambridge-based research team. After the first three years, the programme was extended with a growing network of collaborators around the world and the long-term EP Programme was established.

From an early stage the English RLDs were intended to be innovative with an emphasis on empirical research rooted in data (such as learner corpora), and the collection of representative samples of learner language which could be used to explore language development across the reference levels. This has entailed the setting up of a network of collaborators in different parts of the world who can supply samples of speaking and writing produced by learners.

It is an aspect of the project which has received external funding by the European Commission – see English Profile Network (http://www.english-profile.org) and is now well underway. It has also required technical resources in developing new electronic corpora so that the samples of learner language can be stored and accessed effectively.

The authors of this volume, *Criterial Features in L2 English,* bring together contributions from the research teams at the University of Cambridge (as set out in the acknowledgments) in a concise and readable way. Their own backgrounds in theoretical linguistics and interdisciplinary research projects has enabled them to describe the key points in an accessible way and to provide concrete outcomes which will are relevant and useful to a wide group of English language practitioners.

The book is divided into two main parts. Part 1 (chapters 1 to 5) deals with the background and describes the theoretical basis of the research programme which the authors are reporting on. Part 2 (chapters 6 to 9) deals with the empirical findings, including the *criterial features* referred to in the title.

Chapter 1 provides a comprehensive introduction to the volume by setting out the historical context for the work and summarise what lies ahead in the other chapters. In setting out the background, the authors describe the aims of the English Profile Programme (EPP) as an inter-disciplinary programme which intends to develop RLDs for English to accompany the CEFR; in other words, the aim is to transpose the CEFR for the English language and for teaching and assessment purposes where English is the language being learned. The intended output is a 'profile' of the English language levels of learners in terms of the six proficiency bands of the CEFR – A1 to C2 (see Saville and Hawkey 2010).

In the first phase of the EP Programme the Cambridge Learner Corpus (CLC), as an extensive resource of learner data, has proved invaluable in gaining the insights reported here. It was made available to the research teams in Cambridge and was extensively used to provide the analysis reported by Hawkins and Filipović (see Chapters 1 and 3 of this volume). The CLC consists of learners' written English from the Cambridge ESOL examinations covering the ability range from A2 to C2, together with meta-data (gender, age, first language) and evidence of overall proficiency based on marks in the other components (typically reading, listening and speaking). While lexical analysis has been carried out for many years by researchers in Cambridge ESOL and CUP, error coding and parsing of the corpus have extended the kinds of analysis which can be carried out and have allowed the research teams to investigate a wider range of English language features (see Nicholls 2003 on the error-coding system which has informed EP research). A computational strand of research was introduced into the EPP at the outset and the CLC has been tagged and parsed using the Robust Accurate Statistical Parser

(RASP) by researchers in the Computer Laboratory under the supervision of Professor Ted Briscoe (Briscoe, Carrol & Watson 2006).

Another innovative feature of the EP Programme is the concept of "criterial features". As the title of this volume suggests, this notion is central to the approach taken within the EP to specify the reference levels for English. In chapter 1, Hawkins and Filipović explain what criterial features are and elaborate on the practical and theoretical relevance. In chapter 2 they provide a brief taxonomy of the features which have emerged during the research carried out by them and the other members of the EP team in Cambridge.

As they note, the concept of *criteriality* is not restricted to the lexico-grammatical domain which they have concentrated on, but is applicable to other aspects of language and language learning (phonetics, form-function relations, semantics and pragmatics, etc.). It is hoped that these other strands of the programme will also be developed and published in the EP Studies series.

In addition to describing the "real language" used by learners, the English Profile has sought to investigate *the learning dimension* and to connect the empirical work with relevant SLA and linguistic research. In particular, the EP researchers in Cambridge are interested in "how learners learn English" and how different learning factors interact under various contextual conditions. They have begun to address questions such as:

- how do the different kinds of criterial features (lexical semantic, morpho-syntactic, syntactic, discourse, notional, functional, etc.) inter-relate and cluster together to define learner profiles in English? Which linguistic features realise which language functions across the CEFR levels?
- how does the profile of the learner vary depending on their L1? What are the pedagogical implications of such L1 effects for the learning, teaching and assessment of English?
- which criterial features can be used as diagnostics of proficiency at the individual learner level?
- what are the similarities and differences between adult and young learners of English developmentally and at each stage of learning?
- how does learning to speak differ from learning to write/type? What determines communicative success and comprehensibility in these two language modes?
- what is the role of learner and learning strategies?
- how do all the previous factors interact during language learning? How do they predict likely versus less likely patterns of learner output? What type of learning model can accommodate these multi-factor interactions that underpin language learning?

The emerging performance patterns are informative for our understanding of second language acquisition (SLA), e.g. the order of acquisition of linguistic features and the interaction of factors such as frequency and transfer from the first language.

In chapter 4, Hawkins and Filipović provide a useful summary of the recent literature in the fields of SLA and linguistic theory. They explain the relevance of these theories to the work being undertaken in the EP Programme and potential applicability of the competing approaches (e.g. universal grammar vs. cognitive theories). They also point out that their findings from the EP in turn can contribute to new aspects of theory and provide useful insights for developing a model of L2 acquisition. They deal with this in chapter 5, setting out some principles of learning and illustrating how learner language (interlanguage) develops based on analysis of the CLC data.

Chapter 6 introduces Part 2 and the focus on the empirical findings by re-examining the lexico-grammatical taxonomies in the Threshold series (van Ek and Trim). A useful comparison is made between those earlier descriptions for English (A2, B1 and B2) and the findings from the recent EP analyses. Chapters 7 and 8 provide lists of criterial features which have emerged, covering both the *vertical dimension* (showing how a single feature develops across the proficiency range) and the *horizontal dimension* (showing how the features cluster to characterise a given level – e.g. B1).

In conclusion (chapter 9), the practical and theoretical relevance of the work is discussed, highlighting how practitioners (curriculum planners, materials writers, test developers etc.) might be able to benefit from the findings to date. The authors are careful to point out that some of the findings are still tentative and in "looking ahead" they suggest future directions for the research agenda.

In future volumes of the EP Studies series we hope to publish other aspects of the research now emerging from the EP programme. The concept of "criteriality" is being extended to the analysis to other samples of learner language and in particular to speech. Spoken language data are being collected and corpora are being built with the necessary computational tools to enable the research to be extended in that direction. In addition, a focus on the C-levels continues with the collection of academic English writing samples.

We hope that this new series will make a useful contribution to our field and provide insights in using the CEFR for the learning, teaching and assessment of English.

Nick Saville and Mike Milanovic
Cambridge
March 2012

References

Briscoe, E, Carroll, J and Watson, R (2006) *The second release of the RASP system*, paper presented at COLING/ACL 2006 Interactive Presentation Sessions, Sydney, July 2006.

Coste, D (2007) *Contextualising uses of the Common European Framework of Reference for Languages*, paper presented at Council of Europe Policy Forum on use of the CEFR, Strasbourg 2007.

Council of Europe (2001) *Common European Framework of Reference for Languages: Learning, Teaching, Assessment*, Cambridge: Cambridge University Press.

Green, A (forthcoming 2012) *Language Functions Revisited: Theoretical and Empirical Bases for Language Construct Definition Across the Ability Range*, English Profile Studies volume 2, Cambridge: UCLES/Cambridge University Press.

Little, D (2006) The Common European Framework of Reference for Languages: Content, purpose, origin, reception and impact, *Language Teaching* 39, 167–190.

Nicholls, D (2003) *The Cambridge Learner Corpus – error coding and analysis for lexicography and ELT*, paper presented at Corpus Linguistics 2003 conference, Lancaster 2003.

Saville, N and Hawkey, R (2010) The English Profile Programme – the first three years. *English Profile Journal* 1, available online at <http://journals.cambridge.org/action/displayJournal?jid=EPJ>

Abbreviations

Adj	Adjective
AdjP	Adjective Phrase
AGN	Noun Agreement Error
AGV	Verb agreement
AGV	Verb Agreement Error
AH	Accessibility Hierarchy
ALTE	Association of Language Testers in Europe
AS	Argument Structure
Aux	Auxiliary
BNC	British National Corpus
CAE	Certificate in Advanced English
CAS	Complex Adaptive System
CBN	Communicative Blocking of Negative Transfer
CEFR	Common European Framework of Reference
CLC	Cambridge Learner Corpus
CN	Noun Countability Error
CPE	Certificate of Proficiency in English
CUP	Cambridge University Press
DD	Derivation of Determiner
DY	Derivation of Adverb
E	Extended Meaning
EP	English Profile
EPP	English Profile Programme
EPW	English Profile Wordlists
ESOL	English for Speakers of Other Languages
EVP	English Vocabulary Profile
F	Fixed Expression
FCE	First Certificate in English
FJ	Wrong Adjective Form
FV	Wrong Verb Form
IELTS	International English Language Testing System
Intr	Intransitive
IV	Incorrect Inflection of Verb
KET	Key English Test
LLC	Longman Learner Corpus

MaF	Maximise Frequently Occurring Properties
MaPT	Maximise Positive Transfer
MaS	Maximise Structurally and Semantically Simple Properties
MD	Missing Determiner
MDH	Markedness Differential Hypothesis
MiQ	Minimise Quantitative Load
MLU	Mean Length of Utterance
MQ	Missing Quantifier
MT	Missing Preposition
N	Noun
NP	Noun Phrase
OSLA	Order of Second Language Acquisition
P	Primary Meaning
P, E, F	Primary meaning, Extended, Fixed Expression
PGCH	Performance-Grammar Correspondence Hypothesis
PELCRA	Polish Learner English Corpus
PET	Preliminary English Test
PNT	Permit Negative Transfer
PossP	Possessive Phrase
PP	Prepositional Phrase
RASP	Robust Accurate Statistical Parser
RC	Relative Clause
RLD	Reference Level Descriptor
RCEAL	Research Centre for English and Applied Linguistics
RN	Replace Noun
RQ	Replace Quantifier
RV	Replace Verb
RY	Replace Adverb
S	Sentence
SLA	Second Language Acquisition
SOV	Subject Object Verb
SVO	Subject Verb Object
Tr	Transitive
UG	Universal Grammar
UN	Unnecessary Noun
UQ	Unnecessary Quantifier
USE	Uppsala Student English
V	Verb
Ving	Present Participle Verb Form
VP	Verb Phrase
VPinfin	Infinitival Verb Phrase
WH	WH Words (Who, When, Where, etc.)

WHIZ   WH word + is
XMOD   Modifier of X

Please also see the English Profile Glossary at www.englishprofile.org for concise definitions of key terminology used in this volume.

Part One
Defining the Research Programme

1 Introduction

1.1 Background: The Common European Framework of Reference (CEFR)

The Common European Framework of Reference (CEFR) has had a major impact on the learning, teaching and assessment of foreign languages in Europe. Originally conceived and developed by the Council of Europe the goals and educational options laid out by the CEFR are set out in the Council's 2001 document, *Common European Framework of Reference for Languages: Learning, Teaching, Assessment* (Cambridge University Press). This document describes how a common framework of proficiency scaling came into being, within the context of the Council's larger cultural and educational goals. What is important as a background to the present book is the Council's proposal that it was possible, and useful, to define six levels of proficiency in the learning of different foreign languages. These levels were given the labels shown in (1):

(1) The CEFR Levels: C2 Mastery

C1 Effective Operational Proficiency

B2 Vantage

B1 Threshold

A2 Waystage

A1 Breakthrough

Whenever different stages of learning and attainment are proposed, one needs some way of distinguishing them. The 2001 publication does this primarily in functional terms, i.e. in terms of the different uses to which language can be put and the various functions that learners can perform as they gradually master a second language (L2). Chapter 3 provides a large number of 'illustrative descriptors' for this purpose. At A2, for example, learners can 'understand sentences and frequently used expressions related to areas of most immediate relevance'. At B1 they can 'understand the main points of clear standard input on familiar matters regularly encountered in work, school, leisure, etc.'. At B2 they can 'understand the main ideas of complex text on both concrete and abstract topics, including technical discussions in his/her field of specialisation'. At C1 learners can 'understand a wide range of demanding, longer texts and recognise implicit meaning', and so on. These examples are all taken from the 'global scale' of Common Reference Levels (Council of Europe 2001:24), which is reproduced here as Table 1.1:

Table 1.1 Common Reference Levels: Global scale

Proficient user	C2	Can understand with ease virtually everything heard or read. Can summarise information from different spoken and written sources, reconstructing arguments and accounts in a coherent presentation. Can express him/herself spontaneously, very fluently and precisely, differentiating finer shades of meaning even in more complex situations.
	C1	Can understand a wide range of demanding, longer texts, and recognise implicit meaning. Can express him/herself fluently and spontaneously without much obvious searching for expressions. Can use language flexibly and effectively for social, academic and professional purposes. Can produce clear, well-structured, detailed text on complex subjects, showing controlled use of organisational patterns, connectors and cohesive devices.
Independent user	B2	Can understand the main ideas of complex text on both concrete and abstract topics, including technical discussions in his/her field of specialisation. Can interact with a degree of fluency and spontaneity that makes regular interaction with native speakers quite possible without strain for either party. Can produce clear, detailed text on a wide range of subjects and explain a viewpoint on a topical issue giving the advantages and disadvantages of various options.
	B1	Can understand the main points of clear standard input on familiar matters regularly encountered in work, school, leisure, etc. Can deal with most situations likely to arise whilst travelling in an area where the language is spoken. Can produce simple connected text on topics which are familiar or of personal interest. Can describe experiences and events, dreams, hopes and ambitions and briefly give reasons and explanations for opinions and plans.
Basic user	A2	Can understand sentences and frequently used expressions related to areas of most immediate relevance (e.g. very basic personal and family information, shopping, local geography, employment). Can communicate in simple and routine tasks requiring a simple and direct exchange of information on familiar and routine matters. Can describe in simple terms aspects of his/her background, immediate environment and matters in areas of immediate need.
	A1	Can understand and use familiar everyday expressions and very basic phrases aimed at the satisfaction of needs of a concrete type. Can introduce him/herself and others and can ask and answer questions about personal details such as where he/she lives, people he/she knows and things he/she has. Can interact in a simple way provided the other person talks slowly and clearly and is prepared to help.

Many more detailed descriptors are given in the remainder of Chapter 3 for the different levels and with respect to the five skills of listening, reading, spoken interaction, spoken production and writing. The Council of Europe's intention was to reflect social practices in organising learning and to provide a coherent and transparent framework to enable better practices to emerge. In Appendix D (pp.244–257) the authors also reproduce a set of *Can Do statements* developed by the Association of Language Testers in Europe (ALTE), which were anchored to the descriptors and aligned with the CEFR levels in (1). For example, learners at B1 can 'express opinions on abstract/cultural matters in a limited way or offer advice within a known area'. Learners at B2 'can follow or give a talk on a familiar topic'. And learners at C1 'can contribute effectively to meetings and seminars within own area of work or keep up a casual conversation with a good deal of fluency'.

The illustrative descriptors of the CEFR do not give language-specific details about the grammar and lexis that are characteristic of each proficiency level for each L2. Chapter 5 of the 2001 document on 'The user/learner's competences', for example, which includes discussion of syntax, morpho-syntax and lexis, does not link particular grammatical and lexical properties to the CEFR levels with any degree of specificity. There was a reason for this, however: the authors wanted the CEFR to be neutral with respect to the L2 being acquired and to be compatible with the different languages of Europe. In this way a given level of proficiency in L2 German could be compared with a corresponding level in L2 French or English.

The result of this language neutrality, however, is that the CEFR levels are 'underspecified' with respect to key properties that teachers and examiners look for when they assign learners and candidates to a particular proficiency level and score in a particular L2 (see Milanovic 2009). Learners who perform each of the functions in the illustrative descriptors may be using a wide variety of grammatical constructions and words, and the ability to 'do' the task does not tell us with precision how a learner does it and with what grammatical and lexical properties of English (or of other target languages). It is this (deliberate) underspecification that provides the rationale for this book and that explains its subtitle.

The project described in this book is embedded within a larger applied and theoretical research programme, the English Profile Programme (EPP), which was initiated by the Cambridge ESOL group of Cambridge Assessment in collaboration with Cambridge University Press and other stakeholders in 2005. One of the goals of the EPP from the outset has been to provide 'reference level descriptions' and to add grammatical and lexical details of English to CEFR's functional characterisation of the different levels by using the resources of the Cambridge Learner Corpus (CLC). At the time of going to press this is a corpus of roughly 45 million words of written English from learners around the world at all levels of proficiency. The EPP also builds on the pioneering work of van Ek and Trim, for example in their *Threshold 1990* book, which linked many grammatical and lexical details of English to a rich inventory of language functions and notions in clear and practically useful ways. Van Ek and Trim did not have access to the rich electronic resource of the CLC for the empirical testing of their proposals, however, and nor was their work guided by the search for criterial features at the different levels, which is the aim of this book.

1.2 Specifying the reference levels

The basic idea behind the criterial feature concept is that in addition to whether a learner fulfils the communicative functions required by the task or not, there are certain linguistic properties that are characteristic and indicative of L2 proficiency at each level, on the basis of which examiners make their practical assessments. Since there is a large measure of inter-examiner agreement, and since the illustrative descriptors are underspecified with respect to these L2 properties, we need to discover what it is exactly that examiners look for when they assign the scores they do. Cambridge ESOL has carried out extensive research to help and train examiners to make valid assessments (De Velle 2009, Taylor and Galaczi 2011). It is also reasonable to assume that examiners' collective experience and rater training over many years have led to an awareness of the kinds of properties that distinguish levels and scores from one another. The challenge is to discover what these properties are. This is what the criterial feature concept is all about. If we can make the distinguishing properties explicit at the level of grammar and lexis, and ultimately for phonetics and semantics and form–function correspond-ences as well, then we will have identified a set of linguistic features that will add the necessary specification to CEFR's functional descriptors for each of the levels. This will have considerable practical benefits for teaching/learning, examining and publishing. It can also contribute new patterns and insights to theories of second language acquisition (SLA).

Milanovic (2009:5) summarises the need for this additional specification as follows:

> The CEFR is neutral with respect to language and, as the common framework, must by necessity be underspecified for all languages. This means that specialists in the teaching or assessment of a given language . . . need to determine the linguistic features which increasing proficiency in the language entails . . . Such features are peculiar to each language and so the CEFR must be adapted to accommodate the language in question. . . . A major objective of English Profile is to analyse learner language to throw more light on what learners of English *can* and *can't* do at different CEFR levels, and to assess *how well* they perform using the linguistic exponents of the language at their disposal (i.e. using the grammar and lexis of English).

Putting this another way, we need to know for each European language and for each level which grammatical constructions are used, which words, which syntactic and morpho-syntactic rules are applied and with what levels of success, and which meanings are assigned to individual words and sen-tences. And the basic reason why this is vital is because knowing a language and being a competent native speaker means that one has acquired thousands and thousands of properties of English, or Spanish, or French, including the following:

• the sounds of the language
• meaningful units or morphemes
• words (e.g. the nouns and the verbs)

- precise meanings and usage possibilities of words
- basic grammatical constructions
- productive syntactic and morpho-syntactic rules
- exceptions to these, e.g. lexical idiosyncrasies.

As learners progress, they master more and more of these properties, and move closer to the native speaker's knowledge. Through experience and instruction examiners have learned to recognise this progression and to assign examination scripts to the appropriate level. We shall not delve into the thorny issue of what 'native speaker' can mean in SLA. We simply view it as an ideal towards which L2 learners can aspire even though this ideal may be unattainable for many native speakers, who acquired L1 from birth. For an in-depth view and analysis see Davies (1991).

The Council of Europe is to be credited with reorienting language teaching and assessment away from the 'structure-dominated scholastic sterility' (van Ek and Trim 1991:1) that was inherited ultimately from the teaching of classical languages (see E W Hawkins' 1981 *Modern Languages in the Curriculum*, CUP, for a historical summary of language teaching practices) and 'into a vital medium for the freer movement of people and ideas' with its new emphasis on language use and language functions (van Ek and Trim: ibid.). This functional approach within CEFR and in applied linguistics generally can be traced back ultimately to the highly influential work of John Austin in the philosophy of language, as captured most explicitly in his 1962 book *How to Do Things with Words*. This book was a reaction against a long tradition of research in logical semantics focusing on basic sentence types that carry descriptive or 'truth-conditional' meanings, in favour of a new usage-based and 'speech act' approach (to use John Searle's term which has now largely replaced Austin's 'performative', see Searle 1969). The usage-based philosophy of language provided a theory and a vocabulary for describing the many uses to which language can be put and the manner in which the functions are expressed, whether through 'direct' or 'indirect' speech acts, etc. (see Searle 1975). The influence of this theoretical work on the CEFR, and on the detailed functional taxonomy of van Ek and Trim's *Threshold 1990*, is unmistakable. See Anthony Green (forthcoming 2012: Chapter 2) for a detailed literature review and a historical survey of the origins of the CEFR's language functions going back to Austin, Searle and other philosophers of language.

One reason why we now need to return to a greater focus on grammar and lexis, as part of this added specificity for the different levels in different languages, is because there is, in fact, no simple one-to-one correspondence between functions and linguistic forms. One and the same sentence type can perform many functions. *Can you take out the garbage?* can be an (indirect) request, and also a (direct) question about your ability to do something.

Conversely, one and the same function (requesting or commanding) can be performed by many linguistic structures or single words. Most of the basic construction types of a language, for example intransitive versus transitive versus ditransitive clauses, and most single words and phrases have syntactic and semantic properties that are independent of, though compatible with, a whole range of functions that can be performed using them, and it would complicate matters to make reference to these functions when describing their basic grammar and semantics. Similarly, the types of grammatical errors that learners make at different levels, in inflection, derivation, agreement, word order, etc., are not in general aligned with the kinds of functions they are trying to perform at these levels. There are some clear form–function correspondences, of course, and it is practically useful for learners to have them listed and pointed out. But any functional approach that contains a list of the functions that learners can express at given levels, whether with their common grammatical and lexical exponents or not, needs to be supplemented by a description of the partly orthogonal and autonomous syntactic, morpho-syntactic and lexical properties of the language that are characteristic of the different levels. To quote from Milanovic (2009:5) again:

> We are now in a position to begin a systematic and empirically-based approach to specifying more precisely how the CEFR can be operationalised for English, and this in turn will lead to better and more comprehensive illustrative descriptors . . . In this way the CEFR will become the really useful tool that it was intended to be.

In order to realise this, we need better descriptions of what second language learners actually know as their learning progresses. Let us divide the learning process into six or eight or four stages, or however many the learning data enable us readily to discriminate. The CEFR proposes six, as we have seen, and examining boards have operated with six, prior to and independently of the CEFR. In other words, six levels have been widely regarded as useful. So what are the characteristic properties for a language like English of these six learner levels, in phonetics/phonology, morphology, syntax, the lexicon, semantics, pragmatics and discourse? What do we expect to find at level two or four or six across each of these areas? What phonological skills, lexical-semantic knowledge, morpho-syntactic error types and syntactic patterns correlate at each of the levels? There is, we submit, no theory of SLA that can successfully predict these correlations across the broad range of language mastery skills for each of six levels. Yet this is exactly what we need to specify if learners, teachers, teacher trainers, examiners, curriculum developers and publishers are to do their respective jobs better, guiding learners and teachers more effectively to the next stage, publishing materials that are better oriented to learners' needs, making better assessments, and also training examiners better.

Practitioners have, of course, accumulated considerable knowledge, sometimes implicit sometimes explicit, about these learning stages and their specific properties. Examiners have learned, as suggested above, to agree with one another on the appropriate level to assign to an arbitrary script, based on their training and on years of practical experience assigning scores and passes or fails to exams at various levels. Along with the realisation of specific functions that the task requires, one aspect of performance that they look out for when they make these practical assessments is the details of the grammar, lexis and semantics of English. These linguistic properties can, we submit, often be independent of the functional descriptions of the CEFR, even when the examination level is set within the six-level Common European Framework. The validation systems and statistical tests that support these assessments, certainly for exams administered by Cambridge ESOL, have always been based on the properties of learner English at the different levels and on empirically derived scales and psychometric tests, in addition to the functional descriptors themselves (see Milanovic 2009). In short, as already indicated, we need to specify the reference levels of the Common European Framework for different languages.

Using the Cambridge Learner Corpus

We are fortunate to have at our disposal a rich empirical resource for this purpose, the Cambridge Learner Corpus (CLC), which has been developed over many years by Cambridge University Press and Cambridge ESOL. Roughly half of the CLC's current 45 million words of written learner data is coded for errors. Full details on the CLC and the type of data it contains are given in Chapter 3. The CLC was originally searchable lexically, i.e. on the basis of individual words, and grammatically only to the extent that a rule of English grammar was reflected in an error code. This search capability has now been expanded and the CLC has been tagged for parts of speech and parsed by Ted Briscoe of the Cambridge Computer Lab and Paula Buttery of RCEAL Cambridge using the Robust Accurate Statistical Parser (RASP) developed by Ted Briscoe and John Carroll (see Briscoe, Carroll and Watson (2006) accessible at: http://acl.ldc.upenn.edu/P/P06/P06-4020.pdf). RASP is an automatic parsing system incorporating both grammatical information and statistical patterns, and details of its operation are summarised in Chapter 3. The CLC therefore provides empirical patterns of language use that can inform our search for the specifics of each learner level.

The CLC's error codes have been developed by computational linguists at Cambridge University Press. They classify some 76 error types involving lexical, syntactic and morpho-syntactic properties of English. A small sample is given in (2) together with exemplifying sentences. Note that none of these sentences or other sentences that illustrate error codes in this book are taken from corpus data, but are provided for illustrative purposes only:

(2)   Sample Error Codes in the CLC

RN	**Replace Noun**	*Have a good travel* (journey)
RV	**Replace Verb**	*I existed last weekend in London* (spent)
MD	**Missing Determiner**	*I spoke to President* (the)
		I have car (a)
AGV	**Verb Agreement Error**	*The three birds is singing* (are)
IV	**Incorrect Verb Inflection**	*I spended last week in London* (spent)
FJ	**Wrong Adjective Form**	*The situation got worst* (worse)
UQ	**Unnecessary Quantifier**	*A little bit quite common* (quite common)
DY	**Derivation of Adverb**	*It happened fastly* (fast)

The CLC also contains data from numerous (over 130) typologically and genetically different first languages.

One of the strengths of an empirically based corpus approach to learning such as this is that we can focus not just on errors (i.e. on what learners get WRONG), but on what they get RIGHT. Using the corpus we can quantify, for each learning stage, how many of the thousands of properties that constitute knowledge of English learners actually use. We can also measure how their linguistic performance gradually improves relative to that of native English speakers. In order to compare the learner data with actual English usage by native speakers we can search the British National Corpus (BNC). The BNC comprises 100 million words of modern British English, from a wide range of sources and text types (90 million written, 10 million spoken). It has been tagged and parsed using the same automatic parsing system (RASP) that has been applied to the CLC, making exact comparison between the CLC and the BNC possible.

The CLC gives information for each script on whether the candidate passed or failed and on the candidate's score (A to F). It is important to stress that for the purpose of this research we examined only those scripts with passing grades of A, B and C and filtered the fails. The reason for this is a principled one. We are focusing here on what passing candidates have actually learned, i.e. we are trying to define the criterial features of pass scripts at each CEFR level that learners need to master in order to satisfy the requirements for success at that level. We are aware that scripts that have been graded by examiners as being below the satisfactory band on the mark scheme do also contain correct uses of many syntactic frames and lexical items, but some of these scripts must have been marked as unsatisfactory because fewer correct structures and items were used and more errors were made in general.

We are also fortunate, in our study of learner English, to have the benefit, as stated above, of previous work by van Ek and Trim, specifying the English language functions and notions that can be expressed by learners at different levels together with their suggested grammatical and lexical exponents. Details of the Threshold level for English were set out in van Ek and Trim's *Threshold 1990* published by Cambridge University Press in 1991. *Waystage 1990* was published by van Ek and Trim in the same year, *Vantage* in 2001. The volume *Breakthrough*, specifying CEFR A1 English language level competences, has recently been made available electronically for EPP by permission of John Trim and is accessible via the English Profile website (www.englishprofile.org).

1.3 What are criterial features?

The title of this book promises 'criterial features'. We need to clarify what these are, and exemplify them, at the outset. The basic idea is that we try to find properties of learner English that are characteristic and indicative of L2 proficiency at each of the levels and that distinguish higher levels from lower levels.

For example, Caroline Williams (2007) has identified when the basic construction types of English first appear in the CLC. Simple intransitives (NP-V) and the slightly more complex transitive (NP-V-NP) sentence types are present from the beginning at the **A** levels (Williams examined only data from A2 onwards, but they are there at A1 as well):

A1   *He went.* (NP-V)

A1   *He loved her.* (NP-V-NP)

Modal auxiliary verbs like *may*, *might*, *can* and *must* appear first at **A1** or **A2**, but only in some of their senses. See the English Vocabulary Profile (EVP), previously known and referred to in this volume as English Profile Wordlists (Capel 2010), currently available in preview form via the EP website (www.englishprofile.org). *May* is first attested at **A2** in its epistemic sense of POSSIBILITY, as in the following attested example:

A2   *Then we may go sightseeing.* (POSSIBILITY)

but not yet in its deontic PERMISSION sense (which is **B1**, see below). *Can*, on the other hand, is first attested in the PERMISSION sense at **A1** and in the POSSIBILITY sense at **A2**, as in the following attested examples:

A1   *And if you want, you can bring pencils or pens.* (PERMISSION)

A2   *It is an interesting place because you can see a lot of plants.*
       (POSSIBILITY)

Lexical verbs appearing at the **A** levels are typically among the most basic and frequent verbs of English (see Hawkins and Buttery 2009 for exemplification and a comparative quantification for selected verbs in the CLC and the BNC), and they typically appear first in their most basic and frequent senses. Verbs attested at **A1** include *catch*, *eat*, *give*, *put*, *take* and *walk*. New verbs at **A2** include *break*, *cut*, *fall*, *hit*, *push*, and *stand*, within an expanded total of verbs, again typically in their most basic and literal senses. For *break* this includes its primary physical sense as in the attested:

A2   *I broke a beautiful glass.*

and for *cut* it includes the following attested example of its primary sense:

A2   *First I cut the cake with my mother.*

Properties found at the lower levels of the CLC generally persist through the higher levels. Those that appear first at A2 discriminate only between A1 and all other levels, and their usefulness as criterial features is limited. The new features at B1 are more interesting for criteriality. For example, Williams (2007) found that Object Control structures with an *-ing* verb complement of the type

B1   *I caught him stealing.* (NP-V-NP-V (+*ing*))

appear first at B1 and are criterial for this and for all higher levels, distinguishing them from A1 and A2. Our research has shown that structures with a finite complement clause postposed to the right of predicates like *is true* and *seem* with a subject *it* in so-called 'Extraposition' structures, are also criterial for B1 and higher levels. The following is an attested example:

B1   *It's true* [*that I don't need a ring to make me remember you*] (*it-be*-Adj-S)

The modal auxiliary verb *may* is first used in its deontic sense of PERMISSION at **B1**, as in the following attested example:

B1   *May I borrow your bicycle for the weekend?*

in contrast to its epistemic POSSIBILITY meaning at **A2** above (see the English Vocabulary Profile). A large number of lexical verbs including *divide*, *fit*, *grab*, *spill*, *stick* and *tear*, appear for the first time at **B1** within a further expanded total of verbs. And the meanings of the lexical items that appeared first at A1 and A2 begin to expand from their basic senses above. So *break* appears for the first time in the extended sense of INTERRUPT at **B1**, in the attested example:

B1   *I think the most important aim of a holiday is to break your daily routine.*

Constructions that are criterial for **B2** and the higher levels include 'secondary predications' with object control such as

B2   *He painted the car red.* (NP-V-NP-AdjP, Object Control)

with *red* predicated of the direct object *the car*, as well as another Object Control structure (see Williams 2007):

B2 *I sent him as [a messenger]* (NP-V-NP-*as*-NP, Object Control)

'Subject-to-Subject Raising' constructions appear first at **B2** with most of the higher verbs and adjectives that trigger this rule (see Postal 1974), for example *prove* as in the attested example:

B2 *The car has proved to be one of the most important inventions of our century.* (NP-Aux-V-VPinfin)

New lexical verbs at **B2** include *acquire, capture, drag, rush, spread* and *swallow* within an even larger set of verbs than at B1, and new meanings and uses are attested for the verbs that appeared earlier. For *break*, first attested at **A2**, these include new collocations at **B2** such as *break a promise* or *break the law*, as in the attested example:

B2 *I am very surprised that such a reputable theater [as] yours has been able to break all [the] promises that appeared in the advertisement.*

For *cut*, also an A2 verb, they include new meanings at B2 such as REDUCE in *cut the cost*.

'Subject-to-Object Raising' constructions (see Postal 1974) with the verb *believe* appear first at **C1**, as in the attested example:

C1 *I believe her to be this country's best representative.* (NP-V-NP-VPinfin)

as do passivised Subject-to-Object Raising constructions (Postal 1974) such as the following with *assumed*, again attested:

C1 *. . . the low cost of membership and entry was assumed to be an advantage.* (NP-Aux-V-VPinfin)

New lexical verbs appearing first at **C1** include *accumulate, boast, quote, reassure, shape* and *stain* along with new meaning possibilities for the verbs already introduced. For example, *break* appears first in the idiomatic sense of *break the bank* at **C1**.

New features appearing at **C2** include less common Subject-to-Object Raising constructions with higher predicates such as *presume, declare* and *remember*, as in the attested:

C2 *He presumed work to be the way to live.* (NP-V-NP-VPinfin)

New lexical verbs at **C2** include *limp, raid, saunter, squander* and *sway*. New meanings for *break* at **C2** include original figurative senses such as the attested *break that wall he surrounded himself with*.

One major distinguishing feature of the **C** levels that has emerged from our analysis of the CLC can be seen in the scores for 'negative features' or error types like those illustrated in (2) above. There are significant improvements in a whole range of these syntactic and morpho-syntactic errors at the **C** levels. For many error types at the **B** levels, by contrast, the scores actually get worse. The error codes defined and assigned by our CUP colleagues involve morpho-syntactic errors of inflection, derivation and grammatical form, and syntactic errors of omission, positioning and co-occurrence. It appears that learners at the **C** levels are increasingly mastering these rules of English, whereas **B**-level learners are often not. See Chapter 2.3 for further details.

By enumerating grammatical and lexical details of the learner levels like this we give specificity to the CEFR levels for English in a way that is practically useful and theoretically revealing. We assume in the process that the criterial features of a level are those properties that examiners look out for, consciously or unconsciously, when assessing candidates' performance and assigning grades to them. Are these construction types of English present or absent in a given writing sample? Are certain words and types of word meanings present? Are certain errors made or not made, or made with a certain frequency at a given level? What is the overall complexity level of the sentence structure at a particular level? See Chapter 2.2 for further discussion of the latter.

The goal of the EPP all along has been to provide 'reference level descriptions of English' for all six CEFR levels. The way we have chosen to approach this and to implement it in the present book is through criterial features. These, as indicated in Section 1.2 above, are properties that are distinctive and characteristic of each of the levels, and hence important for both practitioners and theoreticians to know about. They are less than the total describable for each level, first by virtue of their distinctiveness, and second because they constitute a theoretically and practically driven subset of the total number that could be described for a level. Our focus is on important changes from level to level, just as historians of the English language focus on key changes from Old English to Middle English to Early Modern English, like the Great Vowel Shift of Early Modern English. Students of the history of English want to know what changed, when and how, not what stayed the same. Similarly learners, teachers and examiners of English need to focus on key developments from level to level and on significant characteristics of each.

To give a complete description of a language, or a dialect, or a variant, even of an incompletely acquired 'learner language', would in any case be a huge undertaking. The properties of English that native speakers know are vast. Witness the sheer size of Otto Jespersen's (1909–49) seven-volume *Modern English Grammar on Historical Principles*, or of Quirk, Greenbaum, Leech and Svartvik's (1985) *Comprehensive Grammar of the English Language*, or of Huddleston and Pullum's (2002) *The Cambridge Grammar of the English Language*. These descriptions are not complete even for the grammar of English, and they would need to be supplemented by tens of thousands of lexical entries from the *Oxford English Dictionary* in order to make explicit the lexical knowledge that English native speakers routinely carry around in their heads. For the different learner levels, undertaking anything like a full description for each would demand more time and resources than we have available in the EPP. The criterial features approach is in any case, we believe, more revealing, more useful and more interesting for this purpose. The aim of the Programme of which our research is a part is to develop a 'profile', that is 'an analysis representing the extent to which something' (in our case the English language levels of L2 learners) 'exhibits various characteristics; as in a biochemical profile of blood' (Roger Hawkey, personal communication).

In order to find the criterial features of a level we use a mix of inductive and deductive techniques. The CLC reveals many patterns that are not theoretically predictable and that emerge in response to inductive search queries. We also proceed deductively by searching selectively in the corpus for grammatical and lexical patterns that we believe will be distinctive for the different levels, after consulting a broad range of linguistic and psycholinguistic theories that help us make informed decisions about what is likely to be criterial. These theories come from studies of first and second language acquisition, and from relevant work in language processing, grammatical complexity, the lexicon and lexical semantics, and language typology. A set of hypotheses was formulated at the outset of the EPP, by the first author of this book, for emerging patterns in second language acquisition (SLA) derived from these theories. These hypotheses and their predictions have been developed much further in a collaboration with the second author that began in February 2009, and that has resulted in some of the principles of Chapter 5 and in further research towards a Complex Adaptive System model of SLA.

1.4 Practical applications and the theoretical relevance of criterial features

We see our book as having a number of audiences, namely practitioners of different kinds and also theoreticians from different branches of the language sciences. The potential relevance of criterial features to different consumers merits further commentary.

The first sets of practitioners who can benefit from the identification and explanation of criterial features are the learners of English themselves, and those who teach them. If you are going to try and learn a foreign language, like English, it is useful if those who teach you or guide you know the stages through which learners generally proceed on their way to communicative mastery. Learning is aided when your teaching methods and materials are calibrated realistically to the next learning stage. Especially if you are planning to take an exam at this higher level it is vital to know what examiners will be looking for as indicative of success, so that you can optimise your chances of passing. This means focusing on what is criterial, on the new constructions, words and types of word meanings for that level, adding them to your repertoire and learning how to use them, in order to perform the kinds of functions that the CEFR defines for it (see Table 1.1 again). If significant improvements in certain types of errors are criterial for the next level, in the sense that learners typically improve in these areas at this level and examiners look out for these improvements, then these areas need to be specifically targeted in learning and teaching (see Chapter 2.3). Making explicit, and quantifying, the details of each learner level can also lead to improved diagnosis and validation in examining, and to improved examiner training.

Transitional features

These benefits for learners and teachers lead us to make a distinction between criterial features that are 'transitional' and those that are not. Transitional features are those properties that describe the changes from one level to an immediately following level, e.g. from B2 to C1, based on our study of the Cambridge ESOL passing scripts at C1. These transitional features of C1 will generally persist into C2 as well, especially if they are what we call 'positive' or correct properties of the L2, and they will be criterial for both C1 and C2 (i.e. for [C1, C2], to use the square bracket representation for levels that share criteriality). But they will only be transitional for C1. Learners who have already passed a B2 language exam will benefit from focusing their energies on the transitional features of C1, therefore. The more clearly and explicitly that teachers and textbook writers can draw attention to these, the more appropriate their methods and materials can be, and the more successes examinees may have at the respective levels. Hence, transitional features are particularly useful for learners, teachers and textbook writers interested in knowing how learners make the transition to a given next stage and thus what it may be helpful to concentrate on.

Transitional features are also relevant for the training of examiners, and for test validation and assessment purposes more generally. Assessment involves a delicate decision about the appropriate level attained by a candidate, and an even more fine-tuned decision about the right range or score to assign within this level. Discrimination between levels can be greatly aided by an explicit set of criterial features, especially by those which indicate transition from one level to the next.

Relevant language sciences

The fact that learning occurs, and the precise manner and sequence in which target properties are learned, is the subject matter for the scientific fields of first and second language acquisition. Understanding how we learn, how children acquire their native language(s), and how second language learners acquire an L2, has consumed a huge amount of scientific time and effort in recent decades (see Chapter 4). We know a lot at this point, though there is still a lot we don't fully understand, for example about the relationship between biologically given capacities and the data of experience, about the interaction between the various factors that facilitate or impede learning, about the role of transfer from the L1 in L2 learning, and so on, and there are currently many disagreements and uncertainties in these fields (see, for example, Doughty and Long's 2003 *Handbook of Second Language*, Blackwell, for an excellent summary of the state of the art in SLA). In particular, as Ellis (2003) observes, one of the most important tasks in future SLA research is to determine precisely how all the different factors that contribute to success in SLA actually interact, reinforcing or competing with one another. This is exactly what we hope to contribute here and in future English Profile research.

The research project of this book also draws on several other branches of the language sciences, including models of formal syntax, studies of the lexicon and lexical semantics, language typology and cross-linguistic variation, and on psycholinguistics broadly construed as well as computational linguistics. Our findings are, we believe, of relevance to these fields in turn.

The present book has both practical and theoretical goals, therefore. It is a contribution to the applied areas that study the experiences of learners and teachers and examiners with the goal of making proposals that are useful. It is also intended as a contribution to SLA, by providing empirical patterns and principles derived from them that can inform answers to theoretical questions. It is our belief that applications will only be successful if they rest on solid theoretical and empirical foundations. And conversely we believe that the experiences of practitioners, and the data that has been collected by practitioners in pursuit of practical goals, are relevant for theories of learning and use, shedding light on scientific questions that have not yet been resolved.

Defining a research programme

This is perhaps one of the more original features of the present book: the marriage of theory and practice. The CLC is a database of theoretical as well as practical relevance and numerous branches of the language sciences can benefit from the patterns and principles that it reveals. It must be stressed at the outset that we see our results as preliminary and that our primary goal is to define a research method within the English Profile Programme (EPP). We are not presenting a completed research product at this point. Our corpus data, while extensive, are still limited in type (written examination scripts only) and tokens. A new corpus, the Cambridge English Profile Corpus (www. englishprofile.org), is being built to include more types of data responding to more tasks by the EPP research team. More data will enable us to check more reliably for different combinations of features, for the levels at which they appear to be criterial, and for transfer effects from different types of first languages. In the meantime we are striving for the most accurate description that we can achieve of the database as it is at the time of going to press. We have many illustrative criterial features to offer for the learning of English, based on current data, and some partly new principles for describing empirical patterns in the CLC. Subsequent publications from the EPP will provide many more criterial features and theoretical refinements. In the meantime it is our hope that ongoing and future research within this ambitious interdisciplinary programme will be more integrated and focused as a result of our book, and that researchers elsewhere will want to join this venture, and set up similar projects for other languages. We, in turn, have benefited from, and would not have been able to complete this book without, the help of our many EPP collaborators (see the Acknowledgements for details).

1.5 Summary of what lies ahead

The book consists of two parts. The first part lays out the background to this research programme and comprises the more theoretically oriented chapters. The second part is more practical and empirical and contains grammatical and lexical data taken from the CLC exemplifying criterial features of the different levels that will be of interest to learners, teachers, examiners and publishers.

Chapter 2 gives the theory and a taxonomy of criterial features, building on the discussion in this introductory chapter (see especially Section 1.3). Chapter 3 summarises the CLC, its contents, error types and coding, and the automatic tagging and parsing that can be accomplished through RASP. Chapter 4 summarises key points and findings from the current research literature on SLA and from other branches of the language sciences that will be of relevance for the patterns and principles derived from the CLC that are summarised in Chapter 5. In Chapter 5 we present some principles that account for the patterns in these this data.

Part 2 begins with a summary Chapter (6) of some of the pioneering work done by van Ek and Trim, the so-called T series (Waystage, Threshold, and Vantage) with particular reference to their proposed grammatical and lexical features at the different levels. Their data are presented vertically here, rather than horizontally as in their books, and a subset of their proposed features are tested on the CLC. Chapter 7 presents an extensive set of 'positive' criterial features of the CEFR levels, primarily of a grammatical and lexico-grammatical nature. Chapter 8 presents further positive features in the form of a lexical progression profile of new verbs and their meanings at the different levels. Chapter 9 summarises our conclusions and points the way forward to future theoretical and empirical research on criterial features.

2 A theory and a taxonomy of criterial features

2.1 Basics

The major goal of this book is to identify a set of criterial features for each of the CEFR proficiency levels as they apply to English, and more generally to define a broad research programme integrating theory and practice, as pointed out in Chapter 1.4. The present chapter discusses criteriality in more detail and proposes an initial taxonomy of different types of criterial features.

As background, notice that criterial features must be defined in terms of linguistic properties of the L2 as used by native speakers that have either been correctly or incorrectly attained by learners at a given level. The learners whose scripts we focus on in this book are exclusively those who have gained a passing grade at the relevant level. In the case of correct properties we talk of 'positive linguistic features' acquired at a certain L2 level, for incorrect properties we talk of 'negative grammatical features', i.e. of errors and error frequencies characteristic of the different levels. The positive linguistic features can also be examined quantitatively in order to see whether frequencies of use in the CLC do or do not match the frequencies of use by native speakers. If there is a match we can talk of 'positive usage features' in the CLC. If there is not we can refer to 'negative usage features' (cf. Hawkins and Buttery 2010; Salamoura and Saville 2009). Criterial features can also be relativised to particular L1s or groups of L1s. We call these 'L1-specific criterial features'.

Defining what is criterial for each level will necessarily involve multiple factors, i.e. many grammatical, lexical, phonological and discourse features, since there are many properties of these different types that are potentially criterial. The different language functions that learners can perform as they learn English can also be classified in terms of their criteriality for particular levels, as in van Ek and Trim's Chapter 5 of *Threshold 1990* (see Green forthcoming 2012 for an extension of this work for the C levels). Also, criterial properties may not be unique to just one level. A given property may distinguish both of the C levels from the A and B levels. Or it may distinguish both B levels from the A and C levels, or it may be unique to C2, or even to B2. The ultimate definition for what is criterial for a particular level, say C2, will be a cluster of criterial features, each of which distinguishes C2 either uniquely or non-uniquely from other levels. Obviously, the more unique a feature is to C2 alone, the more useful it will be as a diagnostic for that level. But non-uniqueness to C2 is not a bad thing. In fact, it is an inevitable consequence of certain types of criteriality. If learners of English acquire a novel structure at B2, that structure will generally persist through the higher C levels and will be characteristic of all of [B2, C1, C2] and will distinguish them from all lower levels.

It is for this reason that we made a distinction in Chapter 1.4 between criterial features that are 'transitional' and those that are not. A criterial property found in all of [B2, C1, C2] will be transitional for B2 only, the first level at which it is attested and becomes criterial. More generally, a transitional criterial feature will be one that holds for the first level only, in the upward sequence of CEFR levels (cf. (1) in Chapter 1) at which it appears and becomes criterial. All criterial features that are unique to a particular level will be automatically transitional, by this definition. But for those that are non-unique, like [B2, C1, C2], only the first attested level is the transitional one.

The motivation for this distinction is both practical and theoretical. For learners, teachers, examiners and publishers we want to draw explicit attention to those features that change from one level to the next, so that each of these practitioner groups can focus clearly on what should be learned in order to attain the next stage. For theoreticians we need clear statements about the relative sequencing of changes in acquisition, i.e. about what exactly is learned, and when, and in combination with which other features.

The order of presentation in this chapter is as follows. Section 2.2 defines and illustrates positive linguistic features, adding some examples to those given in Chapter 1.3. Section 2.3 defines and illustrates negative linguistic features, and brings errors and error frequencies into the discussion of criteriality. Section 2.4 defines positive and negative usage features for correct properties learned and illustrates how frequency of usage can be a criterial feature for a particular level, as L2 users learn to select from the properties made available by the target language with the same kinds of frequencies as native speakers do. Section 2.5 defines and illustrates some L1-specific criterial features. And Section 2.6 defines a practical rule that we use for deciding when a positive linguistic property first appears and is criterial for a level, in the event that the attested examples in the current corpus are few.

2.2 Positive linguistic features

The label 'positive linguistic features' refers to the correct linguistic properties of English that have been acquired at a certain L2 level and that generally persist at all higher levels. For example, a property P acquired at B2 may differentiate [B2, C1, C2] from [A1, A2, B1] and will be criterial for the former. Criteriality characterises a set of adjacent levels in this case, with P being a transitional criterial feature for B2. Or some property might be attained only at C2 and be unique to this highest level.

Most of the illustrations given in Chapter 1.3 of grammatical and lexical properties of the different levels were of this criterial feature type. For example, Williams' (2007) new verb co-occurrences that appear at **B1**, such as the Object Control structure with -*ing* verbs NP-V-NP-V(+*ing*) (*I caught him stealing*), are criterial for [B1, B2, C1, C2], B1 being the transitional level. Those appearing at **B2**, e.g. the secondary predication structure NP-V-NP-AdjP (*he painted the car red*), are criterial for [B2, C1, C2], B2 being transitional.

Some additional verb co-occurrence features pointed out by Williams (op. cit.) include the following (note that the cited examples from Williams are not taken from corpus data):

The infinitival complement frame plus WH-movement, first attested at B1

B1   *He explained* [*how to do it*] (NP-V-VPinfin, WH-movement)

is joined as a B1 transitional feature by other similar structures with finite or non-finite complements plus WH-movement:

B1   *He asked* [*how she did it*] (NP-V-S, WH-movement)

B1   *He thought about* [*whether he wanted to go*] (NP-V-P-S, WH-movement)

An embedded clause functioning as a direct object of the matrix verb, as in

A2   *They thought* [*that he was always late*] (NP-V-S)

is found at A2, but with a more complex matrix clause containing a prepositional phrase as well, it becomes a transitional feature for B1 and a [B1, B2, C1, C2] feature overall:

B1   *They admitted* [*to the authorities*][*that they had entered illegally*] (NP-V-PP-S)

Infinitival complement structure with verbs like *help* and *like* plus Object Control are also B1 transitional features (see Chapter 7.1.9):

B1   *He helped her* [*bake the cake*] (NP-V-NP-VPinfin , Obj Control)

   I'd like you [*to phone me*] (NP-Aux-V-NP-VPinfin, Obj Control)

A finite verb complement structure with a post-verbal NP rather than a PP, as in

B2   *He told the audience* [*that he was leaving*] (NP-V-NP-S)

is transitional for B2 and a [B2, C1, C2] feature, as is the participial verb complement with Object Control of the type:

B2   *They worried about him drinking* (NP-V-P-NP-Ving, Obj Control)

Since this early work by Williams (2007) it has become clear that we need to add lexical details to particular grammatical constructions, in order to give a descriptively more precise account of the different levels. Different 'raising' constructions (see Postal 1974) in the learner data, for example, appear at very different levels depending on the particular verb or adjective used (see Chapters 1.3, 5.3 and 7.2). This impacts their criticality significantly. Most of the verbs and adjectives that trigger Subject-to-Subject Raising appear first at B2, like *prove*, and are criterial for [B2, C1, C2]:

B2 *The car has proved to be one of the most important inventions of our century.* (NP-Aux-V-VPinfin)

Similar raising examples are found at **B2** with the verbs *appear*, *happen*, *turn out*, and *fail*, and with the raising adjectives *likely*, *unlikely* and *sure*. On the other hand, Subject-to-Subject raisings with the verb *seem* are **B1**:

B1 *They seem to be really interesting.* (NP-V-VPinfin)

As are those with the raising adjective *supposed*:

B1 *I was supposed to go to the English class.* (NP-Aux-Adj-VPinfin)

Passivised Subject-to-Object Raising constructions with many verbs including *assumed* are **C1** transitional features:

C1 *. . . the low cost of membership and entry was assumed to be an advantage.* (NP-Aux-V-VPinfin)

Similar constructions with the passive raising verbs *thought* and *known* occur earlier, however, and are B2 transitional features:

B2 *Your theatre is known to present excellent spectacles.* (NP-Aux-V-VPinfin)

while *presumed* in the passive occurs later, at C2:

C2 *Meetings with people are presumed to give new experiences.* (NP-Aux-V- VPinfin)

We saw also in Chapter 1.3 that modal auxiliary constructions with *can* and *may* appear at different levels. *Can* in its deontic permission sense is already present at **A1**:

A1 *And if you want, you can bring pencils or pens.* (PERMISSION)

May in the same sense is a transitional feature of **B1**:

B1 *May I borrow your bicycle for the weekend?*

And, of course, the first appearance of particular lexical items and their meanings is highly correlated with particular levels as well, as was illustrated in Chapter 1.3 (see Chapter 8 for full details).

Mean length of utterance (MLU) figures

As learners master more and more of these positive features of English, their sentences become more expressive, semantically and pragmatically, as well as visibly longer and syntactically more complex. This will be illustrated in detail in Chapter 7 below, in which we enumerate and exemplify some of the structural types whose usage is acquired or increased as learning progresses. At this point we shall simply document and quantify this added length and complexity with some interesting figures involving mean length of utterance (MLU), an indicator of increasing learning that we have borrowed from the first language acquisition literature and involving numbers of words per sentence, see Andersen (1992:252) for a convenient summary.

In order to calculate MLU scores for the different proficiency levels we selected a random subcorpus of the CLC for manual analysis (with the help of the EPP research team). This subcorpus contained scripts with passing grades of A, B and C by learners speaking four first languages, Japanese, Chinese, Russian and Spanish. We examined five levels, A2 through C2, and selected, again at random, 1,000 complete sentences from each level, 5,000 in all, taken from all four first languages in equal numbers (quantities permitting). We followed the regular conventions of English orthography when identifying the beginnings and ends of sentences, namely full stops (occasionally colons) and capitalisation. We excluded incomplete sentences, namely those with formulaic expressions (*Dear John*, *Love Susie*, *OK*, *Bye for now*, *That's all*, etc.) and those that lacked a verb or predicate adjective (e.g. noun phrase answers to questions like *the man over there*, etc.). We then calculated, with the assistance of colleagues at the University of California, Davis, the MLU for each level. The results are shown in (1):

(1)   MLU figures from the manual corpus
      A2   7.9
      B1   10.8
      B2   14.2
      C1   17.3
      C2   19.0

These MLU figures are quite revealing. Clearly longer sentences are being used at each higher level. But with added length comes added complexity of sentence structure and the generation and use of more complex sentence types. This is reflected in many criterial features: more complex sentence types, like raising constructions and many finite clause embeddings, appear at later levels, see the discussion of complexity in Chapter 4.4 and the detailed illustrations of this in Chapter 7. More generally, Hawkins (1994) has proposed that there should be a correlation between sentence length, measured in terms of words, and the amount and depth of the hierarchical phrase structure that dominates the words of a sentence, and Wasow (2002) has demonstrated that this is indeed the case by examining parsed electronic corpora. According to Wasow (ibid.) it is impossible to distinguish statistically between complexity metrics for a sentence that make use of phrasal nodes and hierarchical structure and those that simply count terminal elements or words. The reason for this is that words 'project to' higher phrase structure categories and nodes (noun phrase, verb phrase, etc.), and hence the more words there are in a sentence, the more structure there is in general, and the more complex the sentence is. An important component of complexity has always involved the amount of structure it contains, ever since Miller and Chomsky's (1963) metric of non-terminal to terminal nodes (see Frazier 1985, Gibson 1998, and Hawkins 1994, 2004 for later refinements of this metric).

Assuming that this correlation between sentence length and structural complexity is also true for SLA and learner data – and the evidence of Chapter 7 suggests that it is (i.e. learners are not just concatenating long strings of unstructured or co-ordinated words, *big red soft ball*, and *big and red and soft*, etc. as their proficiency increases) – then the figures in (1) are of both theoretical and practical interest. Theoretically, they point to an expanding syntactic competence at successive levels, with new criterial features at each higher level. The challenge is to discover exactly what these new features are, and the areas we accordingly concentrate on and test in Chapter 7 are those that we hypothesise, based on the research literature (see especially Chapter 4.4), to involve greater complexity. Practically, these figures provide *prima facie* support for the ability of examiners to discriminate consistently between scripts and between levels. Candidates appear to have been grouped together successfully and assigned to proficiency levels in a way that reflects their expanding syntactic competence.

Obviously there are all kinds of variables that need to be properly controlled for here, including for example the impact of task effects on these learner data, before we can derive reliable conclusions about increasing syntactic ability from the MLUs. But in Part 2 we show that there are indeed clear expansions in syntactically complex constructions at progressively higher levels, and many or most of these cannot plausibly be linked to task effects or to factors other than an expanding syntactic competence. We must also check that the new constructions at higher levels are being used correctly. At this point in the book we simply present these figures as they are, and as suggestive of the growth and expansion of positive linguistic features in learner English from A2 to C2 based on data from the CLC. Data from A1 were not, at the time, available in the CLC so we have taken A1 examples from the English Profile Wordlists.

It is interesting to note finally that Green (forthcoming 2012: Chapter 4) finds evidence for increasing sentence length, measured in words, in the input texts that are given to learners at the different levels. He cites a progression from a mean of 12.5 words per sentence at A2 to a mean of 21.5 at C2. These means are slightly higher than those given in (1), based on learners' actual productions. But it makes sense that complexity targets can be consistently higher than the complexity products at each stage. Green (op. cit.) also shows interesting expansions in the lengths of words, and in various syntactic complexity measures, at higher levels in these input texts.

2.3 Negative linguistic features

There are also negative criterial features, i.e. incorrect properties or errors that occur at a certain level or levels and with a characteristic frequency. Both the presence versus absence of the errors, and especially their characteristic frequency (the 'error bandwidth' as we will call it), can be criterial for the level(s). For example, error property P with characteristic frequency F may be criterial for the B levels [B1, B2]; error property P' with frequency F' may be criterial for [C1, C2].

The error types tagged in the CLC data are based on CUP's error codes and they regularly have different frequency bandwidths at the different levels. As Hawkins and Buttery (2010:16–17) have shown, these bandwidths can be criterial. For example, errors involving incorrect morphology for determiners, as in Derivation of Determiners (abbreviated DD) *Shes name was Anna* (instead of *Her name . . .*), show significant differences in error frequencies that decline from B1 > B2 > C1 > C2. The bandwidths are criterial for B1 versus B2 versus C1 versus C2 here. Errors involving a missing preposition (MT), e.g. *I gave it John* (with missing *to*), show significant frequency differences that decline from [B1, B2] > [C1, C2]. The bandwidths are now criterial for the B levels versus the C levels respectively. Errors involving incorrect inflection of a verb (abbreviated IV), such as *I spended last weekend in London*, show a B1 > [B2, C1, C2] pattern. The bandwidths are now criterial for B1 versus the other levels, which do not show significant differences relative to one another. Noun agreement errors, on the other hand (abbreviated AGN), such as *one of my friend*, show significant differences in frequency that increase from B1 to B2 and then decline again at each of the C levels, resulting in an 'inverted U' pattern of B2 > [B1, C1] > C2. The relevant error scores and bandwidths are criterial for B2 versus [B1, C1] versus C2 here (B1 and C1 being non-adjacent levels grouped into the same criterial feature set on this occasion). These and some other error types and frequencies will be given in Table 2.2 below.

The use of errors as criterial features results in partially different patterns and combinations of levels compared with those we find for positive linguistic features, therefore. The acquisition of a positive (i.e. correct) property of English at a lower level generally persists through all higher levels, resulting in criterial feature combinations like [B2, C1, C2], B2 being transitional. But an error type with a frequency distribution criterial for B2 may cease to be criterial for C1, and instead a different distribution may become criterial for C1. Many transitional features involve changes in error distributions of this type, and it is useful for learners if error counts are presented in terms of

Table 2.1 Percentages of linguistic categories relative to total words at each level

	A2	B1	B2	C1	C2
Verb	24.0	21.5	21.8	20.4	21.1
Noun	20.3	18.6	21.5	23.2	21.1
Adjective	5.3	6.4	5.9	6.4	6.2
Adverb	4.6	6.1	5.6	5.4	6.2
Preposition	8.0	8.6	10.0	10.9	10.2
Conjunction	4.8	5.9	6.9	6.8	7.2
Quantifier	1.0	1.3	1.9	2.0	1.8

transitional features so that they know which error types they should concentrate on and reduce or eliminate if they are going to advance to the next stage in proficiency. Negative criterial features such as those illustrated here may inform learning materials accordingly.

There are many subtle issues, both linguistic and statistical, that arise in any quantification of error types and their bandwidths. We need a revealing way of counting the frequencies with which errors are made. In Table 2.2 below this is done in two ways for an illustrative sample of errors. First of all, the number of errors has been calculated (by the EPP research team at RCEAL) relative to 100,000 words of text at each level. This figure will be shown in square brackets alongside each level, e.g. B1[108], B2[64.5], etc. for verb inflection errors, and it gives us a measure of the change in error rate from one level to another. This is a useful quantification of the direction of change, and also of transitions, since everything is relativised to a common chunk of text, namely 100,000 words. The difference between [B1]108 and [B2]64.5 errors per 100,000 words suggests that there is an improvement at B2, on the assumption that the potential for error is roughly constant per 100,000 words at the different levels. If the numbers of verbs, or of other parts of speech, were to differ per 100,000 words per level, for example, then a decline from 108 to 64.5 might not be significant and might just reflect a difference in overall numbers of verbs, or it might be even more significant, depending on the direction of the difference. For similar reasons this quantification method does not permit us to compare across different parts of speech and say, for example, that verbs are more or less subject to errors than nouns, since there could be different numbers of tokens for the different parts of speech.

It turns out that the rate of occurrence for verbs and nouns per 100,000 words does not fluctuate greatly from level to level in the CLC, and interestingly these two parts of speech have a frequency distribution that is very similar to one another. The same is not true for other parts of speech, however, which have varying frequencies of occurrence across categories and across levels. This is shown in Table 2.1. The raw figures were collected by

Table 2.2 Illustrative error rates and bandwidths (data from Hawkins and Buttery 2010:16–17)

DD	**Derivation of Determiner** *Shes name was Anna*	B1 > B2> C1 > C2
	‖ B1[22.5] ‖ B2[15.9] ‖ C1[10.6] ‖ C2 [5.52] ‖	
	(0.263%) (0.171%) (0.097%) (0.053%)	
	0.217% 0.134% 0.075%	
MT	**Missing Preposition** *I gave it John*	[B1, B2] > [C1, C2]
	‖ B1[288] B2[299] ‖ C1[183] C2[127] ‖	
	(3.297%) (2.998%) (1.684%) (1.253%)	
	2.341%	
MQ	**Missing Quantifier** *I'll call in the next days*	[B1, B2] > [C1, C2]
	‖ B1[17.0] B2[23.8] ‖ C1[11.2] C2[9.12] ‖	
	(1.377%) (1.250%) (0.557%) (0.514%)	
	0.904%	
IV	**Incorrect Inflection of Verb** *I spended last weekend in London*	B1 > [B2, C1, C2]
	‖ B1[108] ‖ B2[64.5] C1[46.5] C2[40.1] ‖	
	(0.498%) (0.296%) (0.228%) (0.192%)	
	0.397%	
RQ	**Replace Quantifier** *It all happened a lot of years ago*	[B1, B2, C1] > C2
	‖ B1[27.6] B2[33.8] C1[26.3] ‖ C2[15.1] ‖	
	(2.234%) (1.777%) (1.312%) (0.851%)	
	1.082%	
RY	**Replace Adverb** *He stayed at her intensively*	[B1, B2, C1] > C2
	‖ B1[159] B2[172] C1[160] ‖C2[117]	
	(2.598%) (3.076%) (2.957%) (1.888%)	
	2.243%	
AGN	**Noun Agreement Error** *One of my friend*	B2 > [B1 & C1] > C2
	‖ B2[207] ‖ B1[113] C1[121] ‖ C2[79.3]‖	
	(0.978%) (0.582%) (0.527%) (0.378%)	
	0.780% 0.453%	
CN	**Noun Countability Error** *I don't have any monies*	[B2, C1] > [B1, C2]
	‖ B2[52] C1[42] ‖ B1[22] C2[22] ‖	
	(0.249%) (0.183%) (0.114%) (0.105%)	
	0.149%	

the EPP research team in Cambridge (RCEAL and Computer Lab), using a subset of the automatically tagged and parsed CLC. We have converted their figures to percentages, showing the percentages for tokens of each category relative to the total set of words at each level. The range for verbs across the different levels is 20.4% to 24.0% (the latter being 1.176 times greater than the former), and for nouns it is 18.6% to 23.2% (the latter 1.184 times greater than the former). The rates of occurrence for these categories per 100,000 words at each level will be in accordance with these percentages.

We have also added to Table 2.1 percentage data for five other common categories, adjectives, adverbs, prepositions, conjunctions and quantifiers. The frequency of occurrence for each of these categories is much lower than for verbs and nouns. For adjectives the fluctuation range across levels is not considerable, 5.3% to 6.4% (a difference of 1.208), but for the other categories it is greater: 4.6% to 6.2% for adverbs (a difference of 1.348); 8.0% to 10.9% for prepositions (a difference of 1.363); 4.8% to 7.2% for conjunctions (a difference of 1.5); and 1.0% to 2.0% for quantifiers (a difference of 2).

The categories that expand their distribution from level to level are those that we would expect to see in the longer and more complex sentence types of the higher levels (recall the MLU data of the last section). Conjunctions (*because*, *since*, *although*, etc.) introduce subordinate clauses, i.e. sentences embedded within sentences, and involve added length and complexity. Prepositions introduce prepositional phrases (*in the garden*, *at the university*, *in an hour from now*, *on account of his stubbornness*, etc.) and these, along with adverbs and adverb phrases introduce the more syntactically optional elements of a clause, as opposed to the more basic and obligatory nouns and verbs. Hence these optional categories can be expected to account for some of the added complexity that is characteristic of the higher levels, and the same applies to quantifier words (*many*, *few*, etc.).

Ultimately we want to know, for each error type, how many errors there are relative to correct instances of the relevant type (verb inflection, noun agreement, etc.) at each level. Again there are subtle issues involved in identifying the relevant universe of comparison, but it is clear, at the very least, that errors need to be quantified separately for each category, given the data in Table 2.1. Error counts must be relativised to the total number of tokens of each category (e.g. verb or preposition) at each level. This has been done (with the help of EPP researchers at the Cambridge Computer Lab) and the results are given as error percentages in parentheses in Table 2.2, i.e. this is our second quantification method, below the figure per 100,000 words. So, 108 instances of verb inflection errors per 100,000 words at B1 corresponds to an error percentage rate of 0.498% relative to the total number of verbs at that level, 64.5 verb inflection errors per 100,000 words corresponds to 0.296% at B2, and so on.

We will say that an error distribution is criterial for a level L if and only if the frequency of errors at L is significantly different from its frequency at the level with the next higher error count. Hawkins and Buttery (2010) applied a quick and convenient test for significance which involves finding a difference of at least 29% compared to the level with the immediately higher error count (which is not always the immediately preceding proficiency level). This guarantees at least one standard deviation from the mean, a minimum requirement for statistical significance. Two or more levels can be grouped together for criteriality if the lower count is not significantly differentiated from the level with the immediately higher error count (i.e. by less than 29%). An error bandwidth is then calculated between each criterial level or levels by splitting the difference between criterial error distributions, as an approximate cut-off point for the different bandwidths. For example, if the lowest error percentage at the B levels ([B1, B2]) were 2.5% and the highest for the C levels

([C1, C2]) were 1.5%, then the bandwidth between them would be set at 2.0%: lower than that would be criterial for the C levels, higher would be criterial for the B levels. Error bandwidths are marked off by '‖'in Table 2.2 together with their defining error frequencies measured in percentages of errors relative to total words of each category.

2.3.1 Error codes and categories

Below we provide definitions and examples of the error types in Table 2.2. Note that these examples are not taken from corpus data, but are provided for illustrative purposes only.

(2) Error types in Table 2.2
Derivation of Determiner (DD)

Where a word RESEMBLES a valid word (i.e. looks feasible) but has been incorrectly derived, usually because it has been given an incorrect affix, it is a Derivation error – D.

> *Playing with yous classmates*   (your)
> *Shes name was Anna*   (her)

Missing Preposition (MT)

Where a sentence or construction requires a word (or words) for completeness and that word has been omitted, it is a missing error – M.

> *Make yourself home*   (at home)
> *I gave it John*   (to John)

Missing Quantifier (MQ)

See definition of M above.

> *I'll call in the next days*   (next few)

Incorrect Inflection of Verb (IV)

Where an attempt at inflecting a word results in a non-valid inflected form, it is an inflection error – I. The learner has made a false assumption about whether a verb is regular or irregular and inflected it accordingly. Most commonly, the error is caused by putting regular inflections on irregular verbs.

> *I was never teached how to handle money*   (taught)
> *I spended last weekend in London*   (spent)

Replace Quantifier (RQ)

Where a valid word in the language has been used AND it is the correct part of speech but not the correct word, it is a replace error – R. A good test for an R code is that the word is a valid word or word form in English. For example, in 'I had a very bored day', 'bored' is a true adjective in English but the wrong adjective for the context.

> *It all happened a lot of years ago*   (many years)
> *There were people of any age there*   (all ages)

Replace Adverb (RY)

See the definition of R above.

> *He lives one mile far*   (away)
> *He stared at her intensively*   (intensely)

Noun Agreement Error (AGN)

When the word is correct and the form of the word used is valid in the language BUT wrong in the context because it does not agree grammatically with its co-ordinates, it is an Agreement error – AG.

> *There are two good reason for this decision*   (reasons)
> *One of my friend*   (friends)

Noun Countability Error (CN)

When a noun can take only one form because it is uncountable but an invalid pluralised form has been used, it is a Countability of Noun error – CN.

> *Please give me some advices*   (advice)
> *I helped John with his homeworks*   (homework)
> *I don't have any monies*   (money)

The classification of learner errors is often difficult. There are many subtle issues of grammatical analysis that arise in this context. For example, what is the precise boundary between derivation and inflection errors, and between the different types of inflection codes? There are big issues in the field of morphology over the precise boundary between derivation and inflection (see Haspelmath 2002 for useful discussion), and this complicates the coders' task. These categories and codes also raise the further question of which form of English they are based on. In many regional varieties of English in Britain and in many versions of English around the world an error in one dialect may be a correct form in another.

Our position on this is as follows. We believe that the great majority of error codes that have been assigned in the CLC are successful in identifying forms or sequences of English that (all or) most grammarians of English would judge to be outside the conventions of standard British or American English, which is the kind of English that many learners around the world use as their target mode. In other words, we believe that while grammarians may take issue with some of the details of these error types, this would not substantially alter the classifications of the relevant words and phrases as errorful, which is the crucial point in this context. These codes also prove meaningful and useful to end users, namely course book writers and lexicographers who make use of the CLC. There is always room for improvement in this area, and as more descriptive linguists and grammarians join applied linguists and computational linguists in the EPP, greater dialogue and interaction can improve all aspects of the programme, but in the meantime we consider these error codes an extremely practical resource.

The more sociolinguistic question about whose form of English should be taught and used worldwide is currently the topic of much debate (cf. Jenkins 2009). We wish to make two brief comments here. First, there is the very practical question of which form of English learners want to learn. The fact is that regional dialects of English, with their distinctive phonologies and sometimes different syntaxes, are not in general the varieties that learners around the world want to learn, and so teachers and textbook writers do need to take account of their consumers and their needs. But secondly, and more theoretically, sociolinguistic discussions often neglect to point out that the number of properties that actually vary across the dialects and registers of English is relatively limited, compared with the tens of thousands that are shared. The vast majority of consonants, vowels, morphemes, parts of speech, co-occurrence restrictions, syntactic rules and meanings etc. that constitute English, and that make it mutually comprehensible among those who call themselves speakers of English, are common to all the variants! And it has to be this way, since otherwise there would be no mutual comprehension, and we would be dealing with quantitative differences of the kind we find between English and Dutch and Frisian and German, etc. It is precisely because English has changed in significant respects from these other (West) Germanic languages, which once shared a common ancestor, that we now have to learn them as foreign languages. The distance between the dialects and variants of English is not (yet) this great, and hence we can legitimately talk about these as being variants of the same language. In the context of our error coding what this means is that the great majority of errors classified as such for standard British or American English will also be errorful in the other varieties as well, precisely because the great majority of the properties and conventions of English, which guarantee mutual comprehension, are shared. Even between English and Dutch and German, etc., there are still many more shared than unshared properties.

In short, while there is always room for improvements in coding, we do not believe that details of grammatical analysis and topics of sociolinguistic debate involving the use of English worldwide undermine the validity or usefulness of this kind of error analysis.

2.3.2 Error patterns

One interesting finding that has emerged from preliminary analysis and quantification of our error data taken from an early subset of the CLC (we are grateful to the EPP research team, and in particular, to Paula Buttery and to Lu Gram for this quantification) is that there appear to be significantly lower error scores at the C levels than at the B levels. This can be seen in the illustrative data of Table 2.2 above. It is almost always the C levels that show the most improvements and the fewest errors, while the B levels have more errors. What varies is whether the B level error rates show a progressive improvement from B1 to B2, or no improvement, or an actual deterioration, before improving again at the C levels.

There are, as mentioned in Hawkins and Buttery (2010:15–17), 'progressive learning patterns' in Table 2.2 in which error frequencies decline at higher CEFR levels as learners improve their command of English. For DD (Derivation of Determiner) there is a significant error reduction at each higher level, i.e. B1 > B2 > C1 > C2. For MT (Missing Preposition) and MQ (Missing Quantifier) the B and C levels are each collapsed and the latter improves relative to the former, i.e. [B1, B2] > [C1, C2]. With IV (Incorrect Inflection of Verb) there is a significant improvement from B1 to B2, but not from this latter to the C levels, i.e. B1 > [B2, C1, C2]. For RQ (Replace Quantifier) and RY (Replace Adverb) C2 is significantly improved relative to C1, which is collapsed with the B levels, i.e. [B1, B2, C1] > C2. These are all cases of progressive improvements in learning, though with different transitional features from level to level, resulting in different combinations of adjacent levels being collapsed for the purposes of significance and criteriality. The general direction in error frequencies is always downwards, however, towards fewer errors at higher levels.

The second major learning pattern evident in Table 2.2 involves 'inverted Us', i.e. errors actually increase after B1 and then decline again by C2 (see also Hawkins and Buttery 2010:17–18). For AGN (Noun Agreement Error) the precise pattern is B2 > [B1, C1] > C2, with error scores starting low at B1, then increasing at B2, declining at C1 to more or less the level of B1, and then later improving at C2. For CN (Noun Countability Error) the pattern is [B2, C1] > [B1, C2], with error scores starting low at B1, then increasing at both B2 and C1, and then declining at C2 to a frequency almost identical to that of B1.

These inverted U error types in second language acquisition are reminiscent of similar patterns found in first language acquisition, for example when children use irregular morpho-syntactic forms correctly at first (*run* versus *ran*, *mouse* versus *mice*), then get them wrong by overgeneralising the productive forms (*run/runned, mouse/mouses*), and later learn the exceptions to productive paradigms and use them correctly again (see Andersen 1992 for a summary of relevant first language research, and Kellerman 1985 and McLaughlin 1990 for second language acquisition). The precise causes of the inverted Us will not always involve such cases of overgeneralisation and of scaling back the productivity of regular rules to take account of irregularities, however. Just as there are multiple interacting principles that explain the learning of positive linguistic features (see Chapter 5), so there are too for negative features or errors. It is an important research area for the future to try and better understand why some of the error types considered in this section show a progressive learning pattern, while others show the inverted U. More empirical research is also needed, and is currently being pursued within the EPP, on all the error types and their frequencies of occurrence within the full CLC.

2.4 Positive and negative usage features

Criterial features can also be defined in terms of frequencies of selection and usage for (correct) properties of the L2. Positive usage features involve frequencies of occurrence for a correct property of L2 that match the normal distribution for native speaking (i.e. L1) users of the L2. The positive usage features may be acquired at a certain level and will generally persist at higher levels and be criterial for the relevant levels, e.g. [C1, C2].

Negative usage features, by contrast, involve usage frequencies for a correct property of L2 that do not match the normal distribution for native speaking (i.e. L1) users of the L2. Their abnormal usage distribution will generally not persist through all the levels, as L2 usage gradually approximates to that of native speakers, and may be criterial for just one or more lower levels, e.g. [B2].

Consider some examples of these two types involving relative clauses formed on subject, direct object, and indirect object/oblique positions. The reader should consult Keenan and Comrie (1977) and Hawkins (1994, 2004) for discussion of the general significance of these relative clause types from a grammatical, typological and processing perspective, and Eckman (1984) and Hyltenstam (1984) for their significance in second language acquisition. These works are summarised in some detail in our literature review Chapter 4.5.1 below. In the present context we shall focus on their relevance for criterial features of a distributional nature. The different relative clause types are exemplified in Table 2.3 (see Chapter 4.5.1 for further details).

Table 2.3 Relative clause types

Subject Relatives	The student who/that wrote the paper
Direct Object Relatives	The student who(m)/that I taught
	The student O I taught
Indirect/Oblique Relatives	The student to whom I gave the book
	The student who/that I gave the book to
	The student O I gave the book to
	The student by/with/after/next to/. . .whom I [Verb]
	The student who/that I [Verb] by/with/after/next to/. . .
	The student O I [Verb] by/with/after/next to/. . .

Table 2.4 gives the frequencies of occurrence for relativisations on these different positions as a percentage of the total within each CEFR level (these data were collected by Paula Buttery and are reported in Hawkins and Buttery 2010).

Table 2.4 Usage of different types of relative clauses as percentage of total within each CEFR level (Hawkins and Buttery 2010:14)

	A2	B1	B2	C1	C2
Subject RCs	67.74%	61.05%	71.11%	70.35%	74.80%
Object RCs	30.65%	37.33%	26.09%	25.02%	20.90%
Ind/obl RCs	1.61%	1.62%	2.80%	4.63%	4.30%

Table 2.5 gives similar usage frequencies for various subcorpora of the British National Corpus (again collected by Paula Buttery and reported in Hawkins and Buttery op. cit.) and so provides a comparison of the learner data in Table 2.4 with data from native speakers of English. The BNC has also

Table 2.5 Usage of different types of relative clauses as percentage of total within subcorpora of the BNC (Hawkins and Buttery 2010:14)

	The Guardian	Mills and Boon	New Scientist	The Law Report
Subject RCs	77.20%	75.63%	80.67%	58.32%
Object RCs	17.02%	20.03%	12.44%	21.98%
Ind/obl RCs	5.76%	4.34%	6.89%	19.71%

been tagged and parsed using the RASP toolkit (see Chapter 3.3), making an exact comparison possible between the CLC and the BNC.

The distributional differences between relativisations on these different positions are striking and roughly in accordance with corpus frequency studies, and with psycholinguistic experimental findings, that have been reported elsewhere (cf. Hawkins 1994, 1999, 2004). It must be stressed, however, that these data are still preliminary at the time of going to press and that an adequate 'gold standard' (i.e. an accurate model for the mechanical parser based on human parsing) for correct recognition and parsing of all relative clauses in the data remains to be set.

With this caveat, notice some interesting usage features of Table 2.4 that can be regarded as criterial at different levels. The relative distribution of indirect object/oblique relative clauses (e.g. *the professor that I gave the book to*) to relativisations on the other clausal positions (subjects and direct objects) departs at CEFR Levels A2, B1 and B2 from that of native speakers of English: 1.61%, 1.62% and 2.80% respectively in Table 2.4 versus at least 4.34% in the BNC (cf. Table 2.5). The distribution at the C levels (4.63% and 4.30%) matches the lowest figures of the BNC subcorpora (4.34%). Hence we have here a positive usage distribution feature for relatives formed on indirect objects/obliques at [C1, C2], but a negative usage distribution feature for [A2, B1] and B2 respectively, each with their characteristic frequency bandwidths.

2.5 L1-specific criterial features

The criterial feature types and illustrations given so far are based on L2 data and on comparisons with native-speaking English data that hold regardless of the L1 of the learner. We can, in addition, define a set of 'L1-specific criterial features', consisting of the same possible types, that hold only for a particular L1 or set of L1s, e.g. for Spanish learners of English, or Chinese learners, or for speakers of languages without definite or indefinite articles learning English. Learners of English whose native language belongs to the Romance language family may acquire some positive property P of L2 English at an earlier level than Germanic speakers or than any other speakers, or speakers of Germanic languages may acquire P earlier, and so on.

More generally, speakers of first languages that share certain typological or genetic characteristics may exhibit distinct criterial features for a given level or levels. They may acquire positive properties of English sooner than other learners, by exploiting the similarities with their own L1 and transferring the relevant properties into L2 English (see the discussion of transfer in Chapter 4.3 and the Maximise Positive Transfer principle proposed in Chapter 5.1). They may exhibit characteristic error patterns, again possibly through influence of the L1 (see the Permit Negative Transfer principle of Chapter 5.5). The positive and negative usage features for correct properties of English L2 may also vary by first language and first language type. Native speakers of some L1s make less use of the Passive construction than native speakers of others, for example French and Russian speakers compared with English, and this may be reflected in the corresponding usage figures for L2 English (see Gilquin 2008 for illustrative discussion and Chapter 4.5.2 below).

A particularly revealing illustration of an L1-specific criterial feature comes from CLC data involving determiners in English, i.e. involving the definite and indefinite article, possessives (*my*, *your*, etc.), and demonstratives (*this*, *these*, etc.). Speakers of languages without definite and indefinite articles have error bandwidths for Missing Determiner ('MD') errors in L2 English that are significantly higher, for all levels, than those for speakers of languages that have articles. Typical errors here are *I spoke to President* instead of *I spoke to the President*, and *I have car* instead of *I have a car*.

Table 2.6 shows Missing Determiner error rates for *the* and *a* at proficiency Levels A2–C2 for French, German and Spanish as first languages (Hawkins and Buttery 2009, 2010). All three languages have an article system not unlike that of English. The figures indicate the percentage of errors with respect to the total number of correct uses. For instance a figure of 10.0% indicates that a determiner was omitted 1 in every 10 times that it should have appeared.

Table 2.6 Missing Determiner error rates for L1s with articles (Hawkins and Buttery 2009:168, 2010:19)

Missing *'the'*				
A2	B1	B2	C1	C2
French 4.76	4.67	5.01	3.11	2.13
German 0.00	2.56	4.11	3.11	1.60
Spanish 3.37	3.62	4.76	3.22	2.21

Missing *'a'*				
A2	B1	B2	C1	C2
French 6.60	4.79	6.56	4.76	3.41
German 0.89	2.90	3.83	3.62	2.02
Spanish 4.52	4.28	7.91	5.16	3.58

We see generally low error rates for the languages of Table 2.6, without significant deviation between levels.

Table 2.7 shows Missing Determiner error rates for *the* and *a* at all levels for Turkish, Japanese, Korean, Russian and Chinese as first languages (Hawkins and Buttery 2009, 2010). These languages do not have an article system. There is generally a linear improvement, i.e. a decline in error rates across the levels with increasing proficiency (shown from left to right). I.e. we see a B1 > B2 > C1 > C2 pattern that makes the relevant bandwidths criterial for these

Table 2.7 Missing Determiner error rates for L1s without articles (Hawkins and Buttery 2009:169, 2010:19)

	A2	B1	B2	C1	C2
Missing _'the'_					
Turkish	22.06	20.75	21.32	14.44	7.56
Japanese	27.66	25.91	18.72	13.80	9.32
Korean	22.58	23.83	18.13	17.48	10.38
Russian	14.63	22.73	18.45	14.62	9.57
Chinese	12.41	9.15	9.62	12.91	4.78
Missing _'a'_					
Turkish	24.29	27.63	32.48	23.89	11.86
Japanese	35.09	34.80	24.26	27.41	15.56
Korean	35.29	42.33	30.65	32.56	22.23
Russian	21.71	30.17	26.37	20.82	12.69
Chinese	4.09	9.20	20.69	26.78	9.79

L1s at the respective levels. Chinese shows an interesting inverted U-shaped progression, especially in the case of missing _a_, with significant improvement only at C2.

2.6 The 10-to-1 rule

It regularly happens, in the course of our searches for constructions and lexical items in the CLC, that the structure or item in question is completely unattested at one level, say A2, and then appears for the first time at the next, B1. Clearly this structure or item is not criterial for A2 in these cases. But when structures or items do appear for the first time at a certain level they often do so in a very tentative way, with just a small number of instances, involving the most frequent exemplars (or for lexical items, with the most common and basic meanings). Whether they should be considered criterial for B1 in such cases, especially if B2 shows many more instances and greater productivity with less frequent exemplars and less basic meanings for lexical items, raises a methodological issue for which we propose the following practical solution. If the ratio between the number of examples is 10 to 1 in favour of the higher level, we place the structure as criterial at the higher level (in this case B2). If the ratio is less than 10 to 1, then the structure is placed at the lower level (in this case B1) for the purpose of criteriality. This is captured in (3):

(3) 10-to-1 rule

At two adjacent levels, if the quantity of occurrences for a property P at one level exceeds that at the other by 10 to 1, relative to comparable word totals, then the level with the higher total wins (i.e. this level is regarded as the criterial one). For any lesser ratio, the level with the lower quantity wins.

The rationale behind this is not so much one of principle as of practice. We need a criterion that we can apply throughout the book in a consistent way so that we can capture the intuition that a certain structure has not really been mastered at a certain level, and is not really characteristic of it, in the event that its occurrence is very limited compared to the level(s) at which everyone would agree that it is completely productive. One of the reasons for what is, in effect, a practical rather than a theoretically grounded procedure here is that we used both the unparsed and the parsed version of the CLC for many positive feature searches and were not able to perform the same statistical analysis for the positive as for the negative criterial features. The statistical analysis for negative criterial features was performed on a smaller portion of the CLC, which was tagged and parsed and available to us at the time of these searches (about 5 million words). Ultimately, we will be able to provide a full and more precise statistical analysis of both positive and negative criterial feature distributions in the next phase of EPP research when we will be able to access a greater amount of data both in the CLC (which is continually growing) and in the new Cambridge English Profile Corpus as this becomes available.

For example, we found only a single instance of the Subject-to-Object Raising verb *known* in the Passive at B1 and 12 examples at B2 (in structures like *Smoking is known to cause cancer*). By the 10-to-1 rule Subject-to-Object Raising with *known* is placed as a criterial feature at B2, not B1 (see Chapter 7.2.3). Similarly, Subject-to-Object Raising plus Passive with *felt* was found once at B2 and 11 times at C1 and was consequently placed at C1. Subject-to-Subject Raising constructions with *seem* (in structures like *John seems to be a nice guy*) occurs 3 times at A2 and 46 times at B1. Thus this is a B1 construction by our rule even though its first occurrence is A2. On the other hand, some examples of poorly attested structures at lower levels did result in criteriality being assigned to these lower levels. For instance, Subject-to-Subject Raising with *certain* was exemplified twice at B2 and 17 times at C1. It therefore stays at B2 by the 10-to-1 rule.

In applying this rule we always took into account the differences in size between the subcorpora of the CLC (A2–C2), because for example the dataset in the A2 subcorpus available to us at the time of doing these searches was significantly smaller than the B1 dataset (1.8 million words for A2 vs. 5.4 million words for B1). The 10-to-1 rule would then apply to a comparison between actual occurrences at B1 and those at A2 augmented by the additional possible instances at A2 that would have occurred had the A2 subcorpus been of the same size. We also made sure that the examples for each observed item came from speakers of typologically different languages and not mainly from languages of the same group or family (such as Romance languages). In this case we increased the reliability of our predictions that the structure in question could be expected to be acquired regardless of specific L1s.

We have to emphasise that our research findings are preliminary at this stage and will need to be checked against the much larger database currently being collected. One reason why we assign criteriality to the level with lower scores in the event there are fewer than ten times more instances at the next higher level is because there is at least the possibility that a larger database will provide significantly more examples at the lower level, to the point where the linguist might judge that the construction or lexical item in question has indeed been genuinely learned at the lower level. Perhaps 10-to-1 is too large a difference and there may be examples in the expanded data that suggest the desirability of a different ratio. This is a topic for the future.

3 A general summary of the Cambridge Learner Corpus (CLC), its contents, error coding, tagging and parsing

3.1 Background

The research presented in this book is based on the Cambridge Learner Corpus (CLC), as explained in Chapter 1.2. This corpus was created and is owned jointly by Cambridge ESOL and Cambridge University Press. The CLC is a unique collection of written learner English, which contains data from over 130 typologically and genetically different first languages.

The CLC currently consists of approximately 45 million words of learner data taken from Cambridge ESOL examination scripts at CEFR Levels A1–C2. About half the corpus (52%) has been error-coded by corpus linguists at CUP. The CLC has also been tagged for parts of speech and parsed (i.e. syntactically analysed) using RASP (Robust Accurate Statistical Parser), an automatic parsing system incorporating both grammatical information and statistical patterns, see Section 3.3 for further details. (For the latest updates on the size and scope of the CLC, the reader is referred to www.cambridge. org/elt/corpus)

Each examination script in the CLC contains the candidate's response to the task(s) in the Writing section of the exam, resulting in an extended piece of text. Information about the writer and the exam is coded, such as gender, age, first language, date and venue of the examination, although all entries have been anonymised. The candidates' overall mark or grade and their marks on the other components (typically Reading, Listening and Speaking) are also included. The tasks to which the candidates responded are available in a searchable sub-corpus.

The CLC consists of Writing section responses from the following Cambridge ESOL examinations. First, there is its Main Suite of General English exams comprising, from CEFR level A2 to C2 respectively: the Key English Test (KET) (A2), the Preliminary English Test (PET) (B1), the First Certificate in English (FCE) (B2), the Certificate in Advanced English (CAE) (C1) and the Certificate of Proficiency in English (CPE) (C2). Second, there is the professional Business English Certificates (BEC) suite, specifically BEC Preliminary (B1), BEC Vantage (B2) and BEC Higher (C1). Third, there is the International English Language Testing System (IELTS), consisting of an Academic module for those wishing to study in English at undergraduate or postgraduate levels and for those seeking professional registration, and a General Training module for people wishing to train or study in English at below degree level and for those wishing to migrate to an English-speaking country.

Fourth, there are the International Legal English Certificate (ILEC) and the International Certificate in Financial English (ICFE). Cambridge ILEC, which assesses English language ability at Levels B2 and C1, was created to meet the needs of both employers and lawyers, and is also suitable for law students intending to follow courses which include a significant English language content. Cambridge ICFE, also set at Levels B2 and C1 can be used as proof of the ability in English necessary to work in an international finance context or to follow a course of accountancy or finance study at university level.

Finally in the CLC there are scripts from the Cambridge ESOL Certificates in ESOL Skills for Life exams, which assess the use of English in everyday life in Britain at five levels – Entry 1 (A1), Entry 2 (A2), Entry 3 (B1), Level 1 (B2) and Level 2 (C1), and scripts from the now superseded Certificates in English Language Skills (CELS, a suite of modular examinations at Levels B1 to C1).

The research results that we present in this book are based on searches and analyses of the Main Suite exam data. These exams are general in nature and are less likely to bias the content towards a particular thematic focus (e.g. related to a professional or academic topic). For A1 we used the Skills for Life Entry 1 data which had been made available for the EPP Wordlists research (e.g. Capel 2010). The Main Suite examination scripts account for approximately 62% of the CLC's total of 45 million words. These exams have been aligned with the Common European Framework of Reference (CEFR, see (1) in Chapter 1.1) from A2 to C2. Details of this alignment are available at the Cambridge ESOL website (www.CambridgeESOL.org/exams/exams-info/cefr.html). See in this connection Table 3.1 adapted from Saville (2009), and also Jones (2000, 2001, 2002) and Taylor and Jones (2006) for accounts of and comment on the empirical validation of the alignment.

Table 3.1 Alignment of the Cambridge ESOL examinations with the CEFR scale

CEFR level	Descriptive title	Main Suite
C2	Mastery	CPE
C1	Effective Operational Proficiency	CAE
B2	Vantage	FCE
B1	Threshold	PET
A2	Waystage	KET
A1	Breakthrough	

3.2 Error coding

The CLC's system of error codes has been developed and implemented by computational linguists at Cambridge University Press. It consists of some 76 codes each containing two parts: the general type of the error (e.g. omission, wrong word, word form error, etc.) and the part of speech of the required word. Examples of some of these error codes were given in (2) in Chapter 1.2 and are repeated here for convenience in (1) (see Chapter 2.3 for others). Note again that none of these examples are taken from corpus data, but are provided for illustrative purposes only.

(1) Sample Error Codes in the CLC

RN	**Replace Noun**	*Have a good travel* (journey)
RV	**Replace Verb**	*I existed last weekend in London* (spent)
MD	**Missing Determiner**	*I spoke to President* (the)
		I have car (a)
AGV	**Verb Agreement Error**	*The three birds is singing* (are)
IV	**Incorrect Verb Inflection**	*I spended last week in London* (spent)
FJ	**Wrong Adjective Form**	*The situation got worst* (worse)
UQ	**Unnecessary Quantifier**	*A little bit quite common* (quite common)
DY	**Derivation of Adverb**	*It happened fastly* (fast)

The codes are inserted according to the following convention:

<#??>wrong form|corrected form</#??>

For example, for a noun countability error, like *I need more informations* abbreviated as CN, the code would be inserted into the text as shown in (2):

(2) I need more <#CN>informations|information</#CN>

Using a combination of these codes together with meta-data about the candidate and simple string searches, error statistics can be collected for each exam level, language group, age, etc. In Chapter 2.5 we gave an illustration of how this could be done with respect to Missing Determiner (MD) errors: candidates were distinguished from one another based on their first language and based on their CEFR level of attainment. The result was a dramatically different set of error scores depending on the type of first language of the candidate, reflecting in this context whether the relevant language had definite and indefinite articles as in English. Similar individual and group characteristics can be distinguished using other demographic variables that have been entered into the data or that will be entered into the new corpus materials currently being collected; see Section 3.5 below.

3.3 The Robust Accurate Statistical Parser (RASP)

The CLC was originally searchable lexically, i.e. on the basis of individual words, and grammatically to the extent that a rule of English grammar was reflected in an error code. Within the EPP this search capability has been expanded and the CLC has been tagged for parts of speech and parsed using the Robust Accurate Statistical Parser (RASP) developed by Ted Briscoe and John Carroll of the Cambridge Computer Laboratory and the University of Sussex respectively, see Briscoe, Carroll and Watson (2006) accessible at: http://acl.ldc.upenn.edu/P/P06/P06-4020.pdf. RASP is an automatic parsing system incorporating both grammatical information and statistical patterns. It applies to raw text (i.e. unanalysed, uncoded samples of everyday written language) and assigns information to it about the parts of speech for individual words, their phrasal grouping (i.e. the most likely 'parse tree'), and grammatical relations that hold between them.

Some details of the operation of RASP are summarised very briefly in this section. These details and most of the examples in the following subsections are taken from Hawkins and Buttery (2009, 2010) and from Buttery (2009). The application of RASP to the CLC was implemented by members of the EPP research team in Cambridge, in particular Briscoe, Buttery and Gram. Applying the RASP toolkit to the CLC makes it possible to conduct more extensive grammatical as well as lexical analyses with a high level of accuracy.

When the RASP system is run on raw text, such as the written sentences of the CLC, it first marks sentence boundaries and tidies up any punctuation errors (so-called 'tokenisation'). The text is then tagged with one of 150 part-of-speech and punctuation labels, on a probabilistic basis. It is 'lemmatised', i.e. analysed morphologically, to produce dictionary citation forms (or lemmas) plus any inflectional affixes. A sentence like *That is a sentence structure* would be represented as (3) initially:

(3) That_DD1 be+s_VBZ a_AT1 sentence_NN1 structure_NN1 ._.

When words are numbered it would look like (4):

(4) That:1_DD1 be+s:2_VBZ a:3_AT1 sentence:4_NN1 structure:5_NN1 .:6_.

3.3.1 Parsing using RASP

Parse trees are constructed from the sequence of tags using a set of around 700 probabilistic Context Free Grammar production rules (of the general form S → VP NP). Features associated with the parse are passed up the tree during construction. A simplified parse for (3) is shown in (5):

(5) (TOP
        (S (DD1 That:1)
          (VP (VBZ be+s:2)
              (NP (AT1 a:3) (NN1 sentence:4) (NN2 structure:5))))
      (. .:6))

which corresponds to the tree diagram in (6):

(6)   T
            top
           / \
         S   .
     sentence   .
       / \
    DD1   VP
    That verb phrase
          /   \
        VBZ   NP
        be+s   noun phrase
              / | \
            AT1 NN1   NN2
             a sentence structure

All the possible parses for a sentence constitute what is called a **parse forest** and RASP ranks these according to the probabilities that are associated with each of the production rules used to derive the tree. The parsing algorithm builds all the parses in the parse forest simultaneously, proceeding from left to right across the tag sequence. It activates all possible rules that are consistent with the partial parses already built and with the next tag in the sequence. This has the consequence that rules can be activated during processing that will not ultimately be used in any valid parse. The parse forest has a dynamic size, therefore, that changes as the parsing algorithm proceeds from one tag to the next. The probabilities were originally calculated by counting rule usage frequencies in a manually annotated corpus.

When a sentence is ambiguous there will be more than one valid parse tree. A sentence like *She saw the boys with binoculars* is ambiguous with respect to where the prepositional phrase *with binoculars* is attached. It can be attached to the noun phrase immediately dominating *binoculars* (structurally [*She* vp[*saw* np[*the boys with binoculars*]]], i.e. the boys that she saw were the boys with binoculars), or to the verb phrase immediately dominating *saw* (structurally [*She* vp[*saw* np[*the boys*] [with binoculars]]], i.e. the manner of her seeing the boys was with binoculars). This ambiguity will result in two possible parses, and the selection between them would ultimately need to be made by accessing information beyond the sentence, which RASP is not currently equipped to do. RASP does not yet model all human parsing capabilities, despite its power and general overall accuracy (see Section 3.4 below), and as a result our searches returned a certain amount of 'noise', i.e. inaccurate or irrelevant data in response to the search query. In order to control for and filter this noise we regularly subjected RASP's searches to a second manual inspection, removing sentences that were not correct instances of the structure we were looking for at the different CEFR levels.

3.3.2 Grammatical relations in RASP

The term 'grammatical relations' is used in a very general sense in RASP to refer to largely theory-neutral binary relations between lexical items. These relations include the kinds of argument structure notions exemplified by subjecthood and objecthood in theories of grammatical relations (see Farrell 2005 for a useful summary) but they also subsume a wide variety of other grammatical combinations and dependencies as well. They are expressed in the general format: (|relation-type| |head| |dependant|).

For example, RASP would annotate sentence (7) with the grammatical relations shown in (8):

(7)   He was buying a house.

(8)   (|subject| |buying| |He| _)

     (|auxiliary| |buying| |was|)

     (|direct-object| |buying| |house|)

     (|determiner| |house| |a|)

Once this annotation has been provided, many detailed grammatical searches can be conducted efficiently, as explained in Hawkins and Buttery (2009, 2010). Building on the example above, imagine we wished to extract all the direct objects of *buying* from the CLC. In the absence of a RASP-type capability we would have to do a string search for the lexical item *buying* and then manually check all the returned concordances for direct objects. This is cumbersome, and it can also lead to direct objects being missed when they lie outside the concordance window (e.g. in a sentence where the direct object is displaced such as *The man was buying, or perhaps we should rather say that he was attempting to acquire, a house*). By collating over grammatical relations, a frequency list can be constructed, as shown for instance in (9):

(9)   Grammatical relation → frequency count

     (|direct-object| |buying| |house|) → x

(|direct-object| |buying| |car|) → y

. . . .

(|direct-object| |buying| |time) → z

With respect to the EP analysis for this specific example, we should expect to find the more frequent literal uses of *buying* to be present at all proficiency levels whereas the more extended and abstract usage (*buying time*) would occur primarily at the higher levels, see Chapter 8.1.

These grammatical relations also make it possible to identify particular grammatical constructions, for example the verb co-occurrence frames discussed in Chapter 5.2. To see how this is done consider the following problem: how do we find all ditransitive verbs in the corpus? From experience we know that the ditransitive verb *give* can occur in the structures shown in (10):

(10)　Simon gave the book to her.

　　　Toby gave the flowers to his girlfriend.

Using these forms as a template we could search in a suitably annotated corpus for the general pattern given in (11):

(11)　SUBJECT gave DIRECTOBJECT to INDIRECTOBJECT

However, this search would fail to return sentences with the alternative ditransitive pattern in English (NP-V-NP-NP) such as *Mary gave Jim the job*. The solution is to search within the grammatical relations annotation for the underspecified pattern that expresses the ditransitive verb frame, as illustrated in (12):

(12)　IF the grammatical relations for a sentence match:

　　　(|subject| ?x ?a _)

　　　(|direct-object| ?x ?b)

　　　(|indirect-object| ?x ?c)

　　　where ?x, ?a, ?b, ?c are variables

　　　AND ?x is a verb

　　　THEN the verb frame for ?x is DITRANSITIVE

3.4 The use of the CLC for research in this book

In this book we have made use of the total set of scripts from the Main Suite of examinations (see Section 3.1 above), both the parsed and unparsed portions, in order to provide relevant data for our research. The parsed version gave us general information about the relative quantities of particular items and structures across the levels. Some of our RASP-based searches, especially those conducted early on in the project, were based on just 5.5 million words of parsed and error-corrected scripts, since not all of the corpus had been parsed and made available to us at the time. This was the case, for example, with the verb co-occurrence frames analysed by Williams (2007). RASP operates more successfully on error-corrected than on uncorrected data. We accordingly double-checked a number of her frames subsequently on the whole unparsed CLC (i.e. the 22.5 million words of the Main Suite data), using lexical cues as well as grammatical search instructions, as illustrated below. Williams recorded only the first instances of particular constructions, whereas we found it necessary in many instances to check for the criteriality of a construction at a particular level by examining a representative set of lexical verbs that 'license' the construction in question. This was supported empirically by the fact that one and the same grammatical construction (for example, a particular verb co-occurrence frame as discussed in Chapter 5.2, using Williams 2007) can occur with very different frequencies for different lexical verbs. It is important to qualify, and quantify, the claim that a particular construction is criterial for a particular level, namely, by conducting both grammatical and lexical searches at the same time (see Chapter 7.2 for a detailed illustration of this with respect to the 'raising' structures of English). We need to know when a particular construction first appears in the CLC (as in Williams' 2007 study), but we also need to know when it becomes really productive, by examining a representative set of lexical verbs, and we need to know which verbs appear in it and when.

An important general point about RASP is that, like any automatic parser, it is not 100% accurate (see Sections 3.3.1 and 3.5 below). This makes it desirable to check the automatic search results manually whenever possible. For example, some verb co-occurrence frames are very similar to one another in their surface structures and RASP is not always able to make the required discriminations, e.g. between minimal pairs like *the wind blew down the street* vs. *the wind blew down the tree*. The first involves the intransitive verb *blow* followed by the prepositional phrase *down the street* containing the preposition *down*, i.e. V-PP. The second consists of a transitive verb plus particle combination (i.e. a phrasal verb) with a direct object *the tree*, i.e. [V-Part]-NP. Notice, as a diagnostic test for this distinction, that one can reorder the particle to produce *the wind blew the tree down*, but not the preposition (i.e. **the wind blew the street down* is ungrammatical in the reading in which *down* is a preposition). This and other subtle grammatical distinctions that elude the automatic RASP parser are responsible for some of its inaccuracies, in addition to some of the ambiguity resolutions referred to in Section 3.3 above. But despite these, RASP is an extremely powerful and useful tool that allows us to identify distinctive and defining trends in the use of verb co-occurrence frames and in other grammatical particulars pertaining to individual levels, as we demonstrate throughout this book, even though there is often 'noise' in the data, which we have tried to control for as much as possible in the data chapters of this book.

In all of our searches for criterial features we analysed only those scripts that were assigned grades that reflect higher ability A, B and C, in order to make sure that they were indicative of success at the relevant proficiency levels. Only those scripts graded A–C were selected in the manual subcorpus as well, as described in Chapter 2.2, almost all of them with the middle range test grade of B, in order to capture the average learner's capacity at each level. The manual corpus was used for mean length of utterance counts and as a basis for hypothesising criterial features for further testing.

With respect to the actual extraction of data from the CLC, this was accomplished using iLexIR Search, a corpus search tool developed by Gram and Buttery (2008) specifically for the EPP. Search terms were designed for each target construction, using a combination of the search options available in iLexIR as described in Section 3.3. The search options included both matching by raw string and matching the information derived from RASP. For example, genitive relative clauses (see Chapter 7.1.13) could be retrieved simply by a lexical search for *whose*. Adverbial subordinate clauses with -*ing* verbs, on the other hand (see Chapter 7.1.18), were extracted whenever the head of a grammatical relation was a verb and its dependent was an -*ing* form. Inevitably, all searches returned a certain amount of 'noise' and irrelevant items were then filtered using both automatic and manual means.

Some important methodological points need to be mentioned in this context. For example, with respect to error correction it needs to be noted that the codes were assigned by adjusting verb co-occurrence frames to the actual verb selected rather than by altering the verb to match the frame. So *he said me that he enjoyed it* would be corrected to *he said to me that he enjoyed it* rather than to *he told me that he enjoyed it* (Williams 2007:4). This fact has an impact on the conclusions that can be drawn from the results in some parts of the research presented here. For instance, the analysis of subcategorisation frames in Chapter 5.2 (which follows Williams 2007) is based on the frames that learners were trying to produce, not necessarily on those they produced with 100% accuracy. So the analysis cannot measure how many of these frames were actually there in the original and how many involved corrections of some kind. This underscores once again the need for double-checking wherever possible.

When it comes to criterial features of a semantic nature, we have focused on the meanings of verbs and verb-particle constructions. In the search for semantic criterial features we were greatly aided by the English Profile Wordlists (EPW) (Capel 2010). EPW is an extensive searchable list of words and phrases in English that are considered to be within the CEFR levels; a preview version is available via the EP website (www.englishprofile.org). For each level (A1–C2) we selected 10 verbs that appeared for the first time at that level and we then traced their meanings and uses in different contexts through the subsequent levels, see Chapter 8. In this way we were able to establish when and how learners acquire different verbs. It is normally a verb's basic physical sense that appears first (e.g. *walk* in the sense of typical bipedal movement), which then develops into a more extended 'accompany' sense as in *walk somebody home*. We also checked for syntactic developments that appear in the process, as when intransitive *walk* becomes transitive *walk*. We also included information about typical constructions or collocations in which the verbs start to appear as learning progresses. For example, while at A2 somebody *gives information* or *gives a ring*, at B2 he *gives (somebody) a chance* and at C2 he *gives (somebody) a piece of his mind* (cf. also Capel 2010:5–6 for an illustration of the progressive learning of the different word senses across A1–B2).

For the levels A1–B2 we made use of the Wordlists data and their word and meaning assignments to particular levels, but for the new lexical items and meanings at C1 and C2 we searched only in the CLC since at the time of our searches Wordlists for the C levels were not yet developed. For A2–B2 words and meanings we also checked all the Wordlists data against the CLC and filtered out any data that appeared to come from candidates of lower ability. The Wordlists include learner examples produced by any candidates who have taken a particular exam. Decisions on CEFR levels in the Wordlists are based not only on the written performance in the CLC but also on a range of other sources, including native speaker frequency of usage and classroom material. Our reason for excluding lower ability candidates is a principled one, as we pointed out in Chapter 1.2. We are focusing in this book on what passing candidates get right, so that learners can ultimately benefit from knowing what successful candidates have succeeded in learning at each level. This filtering of pass vs. fail means that occasionally our level assignment may differ from that given in the Wordlists. It is also due to the fact that we are focusing solely on attested written production, whereas the Wordlists data take into account what is generally known at a given level regardless of how well a particular candidate may have performed and been graded in a particular exam.

Finally, let us comment on the attested data that we have taken from the CLC in this book in order to exemplify our criterial features. We have tried to give as many actually occurring examples as possible. The data used as exemplification in Chapter 1.3, in the four detailed sections of Chapter 7, and in the lexical progression sections of Chapter 8, are systematically taken from the CLC, as are numerous other examples throughout the book that are clearly identified as such. More generally, we reproduce illustrative examples from van Ek and Trim's Threshold series (Chapter 6) and from the work of Briscoe and colleagues on subcategorisation frames (Chapter 5.2) in their original form as cited by these authors. In all these cases the selected examples, whether observed or made up, have contributed significantly to clarifying grammatical structures and error types that the authors define and they have shaped the searches and the resulting classification and quantification that we and others have conducted. It is therefore incumbent upon us, as users of their analyses, to be consistent with all our sources and to reproduce accurately what they are claiming, including their examples. At the same time we do give extensive attested data from the CLC to support the criterial features we propose here, as mentioned above.

3.5 The need for more data

The CLC is currently the largest learner corpus available, for English or any other language, as far as we are aware. A number of other learner corpora have been developed in different centres (we are grateful to the EPP research team at Cambridge ESOL for providing information on these). For example, the Longman Learner Corpus (LLC), with its 10 million words of learner English, is significantly smaller than the CLC. The Longman data come from student essays, including some Cambridge exam scripts. The Hong Kong University of Science and Technology has a 25 million word corpus of English L2 but there is no website giving more detailed information. The International Corpus of English developed at the University of Louvain currently has 3.7 million words from 16 different L1s. The aim of this corpus was to collect data from advanced learners (university graduates). However, their language production has not been independently assessed for level of proficiency, which reduces its usefulness. There are other smaller corpora, such as the Uppsala Student English (USE) corpus of approximately 1 million words, and also, at the University of Lodz, the Polish Learner English Corpus (PELCRA), the Chinese Learner English Corpus (CLEC) (http://langbank. engl.polyu.edu.hk/corpus/clec.html) at 1 million words and the Japanese as a Foreign Language Learner corpus (http://jefll.corpuscobo.net/) at 700,000 words. The CLC is the largest and most comprehensive learner corpus, with its CEFR-based classification according to proficiency level and with the greatest number of L1s (see Salamoura and Saville (2010:107–109) for a more detailed discussion of these advantages). Moreover the size of the CLC (currently around 45 million) is constantly growing as new scripts are added to it.

Despite these advantages the CLC, like all corpora, has some limitations. For instance, as it contains only written data, the claims we can make are restricted to written language (see McCarthy 2010 for EPP developments in the study of spoken production). It is limited in the type of data that it contains, namely written answers to exam questions, and in its size, which is still not as large as we need it to be, especially at the lower levels. Additional written samples, and more varied types of written data going beyond answers to exam questions, are also part of the new data collection initiative.

We must also address the issue of potential circularity in this context, namely that exam candidates are only reproducing the input they receive from their textbooks which are written according to the requirements for each exam level. We do not believe that there is such circularity. First, it cannot simply be that learners are imitating the words and constructions they are explicitly taught in their textbooks, because there are many different textbooks and teaching methods around the world. And secondly learners learn more than they are explicitly taught, from their reading materials, papers, magazines, movies, TV, conversations, and so on.

The research presented in this book is intended as an interim study and as an exemplification of a research method based on a particular learner corpus, the CLC. Our goal is to provide as accurate a description as possible of the corpus as it now is, and as accurate a set of criterial features as we can derive from it at the time of writing (see Chapter 2). We are well aware that new data may remove some of our proposed features as criterial, will add many new ones, and may reassign features to other levels. We have tried to anticipate some of these additions to the corpus by taking seriously even small numbers of relevant examples at lower levels and by not ignoring them in the discussion of criteriality, on the assumption that there is a good probability that more examples will appear later if there are some there now (see the 10-to-1 rule in Chapter 2.6). New data may undoubtedly lead to new and revised criterial features in these different ways, therefore. But despite possible revisions in the assignment of particular criterial features to particular levels, we believe that the **relative** sequencing of the kinds of criterial patterns we are documenting throughout this book will not be significantly affected. In other words, we expect still to see more complex structures and meanings acquired later than simpler ones, less frequent lexical items and constructions later than simpler ones, and so on, as discussed in the principles of Chapter 5 which are supported by the current data in the CLC as well as by extensive findings elsewhere in the research literature (see Chapter 4). We would be surprised if substantial revisions needed to be made, based on new data, to the general progression in positive criterial features, illustrated for example in Chapters 7 and 8, although some differences in criterial feature placement may indeed need to be made in subsequent analysis.

Many of the characteristics of the current CLC have been documented in Williams (2006) and (2007). We reproduce some of her points in what follows.

One important feature of the CLC that needs to be stressed is that the scripts come from a variety of registers and cover many different topics, since the examination questions at different levels vary considerably in the topics that are covered and in the types of texts they elicit. It has been shown (e.g. by Roland and Jurafsky 1998 and Roland, Jurafsky, Menn, Gahl, Elder and Riddoch 2000) that subcategorisation preferences can be skewed to certain topics if only a limited number of topics are considered, which can bias learner data towards certain verb co-occurrence frames. Exam questions or task types can impact the frequencies of syntactic and even morpho-syntactic features, therefore, resulting in a higher proportion of these structures than one finds in a corpus of native speaker English, such as the BNC. Exam questions and task types will also lead to the activation of specific semantic fields (see Lehrer and Kittay 1992) and hence to higher frequencies for certain lexical items (e.g. in the domain of travel, cooking, etc.) and not others (e.g. politics, fashion, etc.). While so-called task effects are present in many data sets, the CLC is actually large enough to minimise such interference since the exam data it consists of were taken in different years and in different locations with enough variety in the topics covered at each level. Importantly, even if there is more activation of some semantic fields than others, this should be reflected primarily in the lexicon rather than in the grammar, on which this study focuses. For these reasons we believe that our results will prove to be only minimally impacted by task effects that smaller data sets or experimental paradigms of data elicitation need to control for explicitly.

The current CLC is not balanced in terms of the relative sizes of the levels. Some levels have twice as many scripts in the CLC as others, while some of the individual examination types contain up to 20 times more words than others. The new dataset being collected is designed to correct or minimise these kinds of imbalances. The proportion of data from different L1s is also currently uneven. The number of words available for languages other than the top 20 is small, sometimes just tens of thousands. The words that can be accessed in each cell (e.g. A2 scripts by Turkish L1 speakers) are then too small for meaningful comparison. Such data shortages complicate our attempts to build grammar profiles for each level and to carry out comparisons between levels. Similarly, there is an unbalanced mix of discourse genres and topics, which is due to the fact that that the task types are largely aligned to the Can Dos in the CEFR and so represent the types of writing that are thought to be relevant and do-able at a given level. At lower levels (A1–B1) topics tend to be transactional and descriptive, focusing on the candidate's everyday life, while at the higher levels (B2–C2) candidates give their opinions on a wide range of topics. Such discrepancies can weaken comparisons of learner grammars between levels, since there is always the question of whether any differences between levels are partially attributable to differences in chosen discourse genres or topics. This observation should inspire further research into task assignment, namely into trying to assign topics across all levels that will enable us to better contrast ability across levels.

Despite these points, the CLC is still the biggest learner corpus we have, and hence it is useful to give a description of its properties at the present time as a basis for more targeted data collection in the future. With new data we can attempt to tease apart what is accidentally absent from the corpus versus absent for principled reasons (i.e. learners have not yet learned the relevant constructions and lexical items), and we can more directly test the learners' command of grammatical and lexical items required for different semantic fields. But all this presupposes a good description of the CLC as it now is, and providing one in terms of criterial features for the different levels is what this book is all about.

The goal of the new data collection project currently underway within the EPP, the Cambridge English Profile Corpus (www.englishprofile. org), is to enrich and complement the existing CLC. New corpus data are being collected from learners of English in classroom settings around the world, together with demographic information and information about the educational and sociocultural settings in which learning takes place. As Alexopoulou (2008:16) points out:

> An important feature of this new corpus is that it will consist of language samples produced by learners *on demand* and *for* the corpus. This provides us with a unique opportunity to collect materials exhibiting a wide range of linguistic features, and, therefore, construct a learner corpus balanced for factors that are normally beyond the control of researchers compiling learner corpora from materials produced for another purpose (e.g. exam, placement test, university essay etc.). This unique opportunity presents, at the same time, a challenge for the design. For most native corpora a wide and diverse sample of existing work (from newspapers and novels to courtroom proceedings) normally guarantees the whole spectrum of linguistic features and vocabulary. For the new learner corpus, however, the burden of eliciting a wide range of linguistic features and vocabulary falls on the design.

With respect to the candidates taking the Cambridge exams sampled in the CLC, we currently know relatively little about the kind of exposure to English that they have had. Nor do we know exactly which textbook or other materials they have used in order to prepare for the exam. Certain types of demographic data are currently coded (e.g. first language, age, sex, years of studying English) but the new data will include additional types of information about candidates (such as type of tuition, purpose of learning English). We also need to bear in mind that exam candidates are writing in such a way as to maximise their chances of passing and of gaining a high mark. As a result they may avoid structures that they find difficult and produce lower error rates than one might expect given their linguistic background (recall Schachter's 1974 discussion of the need to take account of avoidance strategies in the discussion of errors). And of course these CLC data are written texts which the candidate has had the opportunity to edit and correct, which impacts its relevance to discussions of spontaneous online production. The new corpus compilation will also include spoken data and a new subproject is under discussion at the time of writing that will identify criterial features of the CEFR levels in speech as well as writing.

It is our belief that the new data currently being collected will go a long way to remedying some of the limitations that we discuss in this chapter.

Despite these limitations, the current CLC is a unique resource that is large enough for us to propose a set of criterial features for the CEFR levels that can be deemed reasonable and reliable first approximations to the learning stages of L2 English until proven otherwise by subsequent data. It is in this spirit that the patterns and principles of this book are being offered.

4 Some relevant Second Language Acquisition (SLA) and general linguistic research for criterial feature identification

4.1 Background

Second language acquisition (SLA) has been a vibrant research area for several decades now and it has succeeded in identifying numerous factors that determine how, and to what extent, a second language is mastered. The literature is large, too large in fact for a thorough summary within the context of the present book, given our goals as summarised in Chapter 1. There are some major findings in this literature that can help us in our quest for criterial features and in the process provide reference level descriptions for the CEFR levels as described in Chapter 1.3. At the same time there are many unresolved issues in SLA to whose resolution our corpus data can potentially contribute. Data used in EPP research can contribute directly to the resolution of certain theoretical issues in this way. We shall accordingly focus on some relevant findings and issues of a theoretical nature in this chapter, as a background to the principles of learning and processing that we propose in the next chapter. It must be stressed, here and elsewhere in this book, that we are not striving for completeness or complet*ed*ness: our goal is to define a research programme whereby practitioners and theoreticians can begin to work together to discover useful criterial features for the learning, teaching and testing of English at successive stages, and can contribute to theoretical issues in learning and processing on the basis of this data. The aim, after all, is a profile of learner English validated by a good understanding of the relevant theories and supported by well analysed empirical data.

Ellis (2003) defines two major frameworks and approaches to SLA: cognitive and linguistic. Cognitive approaches to second language acquisition (and language acquisition in general) see linguistic knowledge and strategies responsible for its development as 'general in nature, related to and involved in other kinds of learning' (ibid.:347). Linguistic approaches, on the other hand, treat linguistic knowledge as 'unique and separate from other knowledge systems'. The mechanisms that underlie the acquisition process are said to be '(in part at least) specifically linguistic in nature' (ibid.). The predominant linguistic theory on which Ellis focuses is Chomsky's Universal

Grammar, which has inspired much work on second language acquisition. In this chapter we shall briefly summarise and assess some basic tenets of these two approaches and then discuss selected studies of relevance to our goals.

4.2 Universal Grammar vs. cognitive theories

Universal Grammar (UG) is hypothesised to be an innate language faculty that guides the learning of language and limits the extent to which languages can vary, i.e. it defines the notion 'possible human language' (Chomsky 1965, Hoekstra and Kooij 1988). UG theorists reason that the task of learning is greatly reduced if one is equipped with such an innate mechanism (Gass and Selinker 2008:161). In particular, access to UG solves the 'negative evidence problem' (see Bowerman 1988 for a summary of key issues and the relevant literature). Theoretically there are two kinds of evidence available to learners as they make hypotheses about correct and incorrect forms of their language: positive and negative. Positive evidence comes from the speech that learners actually hear or read, negative comes from any information given to learners to the effect that an utterance is deviant with regard to the norms of the language (Gass and Selinker op. cit.:163). The child language literature suggests that negative evidence is, in fact, not that frequent and is often ignored and cannot be a necessary condition for acquisition. But positive evidence alone, it is argued, is not sufficient for the learner to be able to construct a grammar that distinguishes between grammatical and ungrammatical sentences, enabling him or her to make judgments about sentences that have not yet been encountered. There must therefore be an innate, *a priori* constraint on grammar formation, i.e. UG. The main issue that SLA theorists are grappling with is the level of access to UG that adult second language learners have. This level varies in different theories (cf. Bley-Vroman 1989, White 1989). The disagreements come from the fact that success in L2 acquisition varies enormously, unlike L1 acquisition, and that L2 competence is qualitatively different from L1 competence. Bley-Vroman (1989) and Schachter (1988) propose a 'Fundamental Difference Hypothesis' regarding child acquisition and adult second language acquisition, while those arguing in favor of access to UG defend the opposing view, namely that the innate language faculty performs the same role in second language learners as it does in child first language learners (cf. Gass and Selinker 2008:164). For a concise table summarising the similarities and differences between 1st and 2nd language acquisition, the reader is referred to Ellis (2003:107).

One difference between the two, pointed out by Schachter (1988), is that children can learn any language presented to them with equal ease, whereas adults cannot. For Spanish speakers, for example, it is much easier to learn Italian than Chinese. Gass and Selinker (op. cit.:165) conclude that UG is accessed through the L1 and then informs the acquisition of the L2. The other camp, namely the direct access to UG camp (e.g. White 2003), argues that UG is not accessed through the L1, and that UG constrains L2 learners' interlanguage grammars directly. The respective roles attributed to the L1 and to UG as possible starting points for L2 acquisition vary substantially (cf. e.g. Eubank 1996, Schwartz and Sprouse 1996a, 1996b, 2000, Vainikka and Young-Scholten 1994, 1996 for L1-based arguments, and Flynn 1996 and Platzak 1996 for UG-based arguments). For example, a full access/no transfer position within theories that propose UG as a starting point for L2 acquisition predicts that L1 and L2 acquisition will proceed in a similar fashion (regardless of L1) and that learners should be able to reach the same level of competence as native speakers. Any differences are said to be performance-related rather than competence-related. As Gass and Selinker (op. cit.:170) admit, there is conflicting evidence as to whether learners have direct access to the principles of UG, have access through the native language, or have no access at all! The empirical results from research on L2 parameters are also mixed and inconclusive (ibid.:172).

A particular methodological difficulty in the UG approach involves the data collection itself, because these studies describe competence and not performance. Elicited rather than attested data is preferred for this reason, especially in the form of grammaticality judgement tasks. But these tasks have been shown to be problematic in many ways, for both native speakers and for learners. Judgements of grammaticality do not guarantee that learners actually perform linguistically in the way they say they would. One of the difficulties that Birdsong (1989) has pointed out is that speakers may be making their judgements on the basis of the difficulties they have in parsing a sentence and not necessarily on the basis of its grammatical properties. Ellis (2003:441) rightly observes that variability in learners' judgements is a major problem which casts doubt on the reliability of many grammaticality intuitions. Moreover, UG is a theory of implicit knowledge, but giving a grammaticality judgement, Ellis (op. cit:442) argues, encourages the use of explicit knowledge.

As Ellis (2003:440) also points out, many of the principles identified by UG grammarians involve complex sentences and therefore can only be expected to manifest themselves in later stages of development. In this respect, UG-based L2 theories deal with a restricted phenomenon, namely the innately specified competence and abstract knowledge. Empirical research in this strand has produced indeterminate results, as we mentioned, and has been limited to specific and rather narrow areas (e.g. access to the Subset Principle, see Berwick 1985, White 1989).

Some researchers, e.g. O'Grady (2003), accept the idea that there are some innate foundations to language acquisition, but not in the form of a UG as such. This approach is termed general nativism. An innate acquisition mechanism is assumed but specific grammatical constraints like those of UG are rejected. As Myers-Scotton (2006:362) puts it, 'theories of this type hold the view that the mind is geared towards processing information but linguistic information is just one type'.

Unlike linguistically based and UG-inspired theories, cognitive theories have appealed to general principles of learning, processing and cognition in explaining the learner's representation of L2 knowledge and how it changes over time. One of the central topics in this strand of research has been the theory of interlanguages, as outlined in the early days by Selinker (1972), further developed by Corder (1981) and followed by the 'variability' theories of Tarone (1983) and Ellis (1984, 1985). One of the aims of these more recent studies is to account for variation in learners' outputs, as a result of a number of factors that include the distinction between explicit L2 knowledge and implicit learning. While both Tarone's and Ellis's models are psycholinguistic in nature, and include components of attention and planning, Preston's (1989) model incorporates an interactional/social dimension in order to account fully for variation in the interlanguage. The interfaces between form and function, as evidenced in these theories, feature centrally in functionalist theories of second language acquisition. Crucially, functionalist theories, as well as the variability approaches, suggest that syntax should not be considered separately from semantics and pragmatics, and as such they provide evidence of the need for a complementary research programme. The emphasis is not only on how knowledge is represented in the mind of the speaker but also on how this knowledge is put to use. For Larsen-Freeman and Cameron (2008) variability is seen as an essential feature of a complex dynamic system which is what language is according to them. Wide differences within and across speakers occur because learners' systems have self-organised in different ways. Some grammatical generalisations that exist at the group level often fail to be realised at an individual level (Larsen-Freeman and Cameron 2008:147). Namely, even though learners may have been exposed to similar instructional procedures they may exhibit diverging patterns of development, which the authors hypothesise is due to the way that individuals have chosen to allocate their limited resources (ibid.). Furthermore, due to the inherent limitation of resources that can be invested in learning a new skill or solving a task (such as working memory or attention), learners' performance may result in higher proficiency in one dimension, e.g. accuracy, which can detract from performance in others, e.g. fluency and complexity (Larsen-Freeman and Cameron 2008:149). These authors see variation as resulting from numerous factors, L1, cognitive and experiential maturity as well as specific learner factors, age, goals, motivation and others.

One influential cognitive and functional approach is the Competition Model proposed by Bates and MacWhinney (1981, 1982, 1987) and MacWhinney (1987, 2005). Language learning is based on **cue validity**, i.e. on the roles of different linguistic forms in signalling grammatical or semantic information. Different cues have different weights in different languages and they may compete, for example when recognising a grammatical subject. In English, the dominant cue for a grammatical subject is preverbal positioning, whereas word order is not such a strong cue in Spanish and Italian. In Spanish, the object relation is often explicitly marked by a preposition and the subject is the noun that is not marked by that preposition. In German, it is the case marking of the definite article that is a powerful cue for the subject while in Russian the case marking is on the noun. MacWhinney explains that the essential question to be answered for a given language is: what is the relative cue strength for a given form–property linkage and how do these cue strengths interact? More recently MacWhinney (2009) has extended his model to L2 learning and proposed a unified model of language acquisition, whereby the 'mechanisms of L1 learning are seen as a subset of the mechanisms of L2 learning' (ibid.:49). This model is therefore conceptually simpler because even though L1 mechanisms are less powerful in the L2 learner, they are still partially accessible (ibid.). The model relies heavily on transfer from the L1, the basic claim being that 'whatever can transfer will' (ibid.:55).

Other approaches to second language acquisition have been based on the premise that L2 learning is very different from L1 learning. Researchers in this group often argue for the importance of instruction. Some promote the role of explicit learning, others argue that it is implicit learning that is more beneficial to SLA (see Myers-Scotton 2006:356–365 for an in-depth overview). The innate faculty is not active for L2 or at least not active to the same extent as it is in L1 (Myers-Scotton 2006:356). Connectionism is effectively a processing model, centred on the regularities that 'emerge from the language learner's analysis of linguistic input, driven by the frequency and complexity of the form-functions relationships that emerge in the input' (ibid.:357). Their central aim is computer-based modelling of learning stages. Most connectionist work has been focused on L1 though the lack of theory has been plaguing this approach, as argued in Gregg (2003). Myers-Scotton (2006) adds that connectionism is not so far from cognitive theories in some respects, since there is a shared view that 'general learning mechanisms enable humans to acquire language given the necessary environment and motivations based on the functions that language can serve' (p. 357).

Also in the general cognitive tradition and potentially informative for research such as ours into criterial features of L2 are 'emergentist' approaches to SLA, as proposed for example in Ellis (1998), Larsen-Freeman (1997), O'Grady (2005, 2008), Larsen-Freeman and Cameron (2008), Mellow (2008), and most recently in the papers of the Ellis and Larsen-Freeman (2009) edited volume. Most of these studies view language acquisition as a complex adaptive system in the sense of Gell-Mann (1992) in which multiple factors and constraints interact, sometimes reinforcing one another sometimes competing, to produce a range of observable outcomes. The outcomes of the system are in this case the observed data of SLA and different kinds of interlanguages. Larsen-Freeman and Cameron (2008) are explicitly in this tradition. The empirical support for their claims is rather limited, however, and is based in large measure on a longitudinal study of a single learner. The Ellis and Larsen-Freeman (2009) paper on SLA in Ellis and Larsen-Freeman (2009) ('Constructing a second language: Analyses and computational simulations of the emergence of linguistic constructions from usage') uses 'connectionist' modelling techniques in psycholinguistics and complements the more symbolic approach to the formulation of SLA principles which we propose in the next chapter.

The importance of these works in the present context is that they recognise the need for multiple interacting factors in understanding SLA and interlanguage formation. The devil lies in the proposed details of the system, in their predictions for the data, and in the range of data on which they have been tested and found to be supported. This empirical support is encouraging but still limited.

This approach is not without its critics. For example, Gregg (2010) argues that language is not a complex dynamical system because language for him is not a system at all, let alone a complex or a dynamical one. Grammars come to exist in the minds of speakers so it is *the acquisition process* that can be dynamical, not language or a language per se (Gregg 2010:553). It does not help Larsen-Freeman and Cameron's case that they present their theory as a metaphorical bridge for readers (2008:15).

We disagree with Gregg that language cannot be seen in terms of a system, but we agree with his assertion that complexity theory can nonetheless offer novel and useful insights into the concerns of applied linguistics. And this is reflected in some of our principles in the next chapter. Gregg (2010:553) ridicules Larsen-Freeman and Cameron's statement (2008:80) that every use of language 'changes it in some way'. He says there is no *it* to change. In this book we observe and document changes in L2 interlanguages at different levels, and the *it* that changes is both a concrete sample of learners' linguistic abilities, i.e. of their performance, and may also involve some change in their evolving abstract linguistic competence. Gregg points out (p.553) that L2 non-native competence can become 'fossilised' and achieve a steady state, like that of L1 competence. But the abstract competence knowledge of native speakers changes over time, generally resulting in different outputs, just as the evolving competence and performance of second language learners does. He seems to have forgotten about the field of historical linguistics and what it tells us about adaptation and change. In this context we focus on the empirically observable changes in L2 learners' performance and offer precisely formulated and predictive principles that begin to account for them. In this way we avoid the metaphors that Gregg criticises, we offer observable data patterns from L2 English and we make concrete proposals for falsifiable principles that underlie them. Researchers who wish to formulate rules and principles of the competence grammar for each learning stage, and to adopt a UG approach, are encouraged to do so. This is a complementary research perspective to the one adopted here, with possible mutual benefits at a descriptive level. The different explanatory perspectives (multiple causal factors versus innate UG) can then be compared in this area of the language sciences as they have been in others (cf. e.g. Newmeyer 1998, Hawkins 2004).

More generally, both cognitive and linguistic theories, although providing valuable insights, have been mainly directed at explaining a rather limited subset of observed grammatical features in L2. For EP research we can potentially overcome such limitations by accessing a rich empirical database, such as the CLC, and by combining theoretical traditions of research. The patterns in the data can help us refine current principles and can reveal the manner of their interaction and their relative strength. This is our goal in the next chapter (5).

We have to emphasise that learning a language is not just a question of learners adopting certain linguistic forms, but rather these forms exist for the purpose of expressing meanings and for carrying out a wide array of linguistic functions. By the same token, the social dimension in language learning provides a formative influence on language development in the form of what Larsen-Freeman and Cameron (2008:126) call 'co-adaptation', defined as the adjustment of each interlocutor to others and involving the linguistic strategies needed for making that adjustment. See also Atkinson (2002) in this regard for his 'sociocognitive' approach to SLA.

4.3 The transfer issue

One of the main distinguishing features between first and second language acquisition involves the prior existence of a first language in the latter case and the impact that this has on the gradual learning of the second language through transfer effects. Theoreticians are divided over the extent of this impact, and the findings that have been reported in the case studies to date are often puzzling. For some linguistic properties transfer seems to occur productively (phonetic properties, for example), for others it is less common or even unattested. Some L1–L2 pairs reveal it, others do not. It is clear that any theory of transfer and of interlanguage formation (and ultimately we all want a predictive theory that can define possible versus impossible, and preferred versus dispreferred pathways of development) is going to have to take account of multiple factors: the typological relationship between L1 and L2; general principles of learning and critical ages; general principles of language processing (production and comprehension); social factors involving the general environment for learning; and pedagogical factors that include teaching methods and materials and types of assessment.

In MacWhinney's competition model for L2 acquisition transfer plays a central role, as we have just seen. For Pienemann (1998, 2003, 2005), however, its role is much less significant. According to his Processability Theory L1 transfer is constrained by general processing principles, irrespective of the typological distance between L1 and L2. Order of acquisition in L2 is guided by a processability hierarchy that determines if and to what extent L1 transfer can be expected.

This developmental view of transfer is not completely novel (cf. Kellerman 1983, Zobl 1980), but Pienemann proposes an explicit formal framework for defining the constraints. He contends that typological proximity does not guarantee positive transfer and he cites a study by Hakansson, Pienemann and Sayehli (2002) whereby Swedish schoolchildren acquiring German did not transfer a particular word order found in both Swedish and German (namely the so-called V2 position in German, as in 'Today likes Peter milk'). However, as Pienemann himself notes (Pienemann 2005:144) German was the third language for these children, the second being English. It could be that the non-application of V2 transfer was due to influence from English. Another example of transfer that should happen (if the 'anything that can transfer will' prediction of the Competition Model is correct) but does not happen according to Pienemann is subject–verb agreement marking. Such marking exists in Polish (in a 'rich agreement' form as discussed in Hawkins 2004:247–50) and does not exist in Vietnamese, but this does not give Polish speakers an advantage over Vietnamese learners when acquiring English: both learner groups acquire agreement in English late (according to Johnston 1997, cited in Pienemann 2005:145). Finally, a study by Kawaguchi (1999, 2002) found that English learners of Japanese did not transfer their SVO word order when learning Japanese, which is an SOV language, even at the initial stage. According to Pienemann, the early processability of the canonical Japanese SOV pattern is due to its low demands on processing. This is a consequence, he argues, of the fact that word order rules apply within and not across individual phrases, thus reducing the domains that the processor needs to access when assigning grammatical and semantic properties to these phrases (cf. Pienemann 2005:146).

MacWhinney (2005:60) counters that his and Pienemann's model do not differ much if one bears in mind that transfer is item-based and that learners do not transfer whole sentences. This may explain, MacWhinney argues, why Swedes do not transfer all their V2 structures early. Within the competition model, they would first learn to place the subject before the verb, then introduce an adverb to produce 'Peter likes milk today' and finally they learn optionally to place the adverb in the initial slot. According to MacWhinney, learners are not learning and memorising whole sentence patterns, but rather chunks below the sentence level, and thus are not able to transfer whole sentences. MacWhinney also points out that for the same reason early transfer of the English cleft structure into Italian L2 would not be expected, even though that structure is present in both languages (ibid.). In general, according to MacWhinney, we should not expect to see consistent early transfer in the area of morpho-syntax since this is the 'most language-specific part of the target language' (ibid.:60). The competition model predicts that in areas where transfer is poorly supported, the learner acquires the L2 structures directly (MacWhinney 1992:371). As for the lack of negative transfer in the case of early acquisition of L2 Japanese SOV by English learners, he claims that it is the emphasis on the input that fixes the Japanese word order for learners in the very early stages of acquisition (MacWhinney 2005:60).

It may indeed be the case that input plays the crucial role here, but this still does not explain why some L1 speakers transfer their word order preferences into English L2 whereas others do not. We shall return to this problem in Chapter 5.5.

In a similar vein McDonald and Heilenman (1991:331) note that English learners of French L2 abandon their English word order strategies early, particularly in non-canonical orders. And Gass (1987, 1992) reports that English learners of Italian switch to animacy as an early cue to subjecthood rather than sticking to their preferred L1 word order cue, whereas Italian learners of English 'move' in a direction that exhibits an increasing amount of consistency with the dominant word order pattern of English (Gass 1992:193). By the same token, Japanese learners of English acquire SVO very rapidly (Rutherford 1983), just as English learners of Japanese produce SOV order and subject omission early, even though their language is SVO and 'non-Pro-drop', i.e. it does not permit subject omission (Kawaguchi 1999, 2002). Odlin (1990) states that there are relatively few instances of transfer involving basic grammatical word order in the literature and he suggests two possible reasons: a) the lack of research on beginner learner stages which are more likely to exhibit word order transfer, and b) learners are likely to be highly conscious of basic word order as it involves the arrangement of semantically important elements. There is a widespread view in the literature that pragmatic or discourse functions for word order can be transferred from the L1 into L2, but there is disagreement over whether grammaticalised word order patterns can also be transferred and under what conditions (cf. Ellis 2003:316–317). The CLC provides some relevant data on this question, for different learners of L2 at different levels, and the principles we discuss in Chapter 5 provide a possible framework for distinguishing those grammatical word orders that will be transferred from those that will not.

Our CLC data provide ample evidence that Spanish learners of English do transfer their pro-drop patterns along with a number of un-English word orders, such as 'Light NP Shift' ('I like very much sweets') and post-posed subjects ('Yesterday came my boyfriend'), whose motivation is arguably as much or more to do with processing efficiency than with pragmatics (see Hawkins

2004, Wasow 2002). By the same token, Chinese speakers transfer preverbal PPs as in 'He by bus went to town'. We predict that because Japanese is a head-final language, the contrast with the mirror-image word order patterns of English is considerable and transferring 'head-final' patterns into a 'head-initial' language such as English, and vice versa, would significantly impair communication (see Chapter 5.5). This is why it is imperative for Japanese learners of English, and for English learners of Japanese, to acquire basic word order in their L2s early. On the other hand, speakers of L1 languages with flexible SVO like Spanish do not have the same incentive, because even when they transfer from their L1s into a fundamentally similar head-initial English L2, communication is not significantly impaired.

Clearly we need a model of learning and processing that can account for these differences. Canonical SVO word orders should be low on Pienemann's processability hierarchy (cf. Pienemann 2005), yet the effects of this hierarchy can be quite varied for different L1 speakers learning an L2, as our model predicts. Similarly, the strongly SVO input for English should set this word order for Spanish and Chinese learners just as it does for Japanese learners, but this does not happen in many cases, as our data analysis and discussion in Chapter 5 illustrate. If this is an instance of direct L2 learning, then it remains to be explained why transfer operates differently for the three first languages, Spanish, Chinese and Japanese. These learners reap different benefits from direct learning and we need to specify why this is so. The principles we develop in the next chapter are an attempt to do so.

A rather different kind of transfer is evident in the phenomenon of 'avoidance' (Schachter 1974), whereby certain typological patterns in the L2 are avoided by learners of L1s who have no corresponding structure. Schachter pointed to the lower incidence of postnominal relative clause usage by L2 learners whose languages have prenominal relative clauses, as in Japanese whereas speakers of L1s with postnominal relatives like Spanish were able to transfer these structures directly into English. The significance of Schachter's findings is that a contrast between languages need not result in an error as such but in the underuse or avoidance of the semantic and syntactic counterpart in the L2. Much of the literature on transfer has been concerned with finding an explanation for why identical properties in the L1 and L2 do not always transfer at least in the early stages. Conversely, non-identical properties need not always result in error, which was commonly assumed to be the case prior to Schachter's (1974) study. Indeed, the whole basis for the contrastive analysis movement launched by Lado (1957) was to predict areas of difficulty and error for L2 learners based on the premise that cross-linguistic differences result in difficulties.

Another factor that seems to play a role in the presence or absence of transfer is language distance and 'psychotypology', which is the perception that speakers have regarding the similarity and difference between relevant languages. Psychotypology is not fixed, it is revised as more information becomes available. In Kellerman's important 'breken' study (Kellerman 1978) he found higher translatability of the Dutch *breken* constructions into German than into English because German is perceived as being closer to Dutch than English is. Ellis (2003:327) points out, that 'translatability' must not be equated with 'transferability', though the two may correlate. When considerable similarities exist, positive transfer can be expected to be maximised and shared structures transferred. However, the learner may doubt that these similarities are real, as in the case of Dutch learners of L2 English who did not accept phrasal verbs when there was close similarity between Dutch and English, most likely because of their 'disbelief' that another language could have a structure so similar to the 'unusual' Dutch one (Hulstijn and Marchena 1989).

Other reasons offered in the literature for why some expected transfer effects do not appear (e.g. Japanese SOV word order into an SVO language like English) while others do (e.g. Light NP Shift in L2 English by Spanish learners and pre-verbal directional PP transfer from Chinese into L2 English) include the possibility that there is heightened metalinguistic awareness of grammatical properties compared to discourse/pragmatic properties (cf. Odlin 1990). The claim is that learners will be more implicitly aware of these basic grammatical properties, and they will also generally be explicitly taught, with the result that transfer is impeded. Learners will be less implicitly aware of the more elusive pragmatic properties of a language and will generally receive less explicit instruction in these, with the result that transfer is not impeded. This explanation is rather vague and difficult to test, however.

Summarising, the research literature on transfer in SLA provides us with some intriguing examples of transfers that occur productively, and of others that do not occur. It also contains some helpful ideas regarding the role of transfer in interlanguage formation. There is much that is still unresolved at a theoretical level, however, regarding when transfer will occur, and when it will not, and with what L1–L2 pairs. In the next chapter we incorporate and revise some of the ideas that we summarise here and we propose a number of different factors and constraints that hold for second language acquisition in general. It is the interaction between factors that determines possible versus impossible interlanguages and that predicts or permits transfer on some occasions and not others. We return to the transfer issue later in this chapter, in Section 4.5.2, after a discussion of some relevant interacting considerations.

4.4 Markedness, complexity and processing load

An important insight for any model of interlanguage formation and SLA is Eckman's (1977) Markedness Differential Hypothesis (MDH). The MDH claims that L1 structures that are typologically more marked and complex than their L2 counterparts will not be transferred. L1 structures that are less marked and simpler than the corresponding L2 structures will be. So, for example, he shows that English learners have no difficulty in learning that German has no voicing in word-final stops, but that German learners experience considerable problems in learning that English does. From a markedness perspective a voiced/voiceless consonant distinction is more marked and more complex than its absence and many languages, even those with a voicing contrast initially or medially, will devoice final consonants (orthographic gab 'gave' in German is pronounced with a final [p]). In other words, there is no transfer when the L1 is marked and the L2 unmarked, but transfer effects do appear when the L1 structure is unmarked and the L2 is marked. We return to a more detailed discussion of this devoicing pattern in Section 4.5.2. For another example of this type of asymmetry in the domain of L2 acquisition for dynamic spatial relations see Filipović and Vidaković (2010).

The precise predictions made by the MDH do depend on a prior definition of 'markedness', of course, and unfortunately while some phenomena are clear, of the kind summarised here, others are not (see Haspelmath 2006 for a detailed discussion and critique of markedness and an exposée of the many different senses: he lists 12 in which the term is used). White (1987), for example, points out that it is not only the L1 unmarked forms that are transferred into L2: some marked L1 forms may be transferred as well when the L1 has marked structures and L2 does not. She cites the case of the English double object structure (as in *Peter gave Mary the book*), which is frequently transferred from L1 English into L2 French, even though this structure does not exist in French. This issue is unresolvable, however, without a clearer definition of the basic concept. In what sense, for example, is the English double object construction more marked than its French counterpart? Nonetheless Eckman's key insight of an asymmetry in transfer effects, in examples of the type he discusses, remains a useful one and it defines an important limitation on 'negative transfer' effects, i.e. on certain classes of otherwise expected errors.

The more general insight that emerges in this area for language acquisition, both first and second, and from a now substantial body of research involves the role of complexity. 'Simpler' structures and meanings are acquired earlier and involve fewer errors, more 'complex' ones are acquired later and are subject to more errors. The question this poses, however, is: what exactly does 'complex' mean? Let us consider some clear examples first and then consider the bigger issue.

One clear set of constructions involving complexity that are late acquired and errorful are the 'raising' constructions of English: Subject-to-Subject Raising (*John appears to be sick*), Subject-to-Object Raising (*I believe John to be sick*), and Tough Movement (*John is easy to please*), see Postal (1974). Constructions of these types are typologically marked in the sense that they are quite rare or of limited productivity in other languages (Givón 1991, 2001, Hawkins 1986, Müller-Gotama 1994). They also involve complex displacements of arguments from a lower clause into a higher clause in which they do not contract normal semantic relations with the 'matrix' verbs and adjectives that they are adjacent to. Saying that *I believe John to be sick* does not imply that I believe John in any way. And John is not necessarily being claimed to be easy in *John is easy to please*. Instead it is pleasing John (with *John* the direct object of pleasing) that is easy. A further cause of complexity results from the syntactic ambiguity of these constructions with their more common 'control' counterparts in surface structure: corresponding to each raising type is a control structure in which surface arguments contract normal semantic and syntactic relations with their adjacent predicates. Compare, for example, the famous pair *John is easy to please* and *John is eager to please* (Chomsky 1957, Hawkins 1986). The former requires considerable unpacking and processing, corresponding to its more complex syntactic derivation; the latter simply interprets *John* as the subject and agent of eagerness to please, and carries the interpretation of *John* over to the infinitival verb that lacks an overt subject, *to please* (Hawkins 2004:162–4).

The difficulties posed by Tough Movement for child learners of English have been documented in Anderson (2005). Children do initially interpret the surface subject *John* as the subject of *easy* and not as the object of *to please,* moving gradually to adult-like competence. In other words, they first assign the more frequent, and simpler, and unmarked interpretation to this adjacent subject–predicate pair. For second language acquisition Callies (2008) has shown, on the basis of a study using a learner corpus, that Tough Movement structures are acquired late by German learners of English and are significantly underrepresented in the writings of even advanced German learners. Our CLC data indicate that Tough Movement is late acquired, regardless of the L1 (see Chapter 7.2.4).

Relative clauses (*the professor who wrote the book*, *the book that the professor wrote*, etc.) are also syntactically complex constructions in many instances and involve late acquisition and errors. We have significant cross-linguistic data for this structure, as well as numerous studies of their processing, usage and second language acquisition for English and other languages, making this a very revealing and useful construction type to study in this context. We shall return to it in the next section on cross-linguistic predictions for acquisition.

A very interesting case study of relevance to syntactic complexity in the learning of English is Mellow (2008). He shows how a 12-year-old Spanish learner gradually acquires a number of complex syntactic dependencies, including control structures in verb and adjective complements (*he*i *wanted to* Oi *eat it, Mom*i *was getting ready to* Oi *leave*), relative clauses (*a plate*i *of salad that the waiter was carrying* Oi), and various adverbial subordinate clauses (*the baby*i *was very excited* Oi *looking at all the toys*). Complex dependencies like these were late acquired in Mellow's longitudinal study which covered a 201-day period and he documents when exactly the different structures appeared in this time frame.

A theory of complexity needs to be able to rank constructions such as these on a scale according to certain general criteria. It must also be able to apply these criteria to other areas in addition to syntax, i.e. to the phonology, the morphology and also to semantics. There have been several attempts in the literature to do this, and they are directly relevant for our purposes here, precisely because complexity means late acquisition and more errors in general, i.e. complexity can potentially define criterial features for the higher levels of proficiency. For grammars and cross-linguistic variation we have the complexity metrics of Dahl (2004), Hawkins (2004) and McWhorter (2001), for language processing Miller and Chomsky (1963), Frazier (1985) and Gibson (1998), for second language acquisition Rimmer (2006), to name just a few.

One key insight that all these approaches share is that complexity means **more** structural units in the area in question (e.g. voiced in addition to voiceless consonants in final position, longer rather than shorter syntactic structures with more relations of combination and dependency, for example more arguments of the verb in transitive versus intransitive verb phrases), or **more** rules and representations with more complex derivations (as in the raising constructions above). Despite its plausibility, this intuition has proved hard to define. The reader is referred to the lively debate in the papers of *Linguistic Typology* (2001) Vol. 5 – 2/3, responding to McWhorter's (2001) proposal that creole grammars are the world's simplest grammars. The discussion went to the heart of the fundamental question: what exactly is complexity and how do we define it?

Some relevant issues that complicate a general definition are discussed in Hawkins (2009). One involves 'trade-offs': simplicity in one part of the grammar is often matched by complexity in another. For example, English transitive NP-V-NP sequences regularly have an Agent–Verb–Patient interpretation, as in *The king visited his people*. But often they must be mapped onto complex argument structures in ways that many (indeed most) languages do not permit, even other closely related languages like German (see Hawkins 1986, Müller-Gotama 1994). Some less common theta-role assignments to transitive subjects that are grammatical in English but ungrammatical in most other languages are: ***This tent*** *sleeps four* [Subject = Locative]; *A few years ago* ***a penny*** *would buy two to three pins* [Subject = Instrument]; ***The book*** *sold 10,000 copies* [Subject = Theme].

What is interesting about these English transitive clauses is that they are syntactically and morphologically simple. The NP-V-NP surface structure is minimal and contains fewer syntactic categories than alternative semantically equivalent structures with PPs (e.g. *Four can sleep in this tent*), of the kind that other languages use. English also lacks case morphology on its NPs, except residually on its pronouns. The rules that generate these English surface forms are also, arguably, minimal. Yet in any formalisation of the mappings from surface forms to argument structures and semantic representations, the English mappings must be regarded, by anyone's metric, as quite complex. There are more argument structure types to be linked to NP-V-NP than to the corresponding transitive clauses of languages with only Agent–Verb–Patient interpretations. This adds 'length' and complexity to the grammar of English (as discussed in Dahl 2004). It also makes processing more complex. The assignment of a Locative to the subject NP and of an Instrument requires crucial access by the processor to the verbs in these sentences, to their lexical semantics and co-occurrence structure, and also possibly to the post-verbal NP. More disambiguation needs to be carried out by the English processor, and greater access is needed to more of the surface structure for this disambiguation, i.e. the processing domains for these theta-role assignments in English are not minimal (Hawkins 2004).

The SVO orders of English, which are typical of so many inflectionally impoverished languages and of creoles, are not so simple, therefore. Trade-offs like this make it difficult to give a definition of overall complexity for a grammar and result in unresolvable debates over whether some grammars are more complex than others, when there is no clear metric of overall complexity for deciding the matter.

The mapping issue between forms and meanings, exemplified in the theta role assignments to transitive clause, brings up another key insight about linguistic complexity that has been discussed first and foremost by Slobin (1973, 1985) and his associates in the area of first language acquisition. They have documented a clear preference for a one-to-one principle in the acquisition of different languages whereby clearly identifiable surface forms are mapped onto consistent semantic notions. For example, the agglutinative nominal morphology of Turkish (one form, one case, for all nouns) is easier to learn than the many-to-many mappings of rich inflectional languages like Russian (one case property being conveyed by many forms, one form often conveying many case properties). See Andersen (1992:257–62) for a particularly clear summary of the first language research in this area. Evidence for the simplicity of one-to-one mappings has also been replicated in a second language context by Andersen (1984) who states that '[a]n interlanguage system should be constructed in such a way that an intended underlying meaning is expressed with one clear invariant surface form' (Andersen 1984:79).

These difficulties in defining complexity at a general theoretical level, especially overall complexity, should not deter us from appealing to the complexity of certain individual constructions, or meanings, however, when there is ample empirical evidence to back up the complexity claim, as in the raising discussion above. This evidence can come from grammar alone, from cross-linguistic distributional evidence, from processing, and from acquisition. There is an emerging consensus in the literature that complexity does have measurable consequences in all of these areas, in the form of fewer languages with the complex pattern in question, greater processing difficulty, and later and more errorful first and second language acquisition (cf. Hawkins 2004).

One point of interesting disagreement, however, within the SLA community concerns the extent to which the consequences of markedness and complexity for learning are simply the result of processing. In other words, is acquisition difficulty primarily a consequence of processing difficulty, of the kind that mature native speakers will also experience with more complex structures? Or are principles of learning and processing more orthogonal to each other, sometimes overlapping in their consequences, sometimes not? Pienemann's (1998, 2003, 2005) Processability Theory reduces much or most of learning to processing, and more specifically to limited processing capacity. He writes (Pienemann 2003:679):

> The notion of limited processing capacity is a standard assumption in work on human cognition. For instance, short-term memory is thought to be limited in capacity and duration (e.g. Baddely 1990). The assumption that the processing capacity of L2 learners is limited forms the basis of several approaches to SLA. The limited-capacity view of L2 processing constitutes a basic assumption in work on L2 input processing (e.g., Krashen, 1982; VanPatten, 1996), in research on L2 skill acquisition (e.g., McLaughlin, 1987), in work on operating principles (e.g., Andersen 1984), in the 'competition model' (e.g., Bates and MacWhinney, 1981), and in Clahsen's (1984) L2 processing strategies, as well as in my own work on processability.

Pienemann claims further (ibid.) that his Processability theory makes 'testable predictions for developmental routes across typologically different language . . . applies to L2 as well as to L1 acquisition, and . . . delineates the scope of interlanguage variation as well as L1 transfer'. In other words, these central facts about learning are claimed to follow not from a theory of learning as such, but from processability.

We have two comments to make in relation to Pienemann's research programme. First, we share his view that a lot of learning can and should be explained in terms of processing. But it is important not to lose sight of the fact that learning and processing are nonetheless distinct, in principle, and that we do need theories of both, even though their effects may sometimes be hard to tease apart. Equating ease or difficulty of learning with ease or difficulty of processing fails in both directions. For example, semantically transparent forms, with a one-to-one mapping, facilitate learning. But processing is often easier when surface forms are reduced and shorter and less transparent, namely when semantic interpretations can be readily inferred. *John is eager for John to please* is a semantically transparent structure in which the subject of pleasing is explicit and overt in the infinitival phrase, but *John is eager to please* is arguably easier to process since fewer words need to be accessed and parsed and the assignment of *John* as a subject argument to *please* can be inferred clearly and unambiguously (cf. Hawkins 2004:162–4). Conversely, the learning of morphological irregularities is hard (*sing/sang/sung* vs. *walk/walked*, *mouse/mice* vs. *house/houses*, etc.) and children will go through a stage of regularising them (see Andersen 1992 for a literature review), but once learned they are often easy to process on account of their frequency and the entrenchment of irregular forms (see Bybee 2007).

The second point to mention in connection with Processability Theory concerns the central notion of limited processing capacity. It is almost certainly the case that there are such limits, but attempts to define exactly what they are have proven to be notoriously difficult (see Hawkins 1994 for critical discussion of, and counterexamples to, working memory claims of relevance to word order processing). And so, in practice, those who propose such theories generally end up defining a relative ranking of processing difficulty, among the permitted options, rather than a concrete proposal for some well-defined upper limit that excludes certain structural types as unprocessable. This is what Pienemann does as well with his processability hierarchy.

A final issue in this section that will be relevant for our SLA principles in the next chapter concerns the relationship between efficiency and complexity. This is the topic of Hawkins (2009). He argues that metrics of complexity need to be embedded in a theory of efficiency, and that it is efficiency and not complexity that is the larger and more inclusive notion.

Efficiency relates to the basic function of language, which is to communicate information from the speaker (S) to the hearer (H). Hawkins proposes that:

Communication is efficient when the message intended by S is delivered to H in rapid time and with minimal processing effort;

and that:

Acts of communication between S and H are generally optimally efficient; those that are not occur in proportion to their degree of efficiency.

Complexity metrics, by contrast, are defined on the grammar and structure of language. An important component of efficiency often involves structural and grammatical simplicity. But sometimes communicative efficiency requires the use of structures that have greater complexity, for example when the hearer needs more detailed and explicit information about some referent or event. And efficiency also involves additional factors that determine the speaker's structural selections including: *speed* in delivering linguistic properties in online processing; *fine-tuning* of structural selections to frequency of occurrence, accessibility and inference; and *few online errors* or garden paths. These factors interact, sometimes reinforcing sometimes opposing one another, see Hawkins (1994, 2004).

The work of Tomasello (2002, 2003) on L1 acquisition is also relevant here. There is an important parallel between his research findings on L1 acquisition and ours on L2 . He argues that children's early language does not revolve around abstract categories and rules but rather around specific lexical items and expressions. This item-specificity of early L1 is something we have detected in L2 as well. Speakers first acquire constructions with specific verbs, and they are conservative in their use of these verbs in the early stages but start extending the use of constructions to include more verbs as they progress, as our model predicts. We illustrate this point in Chapter 7 in great detail. Furthermore, Tomasello argues (2003) that the driving force behind child language acquisition is not an innate language acquisition device but the *need to communicate and make sense of patterns*. Communication is driven by intention-reading skills whereby interaction is established with the outside world and the essential aim is to convey intentions and understand those of others. The socio-cognitive urge to interpret the intentional and mental states of others drives the learning of language, a socio-cognitive construct itself. Just as children need to interact, express their thoughts and understand those of others in the L1, so do speakers acquiring an L2. Interacting socially and linguistically is central to the acquisition of language. Children sample language, recognise patterns and map labels onto referents as well as forms onto functions and then extend them to new constructions of their own. Tomasello's usage-based model is developmentally conditioned, and grammar is not a prerequisite but a product. The biological adaptation for language in humans resides not in the grammar itself but rather in the sets of cognitive and social skills that lead to the construction of a language.

4.5 Cross-linguistic patterns and their predictions for acquisition

There is a growing body of research that links cross-linguistic universals, especially the more empirically based patterns and correlations of the 'Greenbergian' typological tradition (see e.g. Comrie 1989, Croft 2003, Greenberg 1963, 1966, Whaley 1997), to the data and theories of psycholinguistics, both language processing and first and second language acquisition. Hawkins has been arguing for some years now that the grammatical rules of the world's languages, and parameters on cross-linguistic variation, have been shaped by ease of processing (Hawkins 1990, 1994, 2004) and that there is a correlation between performance preferences for certain structures, evident in languages whose grammars permit choices, and the grammatical conventions themselves. This is referred to as the Performance-Grammar

Correspondence Hypothesis (PGCH) and it is defined as follows (Hawkins 2004:3):

> Grammars have conventionalised syntactic structures in proportion to their degree of preference in performance, as evidenced by patterns of selection in corpora and by ease of processing in psycholinguistic experiments.

Consider relative clauses. Many languages (such as Arabic, Hebrew, Persian and Greek) exhibit both a 'gap' and a 'resumptive pronoun' strategy (resulting in alternations such as *the students [that I teach]* and *the students [that I teach them]*). In other languages there may be an alternation between a structure with and without a relative pronoun (as in English, *the students [whom I teach]* and *the students [I teach]*). One of these strategies may be 'fixed' or 'conventionalised' in certain environments, while there can be optionality and variation in others.

The selection from the variants in performance exhibits patterns. The retention of the relative pronoun in English is correlated, inter alia, with the degree of separation of the relative from its head (Quirk 1957): the bigger the separation, the more relative pronouns are retained (see Hawkins 2004 for a summary of this and other performance patterns). The Hebrew gap is favored with smaller distances between filler and gap, the resumptive pronouns with larger and more complex relativisation domains (Ariel 1999). The fixed variants across grammars also reveals patterns: the distribution of gaps to pronouns follows the Keenan–Comrie (1977) Accessibility Hierarchy (AH), and Keenan–Comrie argued that this grammatical pattern was ultimately explainable by declining ease of processing. Resumptive pronouns are found, in both performance and cross-linguistic grammatical conventions, therefore, in those relative clauses that are harder to process, see the next section for details. This is the kind of correspondence that motivates the PGCH in Hawkins (op. cit.).

The relevance of typology for acquisition was first discussed in a remarkable study by Roman Jakobson, *Child Language, Aphasia and Phonological Universals*, which appeared first in its German original in 1941 and then in an English translation in 1968. His basic insight was that implicational universals, i.e. if a language has some property P then it also has property Q, could be used to make predictions for the order in which properties are acquired and for errors. Property Q, he argued, would be acquired first (stop consonants before fricatives, given that if a language has fricatives then it also has stops) and Q would substitute for P in errors rather than vice versa. The precise logic of Jakobson's predictions has been modified and tested further in Hawkins (1987, 2007). Hawkins points out that implicational universals do not actually predict that property Q will be acquired before property P. They predict only that P will not be acquired before Q (the acquisition of fricatives will not precede that of stops). Hence Q can **either** precede **or** be acquired simultaneously with P (stops will either precede or be acquired simultaneously with fricatives). Jakobson's basic insight about the usefulness of typology for language acquisition studies remains, however, with this caveat. His pioneering work provided an important background for the cross-linguistic approach to first language acquisition initiated by Slobin (1973, 1985) and his associates, which in turn has led to the typologically oriented SLA research of Fred Eckman and colleagues. Hawkins (1987, 2004, 2007) has also used typological universals to make predictions for first and second language acquisition. Eckman, Moravcsik and Wirth (1989:195) propose an Interlanguage Structural Conformity Hypothesis in order to capture the basic assumption that underlies these cross-linguistic approaches to SLA: 'All universals that are true for primary languages are also true for interlanguages'.

The Interlanguage Structural Conformity Hypothesis in conjunction with the Performance-Grammar Correspondence Hypothesis now predicts a rather fascinating convergence between cross-linguistic grammars, native speaker performance, and second language acquisition. It is worth illustrating what this convergence really amounts to with a concrete example, involving relative clauses. This will make clearer how we need to formulate some of the principles and predictions of the next chapter, and it will help us understand some of the difficulties in assessing the role of transfer in SLA and whether it can be claimed to have occurred or not.

4.5.1 Relative clauses

Relative Clause Formation involves a dependency between the head of the relative clause and the position 'relativised on', i.e. the gap, subcategorisor or resumptive pronoun within the clause that is co-indexed with the head and that represents the role that the head noun plays within the relative. The sentence *The professor that the student knows is very accomplished* predicates a claim about the professor, the head of the relative, namely that this individual is very accomplished, and it identifies this individual using the sentence in the relative clause which asserts that the student in question knows this professor. See Hawkins (1999, 2004) for a summary of the different formalisations and theories regarding this structure. Hawkins (op. cit.) argues that various hierarchies can be set up on the basis of increasing 'domain' sizes for the processing of relative clauses, measured in terms of the smallest number of nodes and structural relations that must be computed in order to match the relative clause head with the co-indexed gap, subcategorisor or resumptive pronoun. Processing domains in Hawkins' theory refer to the relevant portions of linguistic structure that need to be processed in order to produce or comprehend a particular construction or structural relation. One of these hierarchies is the Keenan and Comrie (1977) Accessibility Hierarchy, formulated as follows in Comrie (1989) (SU=subject, DO=direct object, IO=indirect object, OBL=oblique, GEN=genitive):

(1) Accessibility hierarchy (AH): SU>DO >IO/OBL>GEN

i.e. subjects are higher than direct objects, which are higher than both indirect objects and oblique phrases (i.e. other prepositional phrases accompanying a verb), which are in turn higher than relatives on genitive positions. Examples of relative clauses of each of these types are given in (2) with co-indexation indicated by the subscript 'i' and the gap by 'O':

(2) the professor$i$ [that Oi wrote the book] *SU*

the professor$i$ [that the student knows Oi] *DO*

the professor$i$ [that the student showed the book to Oi] *IO/OBL*

the professor$i$ [that the student knows his$i$ daughter] *GEN*

(i.e. 'the professor whose daughter the student knows')

A 'filler-gap' or 'filler-subcategorisor' processing domain for relativisation on the direct object position necessarily contains a subject within the relative clause (and more phrasal nodes), whereas a relative on a subject need not contain (and regularly does not contain) a direct object. A relativised indirect object typically contains both a subject and a direct object in the relative clause. It is co-occurrence asymmetries such as these between arguments, coupled with the added phrasal complexity of the lower AH positions (obliques and especially genitives) that plausibly underlie the Keenan–Comrie hierarchy. Whether this is the correct explanation or not, there are clear patterns across grammars, and there are equally clear correlating patterns in both performance and acquisition.

One of the most striking grammatical patterns that Keenan and Comrie (1977) presented in favour of (1) involved languages that 'cut off' at different points down the hierarchy, i.e. their grammars permit relative clauses to be formed on all higher positions above the cut-off, but not on lower positions. Illustrative languages cited by Keenan and Comrie are those in (3):

(3) Rules of relative clause formation and their cut-offs within the clause

SU only: Malagasy, Maori

SU & DO only: Kinyarwanda, Indonesian

SU & DO & IO only: Basque

SU & DO & IO & OBL only: North Frisian, Catalan

SU & DO & IO & OBL & GEN: English, Hausa

A further pattern involved the distribution of gap strategies ([-Case] in Keenan and Comrie's terminology e.g. the professor$i$ [that the student knows Oi]) and resumptive pronouns (as a type of [+Case] strategy e.g. the professor$i$

[that the student knows him*i*]). If a gap is grammatical on a low position of AH, it is grammatical on all higher positions. Resumptive pronouns show the reverse pattern: if a resumptive pronoun is grammatical on a high position, it is grammatical on all lower positions (that can be relativised at all).

This can be seen in Table 4.1, which quantifies the distribution of gaps to pronouns for 24 languages from the Keenan–Comrie language sample that have both structures. Gaps decline down the AH, 100% to 65% to 25% to 4%, pronouns increase (0% to 35% to 75% to 96%).

A plausible processing explanation for this is that gaps are harder to process than resumptive pronouns and prefer smaller structural domains for

Table 4.1 Languages combining [-Case] gaps with [+Case] pronouns (Keenan and Comrie 1977)

	SU	DO	IO/OBLGEN	
Aoban	gap	pro	pro	pro
Arabic	gap	pro	pro	pro
Gilbertese	gap	pro	pro	pro
Kera	gap	pro	pro	pro
Chinese (Peking)	gap	gap/pro	pro	pro
Genoese	gap	gap/pro	pro	pro
Hebrew	gap	gap/pro	pro	pro
Persian	gap	gap/pro	pro	pro
Tongan	gap	gap/pro	pro	pro
Fulani	gap	gap	pro	pro
Greek	gap	gap	pro	pro
Welsh	gap	gap	pro	pro
Zurich German	gap	gap	pro	pro
Toba Batak	gap	*	pro	pro
Hausa	gap	gap	gap/pro	pro
Shona	gap	gap	gap/pro	pro
Minang-Kabau	gap	*	*/pro	pro
Korean	gap	gap	gap	pro
Roviana	gap	gap	gap	pro
Turkish	gap	gap	gap	pro
Yoruba	gap	gap	0	pro
Malay	gap	gap	RP	pro
Javanese	gap	*	*	pro
Japanese	gap	gap	pro	gap/pro
Gaps	24 [100%]	17 [65%]	6 [25%]	1 [4%]
Pros	0 [0%]	9 [35%]	18 [75%]	24 [96%]

Key: gap = *[-Case] strategy*
    pro = *copy pronoun retained (as a subinstance of [+Case])*
    * = *obligatory passivisation to a higher position prior to relativisation*
    0 = *position does not exist as such*
    RP = *relative pronoun plus gap (as a subinstance of [+Case])*
[-Case] gap languages may employ a general subordination marker within the relative clause, no subordination marking, a participial verb form, or a fronted case-invariant relative pronoun. For Tongan, an ergative language, the top two positions of AH are Absolutive and Ergative respectively, not SU and DO, cf. Primus (1999).

the various relations that need to be computed in relative clause processing (Hawkins 1999).

Second language acquisition data on gaps versus pronoun retention in relative clauses have been collected in an influential study by Hyltenstam (1984) for speakers of different first languages (Persian, Greek, Spanish and Finnish) learning Swedish as L2, and these data enable us to test whether patterns of acquisition follow these patterns of grammar and performance. In other words, they enable us to conduct an empirical test of whether SLA data are predictable on the basis of cross-linguistic grammatical and performance patterns. Swedish has relative clauses not unlike those of English: a relative pronoun is co-indexed with the head of the relative and is moved to the left of the relative clause, leaving a gap (or subcategorisor) with no resumptive pronoun. The L1 grammars in Hyltenstam's study differ according to whether they do (Persian, Greek) or do not (Spanish, Finnish) employ resumptive pronouns.

It turns out that the interlanguage data for all the L1–L2 pairs in Hyltenstam's study contain at least some resumptive pronouns, with their occurrence being especially favoured when the L1 also has them. An example of the kind of (ungrammatical) pronoun-retaining relative clause that is produced by Persian learners of Swedish is given in (4), with its Persian counterpart in (5) (cf. Moravcsik 2006:164–5):

(4) *mannen som jag slog honom   (Swedish)
     man-the that I hit him
     'the man that I hit'

(5) mardi ke man (u-ra) zadam   (Persian)
     man that I (him) hit

(4) becomes grammatical when the pronoun *honom* is omitted.

Table 4.2 Gaps and pronouns in Swedish second language acquisition (Hyltenstam 1984)

Gaps	SU	DO	IO/OBL	GEN
PersianLSwedish	100%	42%	25%	8%
GreekLSwedish	100%	58%	42%	8%
SpanishLSwedish	100%	83%	62%	8%
FinnishLSwedish	100%	100%	100%	33%
Resumptive Pronouns				
PersianLSwedish	0%	58%	75%	92%
GreekLSwedish	0%	42%	58%	92%
SpanishLSwedish	0%	17%	38%	92%
FinnishLSwedish	0%	0%	0%	67%

Key: PersianLSwedish= Persian L1 learning Swedish L2 etc.

Hyltenstam's data are reproduced in Table 4.2. They show two specific patterns. First, the frequency of resumptive pronouns in Swedish L2 is greater when the L1 has productive resumptive pronouns, i.e. for Persian and Greek, than when it does not. This is a clear transfer effect. But transfer does not explain the resumptive pronouns in Spanish and Finnish, and hence transfer is not on its own sufficient to explain all the data. What is significant for all four L1s is the second pattern in Table 4.2: gaps always decline from top to bottom down the AH, regardless of transfer, while pronouns increase, and this distribution is systematically correlated with that of Table 4.1. Both tables reveal an ease of processing effect, therefore, reflected in the distribution of gaps to pronouns, with pronouns favoring the lower and more difficult positions of the AH, while transfer may or may not add additional resumptive pronouns to this effect, depending on the L1 and on its particular grammatical conventions. The absolute quantities for L2 pronouns are higher in the L1s that retain pronouns, but the relative distribution of gaps to pronouns is exactly that of Table 4.1, further confirming the processing basis for gaps in smaller and pronouns in more complex environments.

The relative clause data in Tables 4.1 and 4.2 point to the need for both transfer- and processing-based accounts of interlanguage data. They also support the general correspondence between conventionalised grammatical data and acquisition data for which Jakobson, Slobin, Eckman and Hawkins have argued. But they show that this correspondence may operate at a more general, macro, level, rather than on an item to item basis. The pattern of gaps to pronouns differs between each of the different L1s in Table 4.2, and each differs in turn from that in Table 4.1. But the relative distribution is the same throughout. The SLA data suggest further that L1 transfer, when it occurs, asserts itself in such a way as to maintain the same relative patterning that can be found in grammars and performance, increasing the absolute values for retained pronouns in those interlanguages in which the L1 also has pronouns. It is important now to find out whether other factors that facilitate second language acquisition, namely frequency effects, ease of learning, and so on, also operate within the universal hierarchies and constraints motivated by processing, or whether they result in partial mismatches with these.

An interesting case to look at here is the Minimise Forms principle of Hawkins (2004:38), defined as follows:

> The human processor prefers to minimize the formal complexity of each linguistic form F (its phoneme, morpheme, word, or phrasal units) and the number of forms with unique conventionalized property assignments, thereby assigning more properties to fewer forms. These minimizations apply in proportion to the ease with which a given property P can be assigned in processing to a given F.

In adult native speaker processing there is clear evidence for minimal forms of these different types (cf. Hawkins op. cit. for copious illustrations) and these minimisations result in greater ambiguity, vagueness and 'zero specification' and in the greater exploitation of enrichments and inferences in online processing (of the kind discussed by e.g. Levinson 2000). In both first and second language acquisition, however, we have seen in Section 4.4 that there is clear evidence that a unique one-to-one form–property pairing facilitates the learning of the property in question. One can hypothesise that we are dealing with a general learning mechanism here that asserts itself, especially at the earlier stages of language acquisition. But once the properties of the adult or L2 grammar have been identified, the general processing preference for minimal forms, with concomitant reductions in processing effort and greater exploitation of processing enrichments, should gradually take over and we should see later acquisition stages that are more in accordance with native speaker processing and with grammatical conventions.

This is one general issue that is raised by the current state of the art in second and also in first language acquisition, and which deserves further investigation. The facts we have just considered confirm the point we made above in connection with the control structure *John is eager to please* that we need a theory of both (ease of) learning and (ease of) processing, and in the next chapter we assume that both exist and that both play a role in structuring the development of interlanguages, even though their effects frequently overlap and are hard to tease apart.

The empirical evidence presented in this section illustrates a growing convergence between grammatical patterns across languages on the one hand and data from language processing and language acquisition on the other. The relative clause data summarised are of particular interest because they also involve clear complexity differences as discussed in the previous section. Observations such as these support the usefulness of both cross-linguistic patterns and complexity metrics in a second language acquisition context and we will return to formulate a prediction for acquisition data in these terms in Chapter 5.

4.5.2 Back to transfer

This discussion of the correspondences between grammars, performance and acquisition puts a new perspective on the transfer question, and enables us to clarify some rules of argumentation. For some interlanguage data, particularly those involving simpler and less marked forms and structures at variance with the L2, there may be two logically possible explanations: transfer (a prerequisite for which is that the L1 has only simpler and less marked items as well); or an explanation, possibly processing based, derived from typological universals.

These possibilities are nicely illustrated in Eckman's (1984) discussion of interlanguage data in relation to the implicational universal involving final consonant devoicing, discussed briefly above, which he formulates (ibid.:88–90) as: if a language has voiced obstruents word-finally, then it also has voiceless obstruents word-finally. Based on this universal, Hawkins (1987:460–1) makes the following prediction: second-language acquirers of English will either acquire voiceless before voiced obstruents in word-final position or they will successfully acquire both together and dispose of a voicing contrast from the outset (correctly distinguishing *sad* from *sat*, etc.). But there will be no interlanguage stage in which only voiced obstruents are found in word-final position, that is with the implicational antecedent property (P) occurring in the absence of the consequent (Q).

Eckman examined the interlanguage data of Japanese, Mandarin Chinese, Spanish and Persian learners of English. The Japanese and Mandarin Chinese speakers used both voiced and voiceless obstruents in word-final position, the Spanish and Persian speakers disposed of voiceless obstruents only. Both the predicted possibilities occurred, therefore, and none of these groups used voiced obstruents only in final position. There is a ready explanation for this avoidance of voicing word-finally in numerous languages and in some of the interlanguage data, in terms of phonetic simplification and a principle of least effort, i.e. in terms of the processing of sounds (Lindblom and Maddieson 1988, Lindblom, MacNeilage and Studdert-Kennedy 1984, Maddieson 2005). This explanation can account for both the cross-linguistic patterning and for the interlanguage data: languages (including interlanguages) may employ either simpler obstruents only (voiceless ones), especially in low-energy environments like word-final position, but if they employ more complex sounds (voiced obstruents) they will also have corresponding simpler counterparts (voiceless ones).

There is no need for a language-specific transfer explanation for these interlanguages, since they are fully in accordance with cross-linguistic patterns. However, transfer can potentially provide an additional motivation for these interlanguage states in the event that the L1 has parallel properties. Eckman points out that the only L1–L2 pair for which this was a possibility is Spanish-English. Spanish has no voicing contrast in word-final position, and the Spanish acquirers of English produced only voiceless word-final obstruents. Japanese and Mandarin Chinese, by contrast, do not permit any obstruents at all in word-final position, and yet in their renderings of English they produced both voiced and voiceless word-final obstruents, just like native speakers. This L1–L2 contrast eliminates the possibility of transfer. Similarly, even when there is L1–L2 identity, as there was in the case of Persian and English both of which have word-final voicing, transfer was also not found: the Persian learners produced only voiceless word-final obstruents.

This example highlights the need for caution when invoking transfer as an explanation in SLA. There needs to be a convergence between interlanguage (IL) stages and the relevant L1. There was no such convergence between

Japanese, Mandarin Chinese and Persian on the one hand and the IL data from these learners of English on the other, but there was in the case of Spanish, making this a possible, or an additional explanation for the IL data, but not a necessary one. In other words, transfer may not be sufficient, in the event that there is another explanation for the IL, but it is not ruled out either. Evidence for this additional reinforcing effect can come from comparative IL data of the kind we saw in the resumptive pronouns of Table 4.2. There was an added effect of pronoun retention in the Persian-Swedish and Greek-Swedish ILs, compared with the Spanish-Swedish and Finnish-Swedish ones, plausibly due to transfer and L1–IL convergence. Similarly when there is convergence between L1 and L2, transfer can still be a (reinforcing) possibility, in addition to simple learning of the L2, in the event that IL stages conform to both. In the next chapter we shall define a principle of maximising 'positive transfer' effects which we see as resulting, ultimately, from minimised learning effort.

Transfer arguments that appeal to usage frequencies in an IL for certain features or constructions may experience the same difficulty with regard to ultimate explanations. For example, Gilquin (2008:7–8) discusses underuse of the Passive by French and Swedish learners of English. French native speakers do not use the Passive as frequently as English native speakers do, but Swedish native speakers do. Hence the argument that this is a 'negative transfer' effect from French is weakened by the Swedish native language and IL data. Instead the underuse of the Passive may be a universal performance feature of interlanguages which may be related to the general preference that learners have for unmarked rather than marked options (cf. Ellis 2003) or for a personal rather than impersonal style (see Petch-Tyson 1998). However, Gilquin (2008:8) does go on to say that 'the influence of L1 French cannot be excluded, and it is probable that transfer reinforces the effect of other factors'.

Transfers are easier to argue for when the L1 and the L2 contrast, and when the nature of the contrast is of a more idiosyncratic and language-specific nature, and is less closely aligned with implicational universal patterns. Odlin and Alonso-Vásquez (2006) have shown that present or past perfect tense in English can have seemingly distinct meanings in different interlanguages depending on the L1. For example in French, as a result of passée composée influence, the present perfect is used in *I have gone to Rome last year*, while Spanish L1 learners produce more target-like structures as in *I have gone to Rome a few times*. Definite and indefinite articles provide other good examples of L1 transfer, since many languages lack them and there are many language-specific contrasts here, and hence their presence or absence in an IL can often be at variance with the L2 and convergent with L1. Cross and Papp (2008:68) show that Chinese learners of English make significant numbers of errors (they count 20% in their learner corpus) involving the appropriate co-occurrences of verbs with prepositions. These are often lexically idiosyncratic in English. They argue that L1 Chinese is the reason behind the omission or inaccurate use of prepositions since Chinese has fewer words functioning as prepositions and they are used less frequently than in English.

Notice finally in this section that we have also seen some revealing examples of L1–L2 contrasts that do not result in transfer effects. These have been much less discussed in the literature, for understandable reasons, than the cases where transfer does occur, but the non-occurrence of transfer is just as revealing and as significant for theories of SLA, in some ways more so, as its occurrence. For example, Pienemann (2009) gives examples of different L1 learners of Spanish L2 all getting the Spanish PRO-drop structure right from the beginning (studies quoted in Pienemann 2009). Similarly English learners of Japanese acquire the head-final syntactic properties of this language early, while Japanese learners of English master the head-initial properties of English early as well.

We shall return in the next chapter to a discussion of when negative transfers appear to be permitted, in general, and when they appear to be blocked.

4.5.3 Slobin's operating principles for first language acquisition

Slobin (1977) has proposed a set of 'operating principles' based on cross-linguistic comparison of early language acquisition. These operating principles are of interest in connection with the principles of second language acquisition that we propose in the next chapter. They have the status of general information processing constraints of relevance for both language learning and linguistic communication. The four operating principles are given in (6) (Slobin 1977:186–188):

(6) i.   Be clear.
     ii.   Be processable.
     iii. Be quick and easy.
     iv.   Be expressive.

Strömqvist, Hellstrand & Nordqvist (1998:206) comment and elaborate on these principles and observe that they can come into conflict. For example, *Be quick and easy* can put *Be processable* at risk. The first and second operating principles, *Be clear* and *Be processable*, are assumed to be prioritised in early stages of language development, while the third and the fourth have a 'greater relative weight' in later stages of development (ibid.). This is understandable because, as Strömqvist et al (1998:206) put it 'mapping out form-content relations and making yourself understood' are priorities in early language acquisition. The latter two principles can also come into conflict, as the authors show in their study of spoken versus written language acquisition (ibid.). Spoken language is associated with the principles and constraints of online interaction, while a high degree of expressivity demands more grammatical and lexical resources and also more processing effort and planning time. The constraints of online interaction are lifted when one composes a written text. Being quick and easy is traded for being expressive in written narratives.

There is a moral and a precedent in Slobin's principles for the principles we shall propose in the next chapter for second language acquisition, with particular relevance to the EPP. There are multiple factors that appear to be at play in structuring the patterns we observe in the CLC, which sometimes reinforce one another but on other occasions are in conflict. The devil lies in the details of the formulation for these principles, as always. It is to this that we now turn.

5 Some principles of learning and interlanguage formation supported by the CLC

After the review of SLA research in the last chapter, and of other research relevant for our purposes in first language acquisition, language processing, typology and complexity, we are now in a position to illustrate some principles that appear to structure the learner data in the CLC. These principles are not altogether new. What is novel to our approach lies in the breadth of relevant factors to which we appeal, in the details of our proposed formulations, and in the interaction between principles. They define possible versus impossible, and likely versus less likely, acquisition stages and interlanguages and they are offered here as an initial explanation for the relative sequencing of learner data at the six proficiency levels of the CEFR. In other words, they are offered as a framework for understanding the criterial features of different levels. They define principles of second language learning that are on the one hand derived from data provided by the EPP and that contribute on the other to an explanation for why the CEFR levels are differentiated the way they are.

Our principles draw heavily on the current state of the art in the language sciences (see Chapter 4) and are intended as a contribution to the theory of second language learning. In this way our unique and growing corpus collection can give something back to theory, as well as benefiting from it in understanding why we see the criterial features that we do at the different proficiency levels. In particular we hope to be able to shed some light on certain issues, involving especially the relative sequencing of developmental changes in SLA, the presence versus absence of transfer, and the interaction and relative strength of principles.

There is also a practical reason for engaging with theory in this way and for asking why questions in this context. Ultimately, through the EPP, we want to provide learners, teachers, textbook writers and examiners with a large list of criterial features that can lead to improved and more efficient outcomes in learning, teaching textbook-writing and examining respectively (recall Chapter 1.4). But to offer only an uninterpreted and unexplained list would not, we believe, be very helpful. It all becomes more convincing and more useful if the criterial features we define can be shown to make sense in terms of some simple and intuitive principles of learning that blend well with the day-to-day experiences of practitioners and that help them understand what is easy, and what is not so easy, in the learning of English.

5.1 Maximise Positive Transfer

Our first principle is (1):

(1) Maximise Positive Transfer (MaPT)

Properties of the L1 which are also present in the L2 are learned more easily and with less learning effort, and are readily transferred, on account of pre-existing knowledge in L1.

Shared L1/L2 properties should result, in general, in earlier L2 acquisition, in more of the relevant properties being learned, and in fewer errors, unless these shared properties involve e.g. high complexity and are impacted by other factors such as (3) below. Dissimilar L1/L2 properties will be harder to learn by virtue of the additional learning that is required, again in general.

For example, learning the grammar and usage of definite and indefinite articles in English is easier when the L1 has the same grammar and usage. This was illustrated in Chapter 2.5 with sample data involving the presence versus omission of definite and indefinite articles in languages with, and without, articles. Table 2.6 showed that Missing Determiner error rates were very low at all proficiency levels for L1s that had similar definite and indefinite article systems to English (French, German and Spanish). Table 2.7, on the other hand, showed significantly higher error rates and a general linear improvement from B1 to C2 for languages without articles (Turkish, Japanese, Korean, Russian), with Chinese showing an inverted U-shaped progression. In the present context we see these results as supporting principle (1) MaPT, which is in turn motivated by a desire to minimise learning effort. Speakers of French, German and Spanish already know a significant amount about the grammar and usage conventions of definite and indefinite articles in English, because their own languages involve a significant overlap with the grammar and usage of English. There is much less learning of new grammatical rules and usage conventions to be accomplished, therefore, when proceeding from these languages to English. For speakers of Turkish, Japanese and Korean, etc., whose languages do not have definite and indefinite articles, there is much more to be learned and learning is more effortful as a consequence. This is reflected in the error rates in the CLC.

More generally, principle (1) leads us to expect that there will be learning advantages whenever the L1 and L2 share grammatical and lexical properties. However, it must be stressed that the sharing of grammatical and lexical properties between L1 and L2 does not actually guarantee the early transfer of these (positive) properties, on account of other relevant factors with which principle (1) MaPT interacts, such as principles (2)–(4) below. For example, complex consonant phonemes or complex lexical meanings that are shared between L1 and L2 may not be transferred early on account of their complexity, which impacts all aspects of the early proficiency levels in particular. This was illustrated in Chapter 4.5.2 when discussing Eckman's (1984) finding that Persian learners of English did not initially transfer the voiced–voiceless opposition in word-final obstruents from Persian into L2 English. Kellerman (1983) has also argued that more complex and non-core lexical meanings of verbs like *break* are not initially transferred from L1 Dutch to L2 English, even when the two languages share these semantic extensions from the core. Our principles can be in partial opposition to one another like this, and they permit different possible outcomes when they are so, in proportion to their respective strengths. Greater complexity, for example, will resist positive transfer to a greater extent.

Notice also that principle (1) MaPT, in conjunction with principle (5) below for negative transfer, now replace the more general Maximise Transfer principle of Hawkins and Buttery (2009). It is desirable, as we shall see, to separate the predictions that we make for positive transfer (i.e. when a property of L1 is transferred into L2 in a way that is correct in L2) from those we make for negative transfer (when the result is incorrect in L2).

5.2 Maximise Frequently Occurring Properties

A second principle is (2):

(2) Maximise Frequently Occurring Properties (MaF)
     Properties of the L2 are learned in proportion to their frequency of occurrence (as measured, for example, in the British National Corpus): more frequent exposure of a property to the learner facilitates its learning and reduces learning effort.

More frequent properties in the input will result in earlier L2 acquisition, in more of the relevant properties being learned, and in fewer errors, in general. Infrequency makes learning more effortful.

For example, in our discussion of MacWhinney's (1987, 2005) competition model for first and second language acquisition (Chapter 4.2), we saw that typological properties of languages are acquired early when they are used frequently and have high 'cue validity' for the expression of basic argument relations and thematic roles, agent versus patient, etc. Different languages make use of different strategies here, and to a greater or lesser extent, namely basic word order, agreement, animacy, etc., with more or less cue strength and frequency for these different features, and learners are apparently sensitive to these cues and acquire them rapidly. Learning is easier when cues are more frequent. In addition, learners want the meanings of their basic clause types to be readily understood by native speakers, and efficient communication requires rapid learning of cues that are appropriate for the L2 (see the discussion of efficiency in Chapter 4.4 and 5.5 below).

As a further example, learning English nouns and verbs with high frequencies of use is generally easier than learning those with lower frequencies, as illustrated in Hawkins and Buttery (2009): frequent lexical items such as the verbs *see*, *want*, *go* and *need* are overrepresented at first in the lower proficiency levels of L2 English, moving closer to L1 English norms at the higher proficiency levels.

More frequent construction types and 'subcategorisation frames' for verbs in English are also acquired earlier than more infrequent ones. This has been shown in a most interesting, and still unpublished, study by Caroline Williams (2007) using the RASP-parsed corpus. Table 5.1 shows the verb co-occurrence frames that Williams found in the CLC data at A2. This table includes some of the most basic, most frequent and simplest construction types of English, like intransitive sentences (*he went*), basic transitives (*he loved her*), intransitives with a prepositional phrase complement (*they apologised to him*), and so on. Williams describes and numbers the frames using a taxonomy of verb subcategorisation frames originally developed by Ted Briscoe, John Carroll and their colleagues (see Briscoe 2000, Briscoe and Carroll 1997, Korhonen, Krymolowski and Briscoe 2006, Preiss, Briscoe and Korhonen 2007). Table 5.2 lists the new verb co-occurrence types that appear first at B1. They include the less frequent ditransitives (*she asked him his name*) and Subject-to-Object Raising constructions (*I found him to be a good doctor*). Table 5.3 gives the new co-occurrence frames found at B2. They include even more complex structures like *he told the audience that he was leaving* and *he thought about what to do*. Interestingly Williams found no new verb co-occurrence frames at the C levels, suggesting that the basic construction types of English have been learned by B2, in some of their lexical manifestations at least, i.e. with at least some of their triggering verbs. These tables preserve the frame numbering used by Williams and by Briscoe and his colleagues.

Notice here and throughout this section that the example sentences given to illustrate the verb co-occurrences of English, in these tables and in the main text, have been taken from the relevant research literature and are **not** being claimed in the present context to be attested in the CLC in exactly this form. If a co-occurrence frame is listed in one of the tables, this means that Williams (2007) found evidence for the relevant construction type at this level, not necessarily for this token with this particular verb. We will be illustrating

Table 5.1 A2 verb co-occurrence frames

19	NP - V - V (+*ing*) *his hair needs combing*
22	NP - V *he went*
23	NP - V (recip Subj) *they met*
24	NP - V - NP *he loved her*
31	NP - V - NP - PP (P = *for*) *she bought [a book] [for him]*
49	NP - V - NP - PP *she added [the flowers] [to the bouquet]*
76	NP - V - Part - NP / V - NP - Part *she looked up [the entry] / looked [the entry] up*
87	NP - V - PP (P = LOC/*to* *they apologised to him*
104	NP - V - S *they thought [that he was always late]*
112	NP - V - VPinf (Subj Control) *I wanted to come*

Table 5.2 New B1 verb co-occurrence frames

16	NP - V - S (Wh-movement with *how, why, where, when*) *he asked [how she did it]*
17	NP - V - VPinfin (Wh-movement with *how, where, when*) *he explained [how to do it]*
33	NP - V - NP - VPinfin (Obj Control) (infin without *to*) *he helped her bake the cake*
35	NP - V - NP - V (+*ing*) (Obj Control) *I caught him stealing*
37	NP - V - NP - NP *she asked him [his name]*
56	NP - V - NP - PP (P = *to*) (Subtype: Dative Move) *he gave [a big kiss] [to his mother]*
57	NP - V - NP - (To Be) - NP (Subj to Obj Raising) *I found him (to be) [a good doctor]*
58	NP - V - NP - Vpastpart (V = passive) (Obj Control/Raising) *he wanted [the children] found*
63	NP - V - P - Ving - NP (V = +*ing*) (Subj Control) *they failed in attempting [the climb]*
70	NP - V - P - S (*whether* - Wh-move) *he thought about [whether he wanted to go]*
74	NP - V - Part *she gave up*
77	NP - V - Part - NP - PP / V - NP - Part - PP *I separated out [the three boys] [from the crowd] /separated [the three boys] out [from the crowd]*
97	NP - V - PP - S *they admitted [to the authorities] [that they had entered illegally]*
113	NP - V - S (*whether* = Wh-move) *he asked [whether he should come]*

Table 5.3 New B2 verb co-occurrence frames

25	NP - V - NP - AdjP (Obj Control)
	he painted [the car] red
29	NP - V - NP - *as* - NP (Obj Control)
	I sent him as [a messenger]
52	NP - V - NP - S
	he told [the audience] [that he was leaving]
65	NP - V - P - NP - V (+*ing*) (Obj Control)
	they worried about him drinking
73	NP - V - P - VPinfin (Wh-move) (Subj Control)
	he thought about [what to do]
114	NP - V - S (Wh-move)
	he asked [what he should do]
139	NP - V - Part - VPinfin (Subj Control)
	he set out [to win]

in Section 5.3 exactly which verbs are found in some of these constructions in the CLC, for example, and at which level(s). More generally Chapters 7 and 8 provide lots of lexically specific criterial features in addition to grammatical ones, and they also give representative examples taken from the CLC for each criterial feature that we propose. It is important to combine lexis and grammar in this way because a given construction type may appear at earlier proficiency levels with only a limited set of triggering verbs, generally the most frequently occurring ones, in accordance with principle (2) MaF. It is therefore important to document the expansion in usage for constructions by showing which additional verbs are found in the various co-occurrence frames as learning progresses. See Ellis and Larsen-Freeman (2009) for further support of this general point.

Table 5.4 gives the average token frequencies for the verb co-occurrences of Tables 5.1, 5.2 and 5.3 in native English corpora, while Table 5.5 shows their average frequency ranking. These relative frequencies are taken from a number of corpora including the BNC and are reported in Hawkins and Buttery (2009). The relevant data has been extracted from the VALEX lexicon (see www.cl.cam.ac.uk/~alk23/subcat/lexicon.html), which has been acquired automatically from five large corpora and from the web. Clearly, the progression from A2 to B2 correlates with the frequencies of these

Table 5.4 Average token frequencies in native English corpora (including BNC) for the new verb co-occurrence frames appearing at the learner levels (Tables 5.1–5.3)

A2	B1	B2/C1/C2
1,041,634	38,174	27,615

Table 5.5 Average frequency ranking in native English corpora (including BNC) for the new verb co-occurrence frames appearing at the learner levels (Tables 5.1–5.3)

A2	B1	B2/C1/C2
8.2	38.6	55.6

co-occurrence frames in the input. Learners of English are first learning the most frequent constructions used by English native speakers (Table 5.1), and then progressively less frequent constructions (Tables 5.2 and 5.3), in accordance, we would argue, with principle (2) MaF.

5.3 Maximise Structurally and Semantically Simple Properties

The progression in Tables 5.1–5.3 also appears to correlate, in general, with the increasing complexity of these verb co-occurrence frames. Structural complexity and frequency are often inversely correlated in language use, i.e. the more complex a structure is, the less frequently it is used (see Hawkins 2004 and Wasow 2002 for relevant data). Matching this, learners of English first learn the simpler co-occurrence frames of English before they learn more complex ones. But simplicity/complexity and frequency/infrequency are not always aligned, see e.g. Diessel (2004) for discussion of the relationship between them in first language acquisition and for some illustrative dissociations. And definitions of complexity are not always in agreement with one another (see Hawkins 2009), whereas frequency effects are more readily observable and quantifiable, so we do need to define separate principles here for both theoretical and methodological reasons. A third principle is accordingly (3):

(3) Maximise Structurally and Semantically Simple Properties (MaS)
     Properties of the L2 are **learned** in proportion to their structural and semantic simplicity: simplicity means there are fewer properties to be learned and less learning effort is required.

Simpler properties should result, in general, in earlier L2 acquisition, in more of the relevant properties being learned, and in fewer errors. Complexity makes learning more effortful, in general, since there are more properties to be learned.

For example, simpler consonants and consonantal distinctions in a phonological inventory can be acquired earlier than more complex ones (Eckman 1984). In syntax we referred in Chapter 4.4 to Mellow's (2008) case study of a 12-year-old Spanish learner of English whose complex syntactic dependencies were acquired relatively late. We also discussed raising-type structures, which are also late acquired (see e.g. Anderson 2005, Callies 2008): Subject-to-Subject Raising (*John is likely to pass the exam*), Subject-to-Object Raising (*I believe John to be sick*), and Tough Movement (*John is easy to please*). They involve complex displacements of arguments from a lower clause into a higher clause in which they do not contract normal semantic relations with their 'matrix' verbs and adjectives. And they also involve syntactic ambiguity in surface structure between the raising interpretation and the more common 'control' pattern in which surface arguments do contract normal semantic and syntactic relations with adjacent predicates (recall *John is easy to please* versus *John is eager to please*, Chomsky 1957, Hawkins 1986).

It is instructive to summarise at this point what the CLC tells us about raising. In Chapter 7.2 we give example sentences from the corpus showing when raising structures of each of the types are first attested for an illustrative set of raising triggers (and including also Subject-to-Object Raising verbs plus Passive, e.g. *Smoking is known to cause cancer*, see Postal 1974). The results are summarised in Table 5.6. For Subject-to-Subject Raising, for example, the construction first appears at B1, but only with the verb *seem* and the adjective *supposed*. Most of the verbs and adjectives that trigger it occur at B2. This confirms the point we have been stressing that we need to consider both grammatical constructions and their lexical triggers when making claims about criterial differences between levels. Subject-to-Object Raising is found with three lexical triggers at B1 (*expect*, *like* and *want*), but the remaining nine in the set of 12 we looked for are B2 or later. Williams' (2007) classification of Subject-to-Object Raising as a B1 feature is correct, therefore (see her verb co-occurrence frames 57 and 58 in Table 5.2), but this is true only for its first appearance: most instances occur later, sometimes significantly later at C1 and C2. Similarly Subject-to-Subject Raising is first attested at B1, but it would be more accurate to characterise this as a B2 feature overall since a full ten of the 13 raising triggers tested are first found at this level. Subject-to-Object Raising plus Passive is first attested at B2, with most triggering predicates occurring at C1, while most (three) of the five attested Tough Movement triggers in our sample tested are B2.

In the lexicon simpler and more basic meanings for verbs are acquired earlier than more complex extensions from the primary sense, figurative uses, etc. So the verb *break* is attested at A2 in its basic physical sense (*break a glass*). *Break* in the extended sense of INTERRUPT is B1 (*break the routine*) and in the extended sense of END is B2 (*break an agreement*). The idiomatic *break the bank* is first found at C1 while an original figurative use (*break the wall his fears have forced him to create*) is C2. See Chapter 8.1 for many further examples of such lexical progressions.

We referred in Chapter 4.4 to the need to define both a theory of learning

Table 5.6 Raising constructions in the CLC

Subject-to-Subject Raising verbs and adjectives
e.g. *John is likely to pass the exam*
  The noise ceased to get on his nerves

Lexical triggers appearing for the first time in the CLC by level (from a sample of 13 tested):
A2	none (i.e. no raising predicates at all)
B1	*seem* (verbs)
	supposed (adjectives)
B2	*appear, cease, fail, happen, prove, turn out* (verbs)
	certain, likely, sure, unlikely (adjectives)
C1	*chance* (verb)
C2	none (i.e. no new raising predicates in this sample)

Subject-to-Object Raising Verbs verbs (unpassivised)
e.g. *I found him to be an engaging chap*

Lexical triggers appearing for the first time in the CLC by level (from a sample of 12 tested)
A2	none
B1	*expect, like, want*
B2	*imagine, prefer*
C1	*believe, find, suppose, take*
C2	*declare, presume, remember*

Subject-to-Object Raising verbs plus Passive
e.g. *Smoking is known to cause cancer*

Lexical triggers appearing for the first time in the CLC by level (from a sample of 13 tested)
A2	none
B1	none
B2	*expected, known, obliged, thought*
C1	*assumed, discovered, felt, found, proved*
C2	*presumed*

(Not attested: *alleged, stated, understood*)

Tough Movement
e.g. *The book is easy to read*

Lexical triggers appearing for the first time in the CLC by level (from a sample of 7 tested)
A2	none
B1	*easy*
B2	*difficult, good, hard*
C1	none (i.e. no new tough predicates in the sample)
C2	*tough*

(Not attested: *boring, tedious*)

---

and a theory of processing, on the grounds that certain linguistic phenomena are easier to learn but harder to process, and vice versa. There is nonetheless a large overlap between ease and difficulty of learning and ease and difficulty of processing. Infrequent linguistic items and their meanings are harder to learn and harder to access and process, in general. More complex structures are harder to learn and also harder to process, and rarer in corpora as a result.

This makes it difficult to tease the two apart. This book is not the proper context in which to try to contribute to the resolution of this major issue in psycholinguistics. We simply offer here a processing counterpart for principle (3) MaS, namely (3'):

(3')   Maximise Structurally and Semantically Simple Properties (MaS)

Properties of the L2 are ***used*** in proportion to their structural and semantic simplicity: simplicity means there are fewer properties to be ***processed*** in online language use and less ***processing*** effort is required.

In other words, the striving for simplicity impacts online processing, just as it does learning. Word orders, for example, that simplify and shorten the domains for phrase structure processing are selected in native speaking corpora in direct proportion to their simplicity when grammars provide structural choices, which they do in English in post-verbal position (Hawkins 1994, 2004, Wasow 2002). In Chapter 2.4 we showed that structurally complex relative clauses low on the Keenan–Comrie Accessibility Hierarchy (cf. Chapter 4.5.1), namely those formed on indirect object and oblique positions, are used very infrequently in both learner data (see Table 2.4) and in the BNC (Table 2.5). In fact, the rates of occurrence in the CLC are even less than they are for the BNC prior to the C levels, suggesting that both principle (3) involving ease of learning and principle (3') involving ease of processing are operating at the A and B proficiency levels. Second language learners appear to use the complex structures they know even less than native speakers do, gradually moving to native speaker distributions at the higher levels.

5.4 Minimise Quantitative Load

A fourth principle is (4):

(4)   Minimise Quantitative Load (MiQ)

The fewer items and/or properties to be learned in a given grammatical or lexical area comprising data set D, the easier D is to learn, in general.

Small data sets should exhibit fewer errors, (proportionately) more of the L2 properties being learned, and earlier acquisition. Larger data sets will exhibit the reverse.

For example, learning a small number of tense and aspect distinctions expressed inflectionally on verbs as in English should be easier than learning a large number in a language like Latin. Learning a small inventory of argument types expressed morpho-syntactically as cases on noun phrases as in Japanese should be easier than learning the larger number of a language like Finnish. Learning a limited set of (closed-class) properties in some morpho-syntactic area, such as subject agreement on English verbs, tense inflection on English verbs, or the singular/plural distinction on English nouns, should be easier than learning the large (open class) set of lexical verbs and nouns in English with all their semantic and syntactic properties and distinctions.

This last point can be illustrated with the following tests. We expect, first, to see fewer morpho-syntactic errors involving some part of speech, e.g. verbs, than we see lexical choice errors for that same part of speech (as reflected in the 'R' or replacement categories of CUP's error coding), since there is a much larger set of items to be learned in the latter case. Secondly we expect to see a greater improvement (measured by declining error rates) from A2/B1 to C2 in the morpho-syntactic area than in the lexical choice (i.e. the replacement) area, since there are still numerous verbs and nouns to be learned at the later levels.

The first prediction is tested in Table 5.7, which measures the ratios of RV errors to AGV, to IV and to FV errors for ten different first languages at the C2 levels. These different error types are defined below:

Table 5.7 Ratios of RV errors to AGV, IV and FV errors at C2

First language	RV to AGV ratio	RV to IV ratio	RV to FV ratio
Spanish	4.7/1	13.2/1	2.3/1
German	6.5/1	8.6/1	2.2/1
Japanese	2.7/1	7.9/1	2.6/1
Chinese	1.7/1	9.8/1	1.7/1
Korean	2.4/1	11.5/1	2.5/1
Turkish	4.3/1	14.3/1	2.2/1
Arabic	2.5/1	4.7/1	2.5/1
Polish	3.3/1	6.8/1	2.3/1
Russian	3.3/1	6.3/1	2.3/1
French	4.1/1	8/1	2.7/1

RV Replace verb *I existed last weekend in London* (spent)

Where a valid word in the language has been used AND it is the correct part of speech but not the correct word, it is a replace error.

AGV Verb agreement error *The three birds is singing* (are)

When the word is correct (and, JAH) the form of the word used is valid in the language BUT wrong in the context because it does not agree grammatically with its co-ordinates, it is an Agreement error.

IV Incorrect inflection of verb *I spended last weekend in London* (spent)

Where an attempt at inflecting a word results in an invalid inflected form, it is an inflection error . . . The learner has made a false assumption about whether a verb is regular or irregular and inflected it accordingly. Most commonly the error is caused by putting regular inflections on irregular verbs.

FV Wrong verb form *We must bearing in mind that . . .* (bear)

When the word is correct and, the form of the word used is valid in the language BUT wrong in the context, it is a Form error . . . FV covers instances where the base (infinitive without 'to'), -ing and to+infinitive forms of the verb have been confused in any combination.

Error rates were counted per 100,000 words of text in Table 5.7 (see the discussion of error quantification methods in Chapter 2.3). For most (but not all) of the ten languages error rates were also available as a percentage of the total number of verbs used at C2 by each first language. The first prediction was tested on these percentage figures as well and found to be confirmed in each case. Since more languages could be included in the test using error rates per 100,000 words, at the time of going to press, this method of calculation was the one selected for illustration in Table 5.7, and also in Table 5.8 below.

Table 5.8 Declines in RV, AGV, IV and FV errors from A2/B1 to C2

First language	RV decline	AGV decline	IV decline	FV decline
Spanish	21%	55%	41%	49%
German	39%	59%	42%	68%
Japanese	2%	22%	2%	22%
Chinese	44%	*22%	*42%	52%
Korean	15%	36%	33%	55%
Turkish	15%	33%	72%	19%
Arabic	28%	67%	*-21%	50%
Polish	37%	76%	78%	76%
Russian	41%	44%	67%	60%
French	34%	67%	*28%	55%

The **first** prediction is confirmed without exception in Table 5.7. There are always more RV errors than AGV, IV and FV errors at C2 for each of these ten first languages.

Notice that the same relative ratios seen in Table 5.7 obtain at the earlier proficiency levels as well, but are less extreme since morpho-syntactic errors decline more rapidly than RV errors from A2/B1 to C2, see Table 5.8.

The **second** prediction is tested in Table 5.8, which measures the improvements in RV errors from A2/B1 (whichever had the higher error count) to C2, compared with similar improvements in morpho-syntactic AGV, IV and FV errors for these same ten languages. All but four of the 30 predictions illustrated (those marked with a '*') are correct, i.e. the morpho-syntactic errors generally decline by a higher percentage than the RV errors. Learners are apparently improving faster when there are fewer items to be learned, in accordance with principle (4) MiQ.

5.5 Negative Transfer

When L1 and L2 share grammatical and lexical properties, transfers from one to the other result in positive, i.e. correct, properties of the L2 being learned in a simple and efficient way (see section 5.1). When properties are not shared, however, and transfer takes place, the result is negative or incorrect properties in the L2. Positive transfers are maximised, we have argued, because they are advantageous for learning. We would also argue that they are good for processing as well. Processing effort is minimised when transfers are positive, since processing mechanisms that the native speaker adopts in his/her L1 for the production and comprehension of the relevant properties can be transferred directly into the processing of L2.

Negative transfers, on the other hand, present a different picture. Empirically, we cannot say that they are maximized, since we saw in the literature review of Chapter 4, and we observe in the CLC, that sometimes they occur and sometimes they don't. This is one of the big unresolved current issues: when do negative transfers occur, and when not? Our principles must allow for them on some occasions, but not others, and they must be opposed on some occasions and not others. The most important point to make at the outset is that negative transfers are permitted in L2 acquisition, subject to other constraints, but they are certainly not maximised, in the way that positive transfers are. Despite this, we do see their occurrence as having the same kinds of learning and processing motivations as positive transfers in an L2 system that has been incompletely learned. What differs between positive and negative transfers, as we see it, is the inherent limitation on expressive power and on communicative efficiency that can be conveyed by linguistic properties that are not actually part of the L2 and not used by native speakers of the L2. Native speakers can tolerate and compensate for departures from their native language conventions to different extents, and they do so regularly when interacting with L2 learners (see discussion of errors versus creative language use in Cross and Papp 2008). On some occasions, however, learners' outputs depart, or would depart, too radically from the native speaker's conventions and on these occasions learners are not understood. Learners appear to acquire a sensitivity to the needs of their native-speaking interlocutors and it is this, we believe, that ultimately underlies many of the occurring and non-occurring negative transfers in L2 English, in addition to the principles we have defined here that hold for both positive as well as negative transfers.

We accordingly propose principle (5) for negative transfers:

(5)   Permit Negative Transfer (PNT)

Properties of the L1 which are not present in the L2 can be transferred, resulting in errors, in order to achieve an expressive power and communicative efficiency in L2 comparable to that in L1, while minimising learning effort and/or processing effort.

In phonology, for example, substitutions of L1 consonants like [t] or [s] or [f] for L2 [θ] in words like English *thin* minimise learning and processing effort for learners whose L1s do not have this consonant, and succeed in expressing the word in question, generally with communicative success (see Lado 1957 for discussion of relevant languages and interlanguages here). In syntax Spanish Pro-Drop (e.g. **is a beautiful country* instead of *it is a beautiful country*) is often transferred into early L2 English when conveying the predication in question without impeding communicative success. This is a simpler structure than its English counterpart with an overt subject, and transfer is not blocked by principle (3) or (3'). Many article omission errors achieve expressive power and communicative success, while minimising learning and processing effort through the transfer of L1 structures, e.g. *piece of X* for *a piece of X* by Serbian learners. We saw a number of such negative transfers in the Missing Determiner data of Table 2.7 in Chapter 2.5, involving English learners whose native languages were Japanese, Korean and Russian that lack definite and indefinite articles. On the other hand, Chinese prenominal relative clauses do not result in errors converting *man whom the woman loves* into its Chinese prenominal counterpart **the woman loves whom man*, in part at least because this is a complex and typologically 'marked' structure in Chinese, see Chapter 4.4. Complex lexical or constructional meanings in an L1 without an L2 equivalent will not generally transfer negatively, on account of principle (3) or their infrequency (2), just as complex structures and meanings may not immediately transfer from L1 to L2 even when they are shared, in opposition to principle (1).

In other words, principles (2) MaF and (3) MaS can block both positive and negative transfers into L2. The need for communicative efficiency, and the sensitivity of learners to their native speaking interlocutors and their tolerance for errors, results in our proposed principle (6):

(6)   Communicative Blocking of Negative Transfer (CBN)

The transfer of negative properties from L1 to L2 is filtered in proportion to communicative efficiency: the more an L1 property impedes efficient communication in L2, the less negative transfer there is.

Building on the discussion of communicative efficiency in Chapter 4.4 we can say that: **Communication is efficient when the message (M) intended by the speaker (S) is calibrated to the hearer's (H) mental model in such a way as to achieve accurate comprehension of M with rapid speed and the least processing effort compatible with H's mental model** (Hawkins 2004, 2009). This need to communicate efficiently with a given hearer on a given occasion results in sometimes more, sometimes less processing effort, in partial opposition to principles such as MaS (3') above. One hearer may understand the reference of *him* without further specification, another may require the more complex NP *the linguistics professor*, and so on (see Hawkins 1978, 1991). The result is sometimes more, and sometimes less complex expressions.

As an example of the blocking of negative transfer for communicative efficiency consider basic word orders in English and Japanese. These two languages have equally simple and productive but mirror-image word order patterns, head-initial versus head-final: [*went* [*to* [*the cinema*]]] versus [[[*the cinema*] *to*] *went*], see Greenberg (1963), Dryer (1992), Hawkins (1983, 1994, 2004). The negative transfer of head-final orders into L2 English by Japanese learners does not occur (see Chapter 4.3 for literature summary) and is blocked, we argue, on account of its communicative inefficiency: speakers importing Japanese word orders into English would simply not be understood! But Spanish-style head-initial variants of English word order that do not impact efficient communication ARE negatively transferred (e.g. *I read yesterday the book*).

Principle (6) enables us to capture a number of puzzles involving transfer that have been pointed out in the literature (see Chapter 4.3). Errors like the overuse of topicalisation by Chinese learners and by French learners (see Trévise 1986) or underuse of the passive by Hebrew learners (cf. Seliger 1989) can be explained by the fact that they do not affect the ability of learners to make themselves understood by the hearer. Errors that do not affect communication may either be eliminated at later stages or will persist throughout acquisition (e.g. as uses and misuses of articles). Errors that do significantly impact communication will be blocked.

5.6 The order of second language acquisition

We can summarise the cumulative effect of the principles proposed in this chapter in principle (7):

(7)   Order of Second Language Acquisition (OSLA)

The order of acquisition for properties of the L2 is in accordance with the principles and patterns summarised in this chapter that emerge from the CLC data. These principles collectively define possible versus impossible, and likely versus unlikely, interlanguage stages proceeding from a given L1 to a given L2.

In other words, we see these principles as operating in combination to make interesting predictions for the acquisition of L2 properties of English and other languages, and for their relative sequencing. The precise interaction between them is complex, however, both because there are several such principles and because they are ultimately gradient and differ in relative strength. There are different degrees of complexity, and frequency can be higher or lower, etc. It would be desirable for this reason to set up a computer simulation that defines these possible/impossible and likely/unlikely routes from L1 to L2 in the manner of other complex adaptive systems (Gell-Mann 1992). In this way the interaction between principles and their predictions can be defined and tested. Possible and impossible, and likely versus less likely interlanguages and learning stages can be defined precisely in this way, and tested against the learner data of the current CLC and the Cambridge English Profile Corpus now being collected.

Part Two
Empirical Findings

6 Testing some grammatical features in the Threshold series

We explained in Chapter 1.3 that our search for criterial features proceeded both deductively and inductively. We began by setting up certain hypotheses for the sequencing and time course of acquisition that we could test on the CLC. Many of these hypotheses were suggested by current research on SLA and related fields, as summarised in Chapter 4 and as developed further in Chapter 5. Inductive patterns have come from an examination of sample scripts, especially the manual subcorpus described in Chapter 2.2. A further source of patterning and insight was available to us in the 'Threshold series' developed by van Ek and Trim starting in 1971 and culminating in the three volumes, *Waystage 1990*, *Threshold 1990* and *Vantage*. These three volumes contain a detailed list and exemplification of language functions and key semantic notions that are characteristic of these levels, together with their possible grammatical and lexical exponents in English.

This invaluable work by van Ek and Trim focused initially on the Threshold level and was an attempt to describe the kind of language proficiency that would enable users to cross the threshold into language use for communicative purposes in the modern age. This level became associated with B1 as the CEFR levels were developed, see the CEFR distinctions in (1) of Chapter 1 and in Table 3.1 of Chapter 3. Vantage was then associated with B2 and Waystage with A2.

The reason why the functional/notional approach was given centre stage, especially in the CEFR (see the Council of Europe 2001) but also in van Ek and Trim's *T-series* is an understandable and well-motivated one: it was in order to shift the emphasis of language teaching, learning and testing away from the 'structure-dominated scholastic sterility' (van Ek and Trim 1991:1) of the past and 'into a vital medium for the freer movement of people and ideas' (van Ek and Trim ibid.), as explained in Chapter 1.2. As a consequence, language-specific factors and cross-linguistic variation were not the focus of the CEFR descriptors. The Council of Europe needed a matrix that could be used for measuring language learners' performance and assessing their demonstrated ability and knowledge across a whole variety of European languages. In this way the CEFR ensured the widest possible applicability of its learning, teaching and assessment criteria. In other words, the language functions performed by speakers and learners of all languages were a common factor that could be defined at a general level, and subsequently taught and assessed. Van Ek and Trim's books then exemplified the linkage to grammatical and lexical specifics of English, and the EPP, as explained in Chapter 1.1, is an attempt to specify the reference levels of the CEFR even further through empirical use of the CLC and through the search for criterial features.

John Trim explains in a 2009 interview (available in audio format at Cambridge ESOL) that the Threshold level was initially envisaged simply as a specification of the necessary means for independent and satisfactory communication. At the time of its conception, there was no plan to create a multilevel model in a vertical progression, along the lines of the A1 to C2 levels. The T-level was supposed to be a characterisation of valuable knowledge and skills that a learner would accumulate. Once these were mastered, the learner crossed over the threshold into the realm of a foreign language competence. As John Trim explains further (Trim 2007), the decision was made to provide an exemplar rather than a large-scale overall system. Accordingly, the Threshold level was conceived of as defining a point at which 'the learning of particular bits and pieces of language first evolves into an overall communicative competence'. As a result, it represents 'the minimum that a language learner should know and be able to do in order to move as an independent agent in the foreign language environment, in terms of the functions language performs, the concepts or notions, both general and theme-specific, to be expressed and consequently, the grammatical categories and structures, and the vocabulary needed for this purpose'.

In order to understand the significance and novelty of the Threshold concept, we have to remember that until the Threshold level was proposed and widely accepted as encouraging a new approach to language teaching, learning and assessment, the divide between the respective roles and responsibilities of teachers and learners was immense. Teachers were responsible for building learners' grammatical and lexical knowledge (e.g. from simple to complex structures and from more common to less common items respectively), while the use of that knowledge and its application to specific situations was entirely the responsibility of learners (Trim 2007).

Defining the Threshold did not mean that all the listed features had to be mastered to perfection at that level: learners differ with respect to how securely they have crossed the threshold and thus there was a platform for formulating assessment principles based on the quality and quantity of the results achieved from the list of Threshold features. By the same token, the later volumes *Waystage 1990* and *Vantage* indicated pre-Threshold and post-Threshold progress respectively. A very crude way of distinguishing these two stages from the Threshold would be *qualitatively and quantitatively less and more of the same respectively*. With respect to assessment, the alignment of the levels in the T-series with the ESOL examination levels is shown in Table 6.1, repeated from Chapter 3 for convenience (note that the *Breakthrough* level has recently been made available by John Trim in an electronic format).

Table 6.1 Alignment of the Cambridge ESOL examinations with the CEFR scale (from Saville 2009)

CEFR level	Descriptive title	Main Suite
C2	Mastery	CPE
C1	Effective Operational Proficiency	CAE
B2	Vantage	FCE
B1	Threshold	PET
A2	Waystage	KET
A1	Breakthrough	

Even though this alignment has been empirically validated, the precise formulation of how the levels differ criterially in terms of concrete exponents in particular languages is now being documented in the various language profile projects and programmes such as the EPP. Unlike other profile products (e.g. *Profile Deutsch* or *Profilo della lingua italiana*), the English Profile is based on a large learner corpus, and it also focuses on criterial features, as explained in Chapter 1.1. The pioneering work by van Ek and Trim contained chapters which provide us with examples of relevant functions and of the lexical and grammatical properties of English that can express them. We summarise below a number of van Ek and Trim's features of English syntax, morpho-syntax and semantics, divided by level and as contained in their T-series appendices. They are arranged here in this summary, as they are in the appendices, by parts of speech (nouns, determiners, adjectives, etc.) and by phrase (e.g. verb phrase) and clause level type (e.g. adverbial relative clause, WH-question, etc.), together with illustrative words, phrases and sentences of English. These proposed features were an important source of information for us in deciding which properties to search for empirically in the CLC. We have checked a number of them to see when they are found in the CLC. Given that van Ek and Trim did not have access to this modern empirical resource it is remarkable how many of their claims are supported by the corpus. Of course, in some cases their claims do not match the CLC data and we comment on some of these below.

PARTS OF SPEECH	Waystage A2	Threshold B1	Vantage B2
Nouns	Plural: regular vs. irregular formation; verbal nouns; countables vs. uncountables	Plurals: different pronunciation of endings Nouns in singular only Genitive -s different pronunciation	Compound nouns and complex N and NP genitives
Pronouns	Possessive, relative; indefinite pronouns	Reflexive/emphatic (myself, etc.) Gender in 3rd person singular Anaphoric use for non-sex-specific personal nouns (he/him/their, etc.)	

PARTS OF SPEECH	Waystage A2	Threshold B1	Vantage B2
Determiners	Articles and other determiners	The: different pronunciation; differentiating uses: unique, generic A/An frequency (once a day), amount (two pounds a kilo) Identifiers: other/another	
Adjectives	Comparative superlative (regular vs. irregular); ordinal numbers; comparison	V+ing (walking stick) V+ed/en (broken promises) Attributive only (daily) vs. predicative only (alive) Gradable (e.g. polar old vs. young) and non-gradable (married/single) Comparison of gradable Adjs (such, like, the same) Equality/inequality: as . . . as/not so . . . as; different from Complementising Adjs: broader spectrum than A2	
Adverbs	Interrogative uses: who, how, etc.; formation and comparison; regular vs. irregular	Relative uses: Where is your pen? I do not know where it is. Preference: rather than	
Prepositions	Simple prepositions in transparent uses; prepositional phrase; all except relative position (in/on/under/ behind/near)	Complex prepositional phrases: in the centre of, in the neighbourhood of, to the left/right of, etc.	
Verbs Verbs-cont.		Present simple for future reference with adverbs: The train leaves soon. Past perfect: all uses Present cont. with future reference: We are driving to Scotland next week. Past cont. all uses except reporting Present perfect cont. and past perfect cont.: all uses More complex passives: A book was given to me/I was given the book.	
Auxiliaries	May: permission Must: withholding permission Should: advice Will: future reference, requests, intentions; Would	May: possibility Might: all uses, e.g. suggesting a course of action Must: necessity, logical necessity, pressing invitation Should: duty, expectation Will: prediction, capacity	
Conjunctions		As well as As strong as Effect, consequence: It was so hot that (or: so I) took my coat off. Relative: I know what you mean.	

PHRASE AND CLAUSE LEVEL	Waystage A2	Threshold B1	Vantage B2
VP	VP gerund: I hate saying goodbye.	+benefactive: I gave John the letter for Mason +instrumental: Susan opened the door with a key To+INF as subject: To kill people is wrong. Following complementising adjectives and verbs: He is likely/expected to arrive late.; He forgot to lock the door. Gerund as subject: Swimming is good for you.	Phrasal verbs: V+adverbial particle (+NP): What did the wind blow down? The wind blew down the tree. Vs. What did the wind blow down? The wind blew (very hard) down the valley
Adv P	Of degree: He works very hard	Increased complexity: We drove to the seaside by car. Equality/Inequality: He did as well as he could.	
Pronoun P	Relative: that one, bigger one, some of these	PRO+Adjunct: May I have something to drink? Indefinite PRO+Adj.: He told me nothing new. Indef, PRO+relative clause: Susan is someone I met in Spain.	
Adj P		Predicative Adj.+postmodifier: This food is not good enough. Predicative Adj.+adjunct: Smoking is not good for you. Predicative complementising: Apples are good to eat.	Adverbs of degree+gradable adjectives: She is a very beautiful and most intelligent woman. Adjectives+ past participle: This is a very poorly made dress.
Clause level	Subordination: I hope that . . .; I don't mind if you smoke; Tell me where? Short answer to wh-Q (because . . .); Compound and complex sentences	Adjectival and adverbial relative clauses Following It+certain complementising verbs, adjectives and NPs: It does not matter that she is not there. It is likely that it will snow tonight. It is a pity that they cannot come. WH+NP+VP (as subject and following be complement)&WHAT+VP (as subject and object): What I like is watching TV. This is not what I wanted. What interests me most is politics. I know what is meant. NP+to+VPinf.	Nesting of further clauses and phrases

PHRASE AND CLAUSE LEVEL	Waystage A2	Threshold B1	Vantage B2
		I want my son to be a doctor. NP+VPgerund: I remember my brother being born. NP+to be+Adj.: I prefer water to be boiled. NP+VPinf. I saw him drive away. I had the laundry clean my coat.	

When using these syntactic, morpho-syntactic and semantic properties of English as possible candidates for criterial features of the Threshold level (CEFR's B1) it is essential to draw attention to an important point that John Trim makes in the 2009 interview. These properties listed in the *Threshold 1990* appendices are not being claimed to be exclusively associated with B1. Some of them may actually appear first at an earlier level, e.g. A2, and be carried forward. To put this in the terminology of our criterial features discussion in Chapter 2.1, the van Ek and Trim grammatical and lexical properties of the Threshold level are not being claimed to be 'transitional' criterial features of B1 that necessarily appear at this level for the first time. But they are being claimed, in some cases at least, to be criterial for it and appropriate to this level, i.e. to be characteristic of this level and (since these are 'positive' linguistic features) to be known and used at higher levels as well, in general. Conversely, it is possible that some of the Threshold properties could end up as criterial for the next higher level, B2, in the event that learner variability results in only some learners mastering them at B1. Some learners taking a B1 exam may be closer to the borderline with B2, or alternatively to the lower A2 level, which is then reflected in their marks. Cambridge ESOL captures this learner variability quite precisely by having a range of grades within each level (see, for example, the Cambridge ESOL Common Scale for writing (Hawkey and Barker 2004).

What the EPP brings to these van Ek and Trim level descriptions is a more precise empirical test of the features, lexical, grammatical and functional, that are criterial for each level. Having a corpus like the CLC enables us to determine at what level a particular feature is mastered. This technical resource was not available in van Ek and Trim's time, and we are privileged to have access to it now. As mentioned above, it is impressive in retrospect how closely their grammatical and lexical properties do match the criterial features that we are deriving from the CLC for the three levels in question (A2, B1, B2). In what follows we discuss some of their properties in the light of our CLC searches. Assigning particular items to a specific level as criterial is still provisional at this stage and illustrative since the CLC is being further developed and new information currently being added to it may affect some of the level assignments for our features (see Chapter 3.5). New data may shift some features to a higher or a lower level. We do not believe that this will undermine the kinds of principles we are arguing for (see Chapter 5), however, and the general sequencing of L2 learning patterns that we observe, many of which are supported in studies other than our own.

We have checked numerous grammatical and lexical features from the van Ek and Trim summary above, against CLC data, as the reader will be able to see, by comparing this summary, and more generally by comparing the T-series appendices, with our data in Chapters 7 and 8. Some of their proposed properties for Waystage, Threshold and Vantage matched our searches perfectly. For example, reflexive and emphatic pronouns (*myself*, etc.) are indeed present at B1 (as stated in the *Threshold 1990* appendices) and appear to be transitional for, i.e. acquired at, this level. So are indefinite determiners used for frequency or measure such as *once a day* or *two pounds a kilo*. Prenominal -*ing* and -*ed* forms (such as *talking doll* and *loved ones* respectively) as well as uniquely attributive (e.g. *daily*) versus uniquely predicative (e.g. *alive*) adjectives are also well-positioned as transitional features that characterise B1 against the earlier level, A2, where they may occur in isolated instances rather than as overwhelming patterns (see Chapter 2.6 for discussion of our 10-to-1 rule for criterial feature assignment).

Similarly, many properties listed in the *Waystage 1990* appendices are indeed A2, for example verbs with finite complement clauses such as *I think the zoo is an interesting place* (see Chapter 7.1.3); verbs with infinitival complements and Subject Control e.g. *I want to buy a coat* (see Chapter 7.1.4); and direct WH-questions with fronted WH-words e.g. *What are you going to wear?* (see Chapter 7.1.5).

For many of the van Ek and Trim properties that we checked, the assignment to levels matched the CLC data in some respects or for some subtypes but not for others. For example, *it*-extraposition is not acquired in a uniform way. The finite (B1 *It's true that I don't need a ring to make me remember you*) appears to come before the infinitival (B2 *It is amazing to think that I'll meet you*). Therefore we can say that finite extraposition is a transitional criterial feature for B1 (see Chapter 7.1.11), whereas infinitival extraposition is not a B1 feature but a transitional feature for B2 (see Chapter 7.1.19). Similarly, pseudocleft structures like *what I want the most is to swim and sunbathe* (in which *what* functions as the direct object of *want* in the clause in which it has been fronted) appear first at B1 and are criterial for that level (see Chapter 7.1.14). But pseudoclefts like *what fascinated me was that I was able to lie on the sea surface* (in which *what* is the subject of the verb *fascinate*) do not appear before B2 (see Chapter 7.1.20). Adverbial subordinate clauses with

-ing appear at B1 in the back position of a main clause (*I went to the canteen to buy something, leaving my bag on the chair*) and at B2 in the front position (*Talking about spare time, I think we could go to the Art Museum*), see Chapter 7.1.18.

We also looked at the acquisition of raising verbs and adjectives in the CLC. Our terminology is different from that used in the T-series and follows Postal (1974), see Chapters 5.3 and 7.2 for full details. The major types of raising structures given in these sections are Subject-to-Subject Raising (*John is likely to pass the exam*), Subject-to-Object Raising (*I found him to be an engaging chap*) and Tough Movement (*The book is easy to read*). All these types are listed in the *Threshold 1990* appendices as B1 features. Van Ek and Trim give examples that include *She seems to be asleep*, *I prefer water to be boiled*, and *Apples are good to eat* for these three structures respectively. For the Subject-to-Object Raising type Williams (2007) also claims that this is a new B1 feature, and hence a transitional criterial feature in our terms. These claims raise a general methodological problem, however. It is questionable to assert that a whole verb co-occurrence or construction type has been acquired if its first appearance is limited to only a single verb or to a small handful of common verbs. In order to control for this possibility, we tested each of the raising constructions on a sample set of verbs taken from Postal (1974).

Our CLC searches for Subject-to-Subject Raising predicates revealed that most of them are first attested at B2, not B1 (e.g. *appear* as in *The Internet shop appears to be the only one solution in our case*). Some semantically simpler and more frequent verbs do appear in this frame at B1 (e.g. *seems* as in *Monika seems to be good, intelligent teacher*), while one verb in our set (*chance*) appears as late as C1, which is probably due to its infrequency (see Chapters 5.2 and 7.2.1). Similarly most Subject-to-Object Raising predicates are first attested at B2 or higher levels, not B1 (see Chapter 7.2.2), and most Tough Movement predicates are also later than B1, with the exception of *easy* which does appears at B1 (see Chapter 7.2.4). For the modal verbs *may*, *might*, *can*, *must* and *should Threshold 1990* and *Waystage 1990* list either A2 or B1 as the relevant levels for learning, depending on the verb and its precise meaning. For *may*, for example, the 'deontic' permission sense is given as A2 while the 'epistemic' possibility sense is B1. Our searches in the CLC, and in the English Profile Wordlists, show the reverse: *may*-possibility is A2 (*Then we may go sightseeing*) while *may*-permission is B1 (*May I suggest that you book me in for the new accommodation?*), see Chapter 7.4. If these CLC data are representative, then *may*-permission is not an A2 feature. For *might* the T-series gives all uses as B1. According to our searches *might* is used in its epistemic possibility sense at A2 already (*the paint might make our t-shirts dirty*), while its deontic permission sense is attested only later at C1 (*Might I tell you what we discuss?*). This permission sense appears not to be B1, therefore, see Chapter 7.4. *Can* is attested early at A1 in its ability sense, and in asking for permission, and at A2 for epistemic possibility. *Must* is present at A2 in its obligation sense, and at B1 with the epistemic sense of necessity. *Should* is first used for giving advice at A2 and then in expressing possibility at B1. These senses and uses of *can*, *must* and *should* are therefore all present at the Threshold level, as van Ek and Trim claim.

It could be that the nature of the data (written scripts) results in not many instances of deontic meanings for modals at earlier levels since they are perhaps principally characteristic of the spoken medium. This may account for some of the discrepancies with the T-series listing. For *may*, however, the epistemic possibility sense occurs earlier than claimed while deontic per-mission is later. And while we need to bear in mind that some features may appear earlier or later in spoken language, our data do give an interesting progression for modal uses and meanings in written production (see Chapter 7.4 for further discussion of this).

Some further cases in which our CLC searches did not match the listing of features given in the *Threshold 1990* and *Waystage 1990* appendices are the following. Pronoun plus infinitive sequences such as *something to eat* and *nothing to do* are given as B1 features in *Threshold 1990* and not as A2 in *Waystage 1990*. They are, in fact, productively attested at A2 (see Chapter 7.1.6). Indirect WH-questions in finite subordinate clauses are given as A2 fea-tures. In fact, examples like *he asked how she did it* and *he asked what he should do* appear to be B1 (see Chapter 7.1.15). Indirect WH-questions in infinitival phrases (*teach me how to swim*) appear to be not A2, but again B1 (see Chapter 7.1.16). Secondary predications of the type *I prefer water boiled*, which are proposed as B1 in *Threshold 1990*, also appear to be later B2 features.

7 Positive linguistic features of the CEFR levels

This chapter gives a summary of a representative set of positive linguistic features, i.e. correct linguistic properties of English that have been acquired as transitional features at different CEFR levels and that generally persist at higher levels (see Chapter 2.2). These features involve numerous syntactic constructions of English, the grammatical meanings of certain parts of speech like modal auxiliaries, and also new lexical items and phrasal verbs and their expanding lexical meanings. The levels at which these respective features first appear and become criterial are those for which we find evidence in the current version of the CLC, as made available to us at the time of writing. Our focus, in this chapter as in Chapter 8 on lexical progression, will be on *transitional* features since it is useful for learners and teachers to know what they should strive for when moving from one level to the next. We explained in Chapter 3.5 that an extensive new data collection project is currently underway within the EPP, and we fully expect that this larger data set will result in certain revisions to the criterial features proposed here. Some grammatical constructions or words may show up earlier. On the other hand, more data may reveal that some early occurrences in the current CLC are not representative of a larger database and do not satisfy the current rule for criteriality (see the 10-to-1 rule in Chapter 2.6). That rule in turn may need to be revised.

In short, in this chapter and throughout this book we are simply trying to describe the current CLC and its criterial features in the most descriptively adequate way we can. In the process we aim to define and illustrate a research programme that can be applied to the expanded CLC, to other learner corpora, and to second languages other than English. The set of positive features we have chosen to search for is intended to be large enough to be practically useful and theoretically revealing, but it is still a small sample compared with the total set of grammatical and lexical properties that needs to be made available to learners, teachers, textbook-writers and examiners, so that their respective tasks can become more efficient (see Chapter 1.4). Future research papers and edited volumes emanating from the EPP will contain many more criterial features.

In choosing which grammatical properties to focus on we began with a set of hypotheses deriving from current theoretical research on second language acquisition, first language acquisition, language processing, language typology and grammatical theory, as summarised in Chapter 4. We were also strongly influenced by the work of van Ek and Trim in their T-series publications, especially their appendices on grammar and lexis (see Chapter 6). One important insight that emerged in the course of our empirical searches involved the need to combine and integrate grammatical and lexical information when doing research on syntax. For example, early findings and insights by Williams (2007) on the acquisition of basic construction types in English ('subcategorisation frames'), based on the parsed and corrected CLC available at the time, provided interesting data regarding the first appearance of certain syntactic frames at A2, B1 and B2 (see Tables 5.1, 5.2 and 5.3 in Chapter 5.2). But closer inspection revealed that some of these frames were being used with only one or two verbs or adjectives and were not therefore fully productive at the relevant level. Grammatical constructional analysis must therefore be supplemented in these cases with searches for relevant and representative lexical items that 'trigger' the relevant rule or that occur in the relevant construction (cf. also Ellis and Larsen-Freeman 2009). This point is illustrated in some detail in Section 7.2 below, with a discussion of the various 'raising' constructions of English. The first level at which a particular raising type appears is typically not the level at which the majority of raising triggers are found, and hence is not the level at which we would want to say that the rule as such has become criterial. We define criteriality in both grammatical and lexical terms in a case like this and state that Subject-to-Subject Raising is criterial for a particular level in conjunction with a certain verb or adjective or a certain set of verbs and adjectives. Other constructions, like the transitive (NP-V-NP) versus intransitive (NP-V) clause type, are potentially much more general and less lexically sensitive, and for them criteriality can be defined in purely syntactic terms.

When conducting a number of the grammatical searches in Sections 7.1 and 7.3 we were assisted by members of the EPP research team in Cambridge. When conducting the lexical searches we made extensive use of the EPW (Capel 2010, see the preview available via the EPP website, www.englishprofile.org). We also searched the CLC directly for the lexical items and their meanings listed in the next chapter. For C1 and C2 we relied exclusively on the CLC since at the time of writing the C level Wordlists were under development. One important methodological difference between our criterial features and the Wordlists data involves the use of scripts that satisfy the requirements for a particular level and those that do not (what are traditionally called pass versus fail scripts although examiners themselves do not pass or fail scripts per se but give a range of marks that describe learners' performance). We commented on this in Chapter 3.4 and we reiterate the point here. All of our criterial features for A2–C2 are based on data from passing scripts only, i.e. we are trying to define the characteristic grammatical and lexical properties of English at each level that are known by candidates who passed that level, with the result that we can better inform learners, teachers, textbook-writers and examiners about what needs to be known at that level in order to be successful. We are aware of the fact that the scripts which show inadequate performance for a particular level do also contain many correct uses of syntactic frames and lexical items. But the relevant candidates' writing must have been marked as below the required level because they use fewer of these correct items and produce more errors, in general. This filtering of 'pass' versus 'fail' means that occasionally our level assignments can differ from those given in the Wordlists, in which sources other than the CLC (e.g. teaching materials) were used to determine CEFR words and senses. For example, our criterial level for certain complex auxiliaries (Section 7.1.17) or phrasal verbs (Chapter 8.2) may be higher than that given in the Wordlists, as a result of excluding data from the candidates who failed. The distinction between passing and failing is an important one in the context of criteriality. However, the study presented in this book is not meant to be the final word or to have any prescriptive applications at this point (i.e. determining which features the learners MUST know in order to pass exams). The purpose of our study is to illustrate general trends in learner progression and define a research programme for the future. Practitioners will then be able to decide how to implement the findings from both Wordlists and the work presented here.

The organisation of this data chapter is as follows. Section 7.1 presents general syntactic features, 22 in all, based on searches conducted by our EPP collaborators and by us. For each structure at least one representative example is given from the CLC, taken from the relevant level. Section 7.2 presents the raising data as a case study exemplifying the need for lexically sensitive syntax when defining criterial features. Section 7.3 illustrates a syntactic phenomenon that we believe to be significant and of wide applicability when defining criteriality involving complexity differences between levels: double embedding. And Section 7.4 presents modal auxiliaries. The next chapter (8) gives our illustration of the progression in lexical features using 10 new single-word verbs at each level, together with their new extended meanings and usage possibilities at subsequent levels. A representative set of verb particle combinations is also analysed in that chapter.

7.1 General syntactic features

The following syntactic features were examined in the CLC and are proposed as criterial for the levels given, pending further data and analysis. The features of lower levels are presented first and those in ascending levels of proficiency thereafter.

7.1.1 Intransitive clauses

Simple intransitive clauses, NP-V (*he went* and, with a reciprocal subject, *they met*), are present from the beginning. This is given as an A2 structure in Williams (2007), see Table 5.1 (Chapter 5.2), and in van Ek and Trim's *Waystage 1990*:88 (which also subsumes A1 prior to the publication of Breakthrough). Williams did not have access to A1 electronic data, but we can confirm that NP-V is also productively attested at A1. Very often the intransitive NP-V is accompanied by a post-verbal adverb, particle, PP, etc. Examples that cover the intransitive verb co-occurrence frames 22, 23 and 87 in Table 5.1 following Williams (op. cit.) and in the taxonomy of verb subcategorisation frames used in RASP (see Briscoe 2000, Briscoe and Carroll 1997, Korhonen, Krymolowski and Briscoe 2006, Preiss, Briscoe and Korhonen 2007), all of them attested at A2, include:

A2	*We came back*	(NP-V-Particle)
	and went to bed	(Conjunction-V-PP)
	You can go to Yilte Park	(NP-Aux-V-PP)
	You can get there by train	(NP-Aux-V-Adv-PP)
	Can you come to my house at 2pm on Saturday?	
		(Aux-NP-V-PP-PP-PP)
	You write to me soon	(NP-V-PP-Adv)
	We meet in station	(NP-V-PP)

7.1.2 Transitive clauses

Transitive clauses, NP-V-NP (*he loved her*), are also given as A2 structures in Williams (2007), see Table 5.1 frame 24 in Chapter 5.2, and in van Ek and Trim's *Waystage 1990*:88 (*They eat vegetables*). Table 5.1 also includes transitive frames with a following PP, NP-V-NP-PP (*she bought a book for him* and *she added the flowers to the bouquet*, frames 31 and 49 respectively in the RASP taxonomy, see Section 7.1.1 for references). As with intransitives, we can confirm that transitive NP-V-NP is also present at A1. Examples from A2 include:

A2	*I met a lot of interesting people*	(NP-V-PP)
	Now I write a postcard for you . . .	(NP-V-NP-PP, P=*for*)
	I'll give it to you . . .	(NP-V-NP-PP, P=*to*)

7.1.3 Verbs with a finite complement clause

Verbs with a finite complement clause, NP-V-S, are given as an A2 structure in Williams (2007) frame 101 in Table 5.1 (*they thought that he was always late*) and in van Ek and Trim's *Waystage 1990:*89–90 (*I hope (that) you're well*). Both the overt complementiser *that* and its zero equivalent without *that* are indeed attested at A2, as in the following examples:

A2 *I knew that you have a new house too . . .*   (NP-V-S, with *that*)

   I think the zoo is an interesting place   (NP-V-S, with zero)

7.1.4 Verbs with an infinitival complement (Subject control)

Verbs with an infinitival complement and with subject control of the predicate in infinitival form, NP-V-VPinfin, are also given as an A2 structure in Williams (2007), frame 112 in Table 5.1 (*I wanted to come*), and in van Ek and Trim's *Waystage 1990*:89 (*I'd like to go to the theatre*). Attested examples include:

A2 *I want to buy a coat*   (NP-V-VPinfin)

   I would like to sell a book   (NP-Aux-V-VPinfin)

7.1.5 Direct WH-questions

Direct questions with fronted WH-words including *who, what, where, when, how* and *why* are given as A2 features in van Ek and Trim's *Waystage 1990*:91. The following are some attested examples.

A2 *What are you going to wear?*   (Direct WH-question)

   Who would like to buy the English book 'English for Business People'?

   So when are you celebrating your birthday?

   How did you know I liked skateboards?

   Where is the park?

   Why don't we go horse riding if it doesn't rain?

7.1.6 Pronoun plus infinitive

Phrases like *something to drink* and *nowhere to sleep*, in sentences such as *May I have something to drink?* and *I have nowhere to sleep*, are listed as B1 features in van Ek and Trim's *Threshold 1990*:145–6 but not as A2 features in *Waystage 1990*. They are in fact productively attested at A2, in examples such as the following with infinitives modifying pronouns including *something, somebody* and *nothing*:

A2 *You can bring something to eat if you want to*

   . . . I can look for somebody to sing . . .

   . . I'm going to a farm this weekend and there's nothing to do

7.1.7   Ditransitive clauses

Ditransitive clauses with three noun phrase arguments of a verb, i.e. NP-V-NP-NP (*she asked him his name*) are listed as a B1 structure in Williams (2007). This is frame 37 in Table 5.2 and in the RASP taxonomy. Our searches show this to be productive at A2, however. An example from the CLC is:

A2   *I can give you my guitar.*

7.1.8 Postnominal modification with *-ed* and *-ing*

Postnominal modifiers of nouns with participial *-ed* and *-ing* forms, *the boy deprived of his ice cream* and *the boy walking down the road*, are interesting properties to investigate in this context since they are more complex and rarer than prenominal modifiers in native speaker English (*the deprived boy*, *the walking boy*, etc.) but not as complex as full relative clauses. In the early days of generative grammar they were 'derived' from semantically equivalent relative clauses by WHIZ Deletion, i.e. from structures corresponding to *the boy who was deprived of his ice cream* and *the boy who was walking down the road* (see Burt 1971). The *-ed* postmodifier appears to be an A2 feature, though it occurs only with relatively few lexical items at this level (e.g. *called, painted*):

A2   *There are beautiful paintings painted by famous Iranian painters.*

Postmodifiers in *-ing* are productive at B1 and can be considered a B1 feature:

B1   *As I was so desperate I put an advertisement in the newspaper asking if someone had it, but no one answered me .*

7.1.9 Verbs with infinitival complements (Object control)

Williams (2007) lists frame 33 (*he helped her bake the cake*) with an object-controlled infinitival complement as B1, see Table 5.2 in Chapter 5.2 (*her* is understood both as an argument of *helped* and as a subject of *bake the cake*). The infinitival has no *to* in this example. The much more common counterpart with *to* is also productive at B1. An attested example with the verb *order* is:

B1   *I called my assistant and ordered him to gather my men to the hall.*

7.1.10 Verbs with *-ing* complements (Object control)

Williams (2007) lists frame 35 (*I caught him stealing*) with an object-controlled *-ing* complement as B1, see Table 5.2 in Chapter 5.2 (*him* is both an argument of *caught* and a subject of *stealing*). An attested example is:

B1   *Maria saw him taking a taxi.*   (NP-V-NP-VP*ing*)

7.1.11 *It* Extraposition with finite clauses

Van Ek and Trim (*Threshold 1990*:148) list what we here call '*It* Extraposition' structures with finite clause complements as a B1 feature: *It doesn't matter that she is not here*; *It is likely that it will snow tonight*; *It is a pity (that) they cannot come*. The CLC confirms this (though extraposition of an infinitival phrase appears to be later, see Section 7.1.19). The following is an attested example with finite clause extraposition:

B1 *It's true that I don't need a ring to make me remember you* (Finite)

7.1.12 Verbs with a PP plus finite complement clause

Williams (2007) lists frame 97, NP-V-PP-S (*they admitted to the authorities that they had entered illegally*), as B1, with an added level of complexity in the form of the PP compared to the A2 feature NP-V-S in Section 7.1.3. An attested example is:

B1 *He said to me he would like to come back soon* (NP-V-PP-S)

7.1.13 Genitive relatives

Relative clauses formed on a genitive position (e.g. *the professor whose book I read*) are quite complex structures with interesting processing, acquisition and typological correlates of this complexity, see Chapter 4.5.1 for discussion in connection with Keenan and Comrie's (1977) Accessibility Hierarchy. They are first attested at B1 in the CLC, as in the following examples:

B1 *... a biography of this famous painter whose pictures I like so much*
   ... I met a very nice boy whose name's John

7.1.14 Pseudoclefts type (i)

Van Ek and Trim (*Threshold 1990*:149) list what we here call 'Pseudocleft' structures as B1 features. They give two general types, structurally (i) WH-NP-VP within the WH clause, e.g. *What I like is watching football*. This type is further differentiated depending on where the *what I like* clause appears within its containing sentence, e.g. in subject position (*What I like is watching football*) or as a complement after *be* (as in *This is what I like*). The role of the WH element within its immediate clause is that of a direct object in type (i) (i.e. *what* is the object of *like*). According to our searches type (i) is indeed a B1 feature, as in the following attested examples:

B1 (i) WH-NP-VP

   The name is not very original, but what you can do there is great!

I opened the door and what I saw was so amazing.

. . . what I really don't know is if in my bedroom I will have any place to put something new.

7.1.15 Indirect WH-questions in finite clauses

Van Ek and Trim (*Waystage 1990*:90) list indirect questions such as *I will come when you call* and *He will follow where you go*, in which the WH word is positioned at the front of a subordinate and finite clause, as A2 features. Williams (2007), on the other hand, gives frame 16 (*he asked how she did it*) as B1, for the WH words *how*, *why*, *where* and *when*, based on her CLC searches, and frame 114 with *what* (*he asked what he should do*) as B2 (see Tables 5.2 and 5.3 in Chapter 5.2). All of these structures appear to be B1, however. Attested examples from the CLC are:

B1 *Guess where it is.*

I don't know how I could have done it.

I can't understand what she's saying.

In your letter you said that you would like to know what I have bought.

After class he asked me why I was sad and I told him what was the matter.

Do you remember who Lucia is?

7.1.16 Indirect WH-questions in infinitival phrases

Van Ek and Trim (*Threshold 1990*:146) give indirect WH-questions for infinitival phrases, such as *Do you know where to go?* and *Teach me how to swim*, as B1, whereas those in finite clauses are proposed as A2 (see previous subsection). B1 accords with Williams' frame 17 in Table 5.2 (*he explained how to do it*), which is also listed as B1 for WH words *how*, *where*, and *when*. Frame 73 with *what* in Table 5.3 (*he thought about what to do*) is given as B2, however. A *what* within an infinitival phrase is already attested at B1, however, most often in conjunction with the verb do (as in *what to do*), though occasionally with other governing verbs as well. Attested examples of all these types from the corpus are:

B1 *I did not know where to look for it anymore.*

I don't know what to do.

I didn't know what to buy for you.

7.1.17 Complex auxiliaries

Complex auxiliaries such as *would rather* (*I would rather you didn't go to such effort*) and *had better* (*I had better improve my game*) appear to be B1 features, as in the following attested examples:

B1   WOULD RATHER

> *They won't be very happy if you go on holiday with them and then you are bad tempered all the time because you would rather be with your friends.*

B1   HAD BETTER

> *If you don't like to go with them you had better tell them why you don't want to come.*

7.1.18 Adverbial subordinate clauses with *-ing*

Adverbial subordinating clauses with *-ing* verbs occur productively in native speaker English as a means of subordinating one clause within another in an adverbial function, e.g. *walking down the road he bumped into a lamppost.* These adverbial clauses will often precede the main clause, as in the example just given, or follow it, as in *he bumped into a lamppost walking down the road.* Examples of following adverbial *-ing* clauses are found in the CLC earlier than those that precede. Following clauses are found at B1, preceding clauses at B2, as in these attested examples:

B1   *-ing* clause follows main clause

> *He was sitting there, drinking a coffee and writing something.*

B2   *-ing* clause precedes main clause

> *Talking about spare time, I think we could go to the Art Museum.*

7.1.19 *It* Extraposition with infinitival phrases

Van Ek and Trim (*Threshold 1990*:146) also list *It* Extraposition structures with infinitival phrase complements as a B1 feature (*It is likely to rain tomorrow*; *It is wrong to kill people*). Our searches suggest instead that this is a B2 feature, as in the following attested example:

B2   . . . *it would be helpful to work in your group as well*   (Infinitival)

7.1.20 Pseudocleft type (ii)

In Pseudocleft type (ii), WH-VP, e.g. *What interests me is politics* (Van Ek and Trim *Threshold 1990*:149), the *what interests me* clause may appear in various positions within its containing sentence, e.g. as subject (*What interests me is politics*) or as object (*I know what interests me*). The major difference between type (ii) and type (i) (Section 7.1.14) appears to be that in type (ii) the WH element functions as grammatical subject of the verb within its immediate clause (*what is the subject of interests me*), not as non-subject. Type (ii) is attested later than type (i) in the corpus, and is a B2 feature, as in the following example:

B2 (ii) WH-VP

> *. . . what fascinated me was that I was able to lie on the sea surface and read this newspaper.*

7.1.21 Verbs with an NP plus finite complement clause

Williams (2007) lists frame 52, NP-V-NP-S (*he told the audience that he was leaving*), as B2. Attested examples are:

B2 *She told me that she had worked for summer camp for children.*
I told him I loved his songs.

7.1.22 Secondary predications

Structures like *he painted the car red* are referred to here as 'Secondary predications' since *the car* is both the object of *painted* and it contracts a secondary relation with the following predication *(is or becomes) red*. This is frame 25, NP-V-NP-AdjP (Object control), in Williams (2007), and it is listed in Table 5.2 as a B2 feature (see Chapter 5.2). Van Ek and Trim (*Threshold 1990*:149) cite a similar example as B1, *I prefer water boiled* which alternates with *I prefer water to be boiled*. An attested example of frame 25 at B2 is:

B2 *But if you don't want to take any risks, just go and paint the houses yellow and blue if you think that'll do.*

7.2 Raising constructions

We discussed raising structures in English in Chapters 4.4 and 5.3 and summarised relevant research literature on their grammar, distribution across languages, their inherent complexity and their acquisition. In this section we summarise the data patterns in the CLC and give numerous attested examples. We distinguished four construction types in our data summary of Table 5.6: Subject-to-Subject Raising verbs and adjectives; Subject-to-Object Raising verbs (unpassivised); Subject-to-Object Raising verbs plus Passive; Tough Movement. Relevant data are presented in Sections 7.2.1 to 7.2.4 respectively. These constructions all appear first with a limited set of verbs or adjectives before the frame is extended to others. This is in line with what has been observed in first language acquisition by Goldberg (2006). Complex constructions are first learned and used with a small number of relatively frequent and simple predicates before the construction as a whole is generalised to include the full array of exemplars. It becomes much more useful under these circumstances to define criterial features not just for the first appearance of the construction, but for a given construction with particular sets of 'triggering' predicates, i.e. with those that occur in the relevant verb co-occurrence frame and that trigger the application of the relevant raising rule(s), as discussed for example in some detail by Postal (1974). We searched for a representative sample of the triggering predicates for each of these raising constructions and in what follows we present the results of these searches in the current CLC.

7.2.1 Subject-to-Subject Raising verbs and adjectives

These are structures of the type *John is likely to pass the exam* and *The noise ceased to get on his nerves*, in which the subject of the subordinate clause (*John* and *The noise* respectively) has been raised out of this clause and into the subject position of the main clause: John is the logical subject of passing the exam and this whole event, but not John himself, is then claimed to be likely; *The noise* is the logical subject of getting on his nerves and this whole event is then claimed to have ceased, though not necessarily the noise itself, see Chapter 5.3. Both the syntactic displacement and the fact that the subject does not contract normal semantic relations with its closest and 'immediate' predicate (see Hawkins 1986: Chapter 5) makes this a complex structure for learners. Van Ek and Trim (*Threshold 1990*:146) list *She seems to be asleep* as a B1 structure, and indeed Subject-to-Subject Raising is attested with *seem* at B1, but this structure as a whole only becomes productive at the next stage, B2, as shown in the following summary of attested examples.

Lexical triggers appearing for the first time in the CLC by level (from a sample of 13 tested):

A2 none (i.e. no raising predicates at all)

B1 *seem* (verbs)
       supposed (adjectives)

B2 *appear, cease, fail, happen, prove, turn out* (verbs)
       certain, likely, sure, unlikely (adjectives)

C1 *chance* (verb)

C2 none (i.e. no new raising predicates in this sample)

B1 SEEM
       Monika seems to be good, intelligent teacher, but I have a bad feeling about Paula.

They seem to be really interesting and what I like best – very open and easy going.

B1 SUPPOSED

It looks like I have a rehearsal for the 'Yamaha-Concert' at the same time I was supposed to go to the English class . . .

B2 APPEAR

. . . the Internet shop appears to be the only one solution in our case . . .

B2 CEASE

All her treasures and beloved ones had ceased to exist because of her cowardness.

B2 FAIL

To my regret, the evening totally failed to live up to my expectations.

B2 HAPPEN

The plays as well as the films happens to be very popular, that's why I might say some more of these would be better.

B2 PROVE

My worries proved to be wrong.

B2 TURN OUT

Unfortunately for me, the situation turned out to be opposite to what I thought it was.

B2 CERTAIN

We have known each other for a real long time now and you can be certain to be one of the best friends of mine.

B2 LIKELY

And whenever money is involved, some problems are likely to happen.

B2 SURE

Furthermore, by bicycle, you don't spend your time into traffic-jams and you are sure to arrive at work in time.

B2 UNLIKELY

As soon as he starts to see the Vienna that lived through a war, money and success become more unlikely to appear . . .

C1 CHANCE

Dear Sirs, I chanced to know about your Competition from an international magazine.

7.2.2 Subject-to-Object Raising verbs (unpassivised)

These are structures of the type *I found him to be an engaging chap*, in which the subject of the subordinate clause (*him*) has been raised out of this clause into the object position of the main clause: the person referred to by *him* is the logical subject of being an engaging chap and is not in a semantic relation with the higher verb *found*, i.e. I did not find him in the literal sense of *find*. As in the case of Subject-to-Subject Raising, both the syntactic displacement and the absence of normal semantic relations between the higher verb and its direct object make this a complex structure for learners (see Hawkins 1986: Chapter 5). Williams (2007) lists *I found him to be a good doctor*, NP-V-NP-(To Be)-NP i.e. frame 57 in Table 5.2 (see Chapter 5.2), as B1, with the higher verb *find*. This raising type is indeed first attested at B1, but the triggering verb *find* does not occur before C1 (see below). Williams also lists frame 58 with the higher verb *want* in *he wanted the children found* and reduction of the predicate in the subordinate clause (see Table 5.2). Van Ek and Trim (*Threshold 1990*:149) list a similar example with a higher *want* as B1 (*I want my son to become a doctor*) and with a higher *like* (*I do not like my children to smoke*). Both *want* and *like* are indeed attested at B1 as Subject-to-Object Raising triggers in the CLC, but most of the other triggers occur later, at B2, C1 and even C2, as shown in the following summary of attested examples.

Lexical triggers appearing for the first time in the CLC by level (from a sample of 12 tested):

A2 none
B1 *expect, like, want*
B2 *imagine, prefer*
C1 *believe, find, suppose, take*
C2 *declare, presume, remember*

B1 EXPECT

Sara told me she would come, but I didn't expect her to come so early.
I expect you to be a little bit surprised, aren't you?
I am doing fine, I expected it to be more difficult, but it is not so hard.

B1 LIKE

I would like you to spend a weekend at my house too.

B1 WANT

Finally I want you to say hi to everybody and I am looking forward to seeing you.

B2 IMAGINE

You were so kind and friendly that I had never imagined myself to have visited far foreign country, Alaska.

B2 PREFER

I would prefer my accomodation to be in log cabins, because I am alergic to some insects that might go in the tent.

C1 BELIEVE

> *Being born and raised in Mexico, I believe her to be this country's best representative in the world.*

C1 FIND

> *I found the legroom to be far to small, and several of the safety-belts were broken.*
>
> *I find this to be more interesting than the walking route to Lake Hawksmere, . . .*
>
> *Overall I found this to be pretty satisfying as it does fulfill most of the students' wishes.*

C1 SUPPOSE

> *I can assure you that the strike isn't as worrying as you suppose it to be.*

C1 TAKE

> *They take care of our health but nobody doesn't take it to be important.*

C2 DECLARE

> *They declare some products to be the hits of the season, thus creating fashion, and few of us want to be unfashionable.*

C2 PRESUME

> *He presumed work to be the way to live.*

C2 REMEMBER

> *Plus, I remember my classes to be very participative, and dynamic.*
>
> *She remembered her father to be a lively, tall and broad shouldered man with a beard that tickled when he bent down to kiss her goodnight.*

7.2.3 Subject-to-Object Raising verbs plus Passive

These are structures of the type *Smoking is known to cause cancer*, in which the subject of the subordinate clause that has been raised into the higher object position (i.e. *smoking* as in *We know smoking to cause cancer*) is then further promoted to subject position in the main clause by the operation of Passive. On some occasions this additional Passive is obligatory, in the sense that if Subject-to-Object Raising applies without it the sentence is of questionable grammaticality (see Postal 1974). Compare *The student was thought to be drunk*, which is well-formed in English, with the more questionable *?We thought the student to be drunk* (cf. the completely well-formed *We thought the student was drunk*). Van Ek and Trim (*Threshold 1990*:146) list a structure of this type as a B1 feature with the higher verb *expected*: *He is expected to arrive late*. In fact, according to our searches Subject-to-Object raisings plus Passive do not occur before B2, as shown in the following summary of attested examples.

Lexical triggers appearing for the first time in the CLC by level (from a sample of 13 tested):

A2 none

B1 none

B2 *expected, known, obliged, thought*

C1 *assumed, discovered, felt, found, proved*

C2 *presumed*

Not attested: *alleged, stated, understood*

B2 EXPECTED

How many hours a day should I be expected to work?

B2 KNOWN

Your theatre is known to present excellent spectacles.

B2 OBLIGED

So zoos could be the only place where people could spend their time avoiding the pollution we are obliged to live with every day.

B2 THOUGHT

Woods is thought to stand for all of white people and this book could have an influence on them.

C1 ASSUMED

Secondly, the low cost of membership and entry was assumed to be an advantage as well.

C1 DISCOVERED

more and more athletes from the former GDR were discovered to take steroids.

C1 FELT

The children stories were felt to be the best idea for kids, after of course the pony rides.

C1 FOUND

A more modern style of accommodation was found to be represented in the Arnewood Hotel.

C1 PROVED

Internet is a valuable tool which can be proved to be the most important aspect in the learning process.

C2 PRESUMED

Not only meetings with people are presumed to give new experiences.

7.2.4 Tough Movement

These are structures of the type *The book is easy to read* in which the object of the subordinate clause (*the book*) has been raised out of this clause and into the subject position of the main clause: the book is the logical object of reading and this whole event (reading the book) is claimed to be easy, not necessarily the book itself (the book could be easy to read but hard to carry, for example). More generally, the raised noun phrases in Tough Movement structures are not limited to direct objects, but cover other non-subject possibilities as well, as in *The student is easy to study with* (i.e. studying with the student is easy), see Hawkins (1986: Chapter 5). As in the other raising structures of Sections 7.2.1–3, both the syntactic displacement and the fact that the raised noun phrase is linked semantically with a lower predicate, in a different grammatical relation on this occasion, and not with the higher predicate makes this a complex structure for learners (see Chapters 4.4 and 5.3). Van Ek and Trim *(Threshold 1990*:144) list a structure of this type, *Apples are good to eat*, as B1. In fact, the only instance that occurs in the CLC at B1 is with the higher predicate *easy*, which is the second most common *'tough'* predicate cited in Mair (1987, 1990) (*difficult* being the most frequent). See the following summary of attested examples:

Lexical triggers appearing for the first time in the CLC by level (from a sample of 7 tested):

A2   none
B1   *easy*
B2   *difficult, good, hard*
C1   none (i.e. no new tough predicates in the sample)
C2   *tough*

Not attested: *boring, tedious*

B1   EASY

The problem you have is not very easy to solve.
The train station is easy to find.

B2   DIFFICULT

The first Restaurant is 'Mexico', it is situated near the metro station and is not very difficult to find.

B2   GOOD

On the other hand car is good to go everywhere, to go across another place quickly, to an emergency and to get fun.

B2   HARD

The grammar and vocabulary are a bit hard to learn.

C2   TOUGH

What she knew would be really tough to live with was the reason of his death.

7.3 Double embeddings

We commented in Chapter 2.2 on the quite dramatic expansion in mean length of utterance (MLU) figures as learners gain in proficiency from A2–C2, based on our examination of the manual subcorpus conducted with the assistance of colleagues at the University of California, Davis. The figures are repeated here for convenience:

(1)   MLU figures from the manual corpus

A2	7.9
B1	10.8
B2	14.2
C1	17.3
C2	19.0

These figures expand because the sentences that learners are using grow visibly in both length and syntactic complexity down the levels. The criterial features we have enumerated in Sections 7.1 and 7.2 provide some of the syntactic details that underlie these figures and that result in added length and complexity. For example, the kinds of complement and subordinate clauses illustrated in Sections 7.1.9–7.1.22 add syntactic depth and breadth to sentences at the B levels compared with the simpler and shorter structures of A2. The raising structures in 7.2 are also complex structures that are first attested at the B levels, and some of them only become productive at the C levels (see 7.2.2 and 7.2.3). But in addition to these expansions in individual rules and their lexical realisations, there is a very general feature of syntactic development that we notice in the CLC and that we wish to define and illustrate here: 'double embedding'.

Double embedding refers, very broadly and loosely, to sentences with more than one instance of a given phrase or clause, the one being properly contained within the other, for example one finite subordinate clause within another (*I believe* [*that Harry knows* [*that Martha is sick*]]), or one infinitival phrase within another (*I want* [*to tell Johnny* [*to behave*]]), or a relative clause within another relative clause (*the professor* [*who wrote the book* [*which the student read*]], or a genitive within a genitive (*the beginning* [*of the end* [*of civilisation*]]), and so on. We also allow, in the definition of double embedding to be proposed here, for one phrase or clause to be properly contained in a similar but not necessarily identical phrase or clause, for example a finite complement clause within an infinitival complement (*I want* [*to tell Johnny* [*that he must behave*]]), or an adverbial subordinate clause within a finite or non-finite complement clause (*I believe* [*that Harry was unhappy* [*when he was a child*]]), or an *-s* genitive phrase within a higher *-of* genitive (*the beginning* [*of* [*the professor's*] *book*]), or an *-of* genitive within a higher *-s* ([*the king* [*of England*]*'s*] *war*).

There has been much discussion of embedding structures of these kinds going back to Miller and Chomsky (1963) and Chomsky (1965), and significant experimental and corpus work on their language processing and performance has been done since then. In this context suffice it to say that there are numerous factors that have been shown to degrade their acceptability and grammaticality, e.g. whether the lower phrase is 'right-branching' or 'left-branching' (compare *the pen* [*of the guardian* [*of my nephew*]] with [[*my nephew's*] *guardian's*] *pen*), whether the lower phrase is 'centre embedded' or 'nested' (meaning that there are items to both the left and right of the lower phrase within the higher phrase, as in [*the king* [*of England*]'s] *war* and *I believe* [*that Harry announced* [*that Martha was sick*] *to Sue*]), whether the lower phrase is 'self-embedded' (as in *the student* [*who the professor* [*that taught the linguistics class*] *examined*]), and so on. In general, right-branching structures are more common and easier to process than left-branching ones, centre embedding degrades acceptability in proportion to the length and acceptability of the centre embedded phrase, and self-embeddings are often downright ungrammatical. In the present context what is significant and in need of discovery and analysis is (a) whether double embeddings of the types that are acceptable and used by native speakers occur at all in the learner data at different levels, and (b) what the actual combinations of phrases and clauses are that occur in double embedding structures at the different levels.

We define double embedding as follows:

(2) **Double embedding**

A double embedding structure is one in which a phrase A is properly contained within an A' of a similar or identical category type, both being properly contained within a sentence.

Our general expectation is that as sentence length and complexity increase at higher levels, the range and size of double embedding types will increase also, with different A and A' combinations being criterial for different levels. This is illustrated with a sample set of data here involving double embeddings of genitives.

English has two genitive constructions: the *of* genitive following a head noun within a prepositional phrase (PP), this head noun and PP being immediately contained within an NP; and the *-s* genitive which precedes its head noun within a possessive phrase (PossP), the head noun and PossP being both immediately dominated by NP. These two options are shown in (3a) and (3b) respectively:

(3) a. np[*the king* pp[*of England*]]
     b. np[possp[*England's*] *king*]

When one of these is properly contained within the other there are four double embedding possibilities: one *of* genitive (PP) within another, see (4a);

one -*s* genitive (PossP) within another (4b); an -*s* genitive (PossP) within an *of* genitive (PP) (4c); and an *of* genitive (PP) within an -*s* genitive (PossP) (4d):

(4) a. np[*the beginning* pp[*of the end* pp[*of the war*]]]

   b. np[possp[possp[*the king's*] *cousin's*] *mistress*]

   c. np[*the beginning* pp[*of* possp[*the professor's*] *book*]]

   d. np[possp[*the king* pp[*of England*]'*s*] *war*]

Table 7.1 below shows the rates of occurrence per 100,000 words for these four double embedding types from A2 to C2. Identifying these different types within the CLC using RASP was not straightforward and we are grateful to both Stephen Spencer and Andrew Caines of RCEAL, Cambridge, for their assistance with these searches. The structures identified automatically were then subjected to further manual inspection by both them and us in order to arrive at the quantities shown in Table 7.1. In the process we eliminated phrases such as *a lot of* which are really complex determiners rather than instances of an *of* genitive following a head noun immediately contained within NP.

Table 7.1 Double embeddings: Genitives

	[*of* [*of*]] (4a)	[*of* [-*s*]] (4c)	[[*of*] -*s*] (4d)	[[-*s*] -*s*] (4b)
A2	3.518071	0	0	0
B1	6.117444	3.129855	0	0
B2	21.051038	5.156322	0.047306	0
C1	39.948976	14.946427	0.137755	0.413274
C2	37.849294	24.424487	0.086612	0.692893

Instances of each of the double embedding types shown in (4) per 100,000 words of text

The figures shown in Table 7.1 reveal clear frequency increases in general down the levels for the different double embedding types. By the 10-to-1 rule for criteriality (see Chapter 2.6) we should regard the [*of* [*of*]] embedding of (4a) as already present at, and criterial for, **A2**. This type then becomes more and more frequent down the levels and illustrates the added structural complexity that underlies the expanding MLU figures in (1), in accordance with the Maximise Structurally and Semantically Simple Properties principle of Chapter 5.3.

The [*of* [-*s*]] type (4c) starts to become productive at **B1**, increasing gradually from B2 through C2. The addition of an -*s* genitive to an *of* genitive (*the beginning of the professor's book*) makes (4c) harder to process than (4a). There are severe limits in native corpora for even single prenominal -*s* genitives of just 2 or 3 words in length (see Hawkins 2004:129–130 for figures and for the references cited therein). By the 10-to-1 rule B1 must be considered the criterial level here, with attested instances increasing at each higher level.

The type [[*of*] -*s*] (4d) exemplified by *the king of England's war* is extremely rare compared with (4c) for reasons having to do with the sizes of the respective processing domains for this structure (see the Minimise Domains principle of Hawkins 2004: attaching the -*s* to the whole *king of England* phrase introduces a very long and complex domain for the processing of the -*s* genitive relation). Although the numbers are small we assume that [[*of*] -*s*] (4d) is criterial for **B2**.

The [[-*s*] -*s*] type (4b) involves two left-branching genitives. There are no examples at A2 and B1, and only questionable and ungrammatical instances at B2. This double embedding begins to be productive at **C1**, and hence this should be the criterial level for this structure. There is an increase from C1 to C2, as expected, but the relative rarity of the structure accords well with its processing difficulty.

The following examples from the CLC illustrate each of the double embedding types in (4) with data taken from the levels at which these structures become criterial.

A2 [*of* [*of*]] (4a)

I like the colours of the back of the mobile phone . . .

B1 [*of* [-*s*]] (4c)

I am a big fan of the world's most famous British secret service agent.

B2 [[*of*] -*s*] (4d)

After this I went to a friend of mine's house where I spent one week.

C1 [[-*s*] -*s*] (4b)

After spending the first day of their marriage in the bride's family's house . . .

What is interesting about these data is that they reveal the potential of the double embedding concept for the analysis of progressive structural complexity at the higher proficiency levels. Each of the four double embedding types illustrated here becomes criterial at a different level. We suggest that many more such combinations should be investigated in future research as a way of defining the different proficiency levels structurally and of revealing the precise differences between levels that underlie the MLU figures in (1).

7.4 Modal auxiliary verbs

In this section we present criterial features involving the following modal auxiliaries in the CLC with their respective meanings: *may, might, can, must,* and *should*. For A2–B2 levels we have made use of the search data in Wordlists, which identifies the first significant appearance of these modals and classifies and labels their intended meaning(s). For the C levels we checked the CLC directly, since Wordlists did not include data from the C levels at the time of writing. For A2–B2 we also checked Wordlist entries against the CLC in order to ensure that they were not impacted by the presence of any scripts graded at the lower end of the scale (see the discussion of this point in Chapter 3.4 above).

Van Ek and Trim's *Waystage 1990* and *Threshold 1990* volumes contain quite specific proposals for the learning of modals and modal meanings at A2 and B1 respectively, which we have tested in our searches.

For the modal *may* Van Ek and Trim (*Vantage 1990*:85 and *Threshold 1990*:138) give the permission sense as an A2 feature (e.g. *May I smoke? Yes you may*) and the possibility sense as B1 (*It may rain this afternoon*). Our searches show the reverse, as in the following attested examples:

MAY

A2 Possibility (Epistemic)

Then we may go sightseeing.

B1 Permission (Deontic)

May I suggest that you book me in for the new accommodation?

For *might* Van Ek and Trim (*Threshold 1990*:138) give a 'suggesting a course of action' meaning as B1, with no reference to any uses at all at A2 (*Vantage 1990*). Our searches show the possibility meaning as A2, with a permission sense much later, at C1:

MIGHT

A2 Possibility (Epistemic)

. . . the paint might make our t-shirts dirty.

C1 Permission (Deontic)

Might I tell you what we discuss?

For *can* Van Ek and Trim (*Vantage 1990*:85) give a full set of both deontic and epistemic shades of meaning as A2 (e.g. permission as in *Can I go out this evening?*, and possibility in *He can't be 60 years old* which is equivalent to 'it is not possible that . . .'), and our searches confirm that *can* is indeed attested in both deontic and epistemic senses by A2, the former even earlier at A1, as in the following examples:

CAN

A1 Ability implicating Permission (Deontic), see Searle (1975)

So please, can you make me a big sala[d]?

A2   Possibility (Epistemic)

We can meet at our school.

For *must* Van Ek and Trim (*Vantage 1990*:86 and *Threshold 1990*:138) show a deontic (permission) sense at A2 already (*You must not drive too fast*) and epistemic senses involving various types and shades of necessity as B1 (*He speaks Flemish and French – He must be Belgian; We must all die sooner or later*). Our searches confirm this, as in the following examples:

MUST

A2   Obligation (Deontic)

We must be there at 7 o'clock in the morning.

B1   Necessity (Epistemic)

She must be feeling so happy!

We plan to see 'Cell', a new film, which must be really good.

For *should* Van Ek and Trim (*Vantage 1990*:86 and *Threshold 1990*:139) propose similarly that the deontic meaning is A2 (e.g. the advice sense in *You should see a doctor*) while the epistemic meaning is later at B1 (e.g. the expectation sense based on probability in *The train should be there by now*). Our searches confirm this, as in the following examples:

SHOULD

A2   Advice (Deontic)

You should wear old clothes because we will get dirty.

B1   Probability (Epistemic)

I have invite[d] all his friends, [so] we should be 28 people.

8 Lexical progression

In this chapter we illustrate the progressive learning of lexical items and their meanings, focusing on verbs and the other categories with which they co-occur. The selection of particular verbs was based, in part, on their frequency (including high, medium and low frequency items) and on their range of meanings in English native speaker usage (e.g. including dimensions like *literal/metaphorical* or *concrete/abstract*). We wished to identify, first, the initial appearance of a set of verbs at each of the CEFR proficiency levels, and second to document the expanding meanings and co-occurrence possibilities at higher levels for all the verbs that had appeared earlier. This resulted in a vertical profile of lexical progression with criterial features defined for individual verbs and stated in terms of first appearance and semantic type. It was not practical to use the 10-to-1 rule here (see Chapter 2.6) given the size of the current corpus, the infrequency of individual lexical items compared with grammatical structures, and the inability of the parser to differentiate and quantify different word senses. Documenting the first appearance in a corpus is straightforward. Analysing and classifying the semantic progression is much less so. Indeed, any attempt to do a serious semantic analysis of the expanding lexicon of learners raises all the deep issues that are currently being researched, and fought over, in the various branches of lexical semantics and lexicography.

For example, we could talk about the progression from more concrete to more abstract meanings, from literal to metaphorical or from semantically simple to semantically complex (e.g. in terms of some version of feature analysis). E.g. *walk* is semantically simpler than *stagger* since *stagger* effectively includes walking and can be defined as 'walking in a specific manner'. We would accordingly predict that *stagger* is acquired later than *walk*, by the principle of Maximise Structurally and Semantically Simple Properties in Chapter 5.3, which is indeed the case (see below). An approach such as this, in terms of meaning components and features, can capture the lexical semantic progression within different semantic fields (e.g. motion) and reveal how more complex units of meaning within a given semantic field are learnt. However, the expanding meaning possibilities for different verbs are also hugely dependent on the company that these verbs keep. Compare Keenan's examples of the different meanings that verbs (and other 'function categories') can have in combination with different direct objects (or more generally different 'arguments'): *run the race, run the water, run the advertisement, run a business*, *run a good election campaign*, and so on (see Keenan 1979). In the learner corpus these kinds of expanding usage and meaning possibilities are found at later and later levels.

In what follows we illustrate a way of capturing the first appearance of new verbs, and expansions in their meaning, some of which are quite construction-specific (i.e. conditioned by a certain co-occurrence such as *run the advertisement*). We chose 10 new verbs that appear for the first time at each level (A1–C2) and followed their semantic progression upwards (shown left to right in the grids in Section 8.1 below). With respect to labelling the semantic types, we adopted the most minimal possible theory that would not force us to make decisions about 'figurative', 'metaphorical', 'idiomatic' uses, etc., and that did not require a commitment to any particular theory of lexical semantics (e.g. based on constructs such as frames or scripts or mental spaces). Instead we operated with just three descriptive categories, indicated by P, E and F respectively. We assume (and for the 60 verbs in Section 8.1 below it was not difficult to identify) a primary meaning **(P)**, semantically simpler than others and involving a mainly physical sense that is easy to map onto universally perceptible kinds of actions (the same holds true for core meanings of nouns and for object-naming). Any departure from, and extension beyond, this core or primary meaning we labelled simply extended **(E)**, whether the extension was minor (as in *take a bus* extending from the basic physical meaning of taking something) or major (as in *take a chance*). There is a continuum here, involving degrees of expansion from the core, with different qualitative and quantitative aspects for different verbs that makes it extremely difficult to apply a more fine-tuned taxonomy consistently, at a general level. On the other hand, if we were simply to list the individual details for different verbs, our whole discussion would be anecdotal, would not generalise to other verbs, and would not link in to general discussions of complexity and frequency as they impact the lexicon (see Chapter 5.2 and 5.3). Even this very minimal (P) versus (E) classification reveals a very interesting pattern that is immediately apparent in the grids below: P is almost always among the first attested meanings and the progression for each lexical verb is from P to E. The **(F)** category, standing for 'fixed expression', is assigned to those items which are either non-productive syntactically (as in *make sure*) or non-compositional semantically (i.e. the meaning of the whole is not derived from the sum of its parts, as in *cut the mustard*).

In this way we manage to capture some general patterns of lexical semantic progression and to rise above idiosyncratic differences and points of meaning that hold for individual lexical items. We are aware that it is possible to provide a more subtle classification within the categories we propose. For instance, the extended (E) category can be further subdivided into simple and complex, or into figurative and metaphorical, etc. Our main focus is on general points of development where crucial differences in the syntax or semantics of the lexicon occur for individual items. The precise distribution of Ps, Es and Fs for each item will vary depending on numerous factors, such as frequency, syntactic and semantic complexity as well as specific task demands. Despite these differences, we see clear patterns that are in accordance with the general predictions we make in Chapter 5.2 and 5.3, namely Ps almost always come before Es and syntactically and semantically simpler Es come before syntactically and semantically more complex Es. More frequent and less complex Fs (e.g. *take place*) also appear before less frequent and more complex Fs (e.g. *paint the town red*).

8.1 Single-word lexical items

This section gives summary grids for single-word verbs, plotting their first appearance by level and subsequent semantic progression. Ten new items per level are shown as an illustration of this research method. First occurrences of these words, and their new meanings or co-occurrence possibilities at subsequent levels, can be considered criterial features for the respective levels. The A1–B2 data were taken from the Wordlists, and checked against passing scripts only (with the exception of the first level, A1, for which electronic data were lacking). The data from C1 and C2 were taken directly from the CLC. These grids distinguish transitive from intransitive uses of these verbs. Some verbs, e.g. *stand*, which is listed as occurring from A2, can be both intransitive and transitive. The example sentences given are intended to be indicative of the uses that occur at the level in question. If no transitive example is given for *stand* at A2, for example, this indicates that only the intransitive use is found at that level. The first attested appearance of transitive or intransitive use in these cases is shown by (Tr.) and (Intr.) respectively alongside the example.

A1

	A1	A2	B1	B2	C1	C2
Catch Tr.	ECatch a bus	ECatch a cold	PCatch a big fish	ECatch smb's attention/ interest	ECatch a glimpse of sth.	ECaught in a terrible trap
			FCatch fire			ECatch the reader's eye
Eat Tr.	PEat a big chocolate cake	Same	Same	Same	Same	Same
Give Tr.	PGive sb sth	PGive information	EGive an opinion	EGive a chance	EGive a healthy solution to the problem	FGive vent to our emotion
		PGive a ring	EGive a party	EGive a talk		Give me a piece of her mind

	A1	A2	B1	B2	C1	C2
Kick Intr. & Tr.	PKick the ball (Tr.)	None	PKick the door	FKick the bucket	EAll [the machine] did was to kick back at me	EKick us to depression
				PHe turned around and kicked at something hard. (Intr.)		
Make Tr.	PMake a quick snack	EMake a call/a mistake	FMake friends	FMake fun of	FMake the point of	EMake my spirits high
		FMake sure		FMake sense	FMake an exception	Make a scene
						Make room
Paint Intr. & Tr.	PI like to paint. (Intr.)	PPaint my bedroom (Tr.)	Same	EHer kindness is always painted at her wrinkled face.	FPaint the town red	EPaint a sad picture of a future world
Put Tr.	PPut them in the room	PPut my name on the list	EYou helped me to put it together.	EPut an end to	ETo put it mildly	EPut one's mind into sth.
					Put into practice	EPut it into words
Run Intr. & Tr.	PChildren can run everywhere. (Intr.)	Same	ERun a business (Tr.)	EA service bus runs every 15 minutes	FTempers were running short	FRun the risk
					ERun against the clock	Days ran
						EA chill ran down her spine
Take Tr.	PTake a book	ETake a bus	FTake part	ETake a deep breath	ETake this matter further	ETake keen interest
	ETake a picture	ETake an exam	ETake a nap	ETake a chance		ETake thing seriously
		FTake care	FTake place			
Walk Intr. & Tr.	PI like to walk by the river. (Intr.)	PYou will like it, because a lot of people walk their dog in there every day. (Tr.)	PSame	PWalk a few blocks	*Walk along the aisle	EHe walked the maid out of the room/the bride down the aisle/me home

A2

	A2	B1	B2	C1	C2
Break Tr.	PBroke a beautiful glass	EBreak the routine	EBreak a record	FBreak the bank	EBreak their calmness EBreak the wall that surrounds him
Brush Tr.	PI really need it to brush my hair tomorrow.	EI enjoy the cool and refreshing breeze brushing gently across my face while cycling by the lake.	EA soft, cool breeze brushed my skin.	EA good opportunity for me to brush my skills	ECompletely concentrated, with one hand on his chest and another just ready to brush the strings, Jimmy nodded to the technician.
Climb Tr.	PWe can go climb some mountains	PWe climbed a tower and had a magnificent view over the town	ELife is not [about]climbing the rungs of society.	EClimb the ladder of success	EClimb out of the boxes we've been stuck in
Cut Tr.	PI cut the cake.	PThe robot had cut its hand.	ECut the telephone line	FCut our losses FCut the mustard FCut a long story short	EThe war had cut her life into two. EI would not cut their wings.
Fall Intr.	PSome ink will fall on them	FFall asleep/ ill/in love	EScience had already fallen in wicked hands.	FFall into temptation FFall short of	EFall into desperation FFall into a trap
Hit Tr.	PHit smb.	PTyphoon hit my city	ESuddenly, it hit her: 'it is now or never' she said and signed the paper on her desk.	FHit the roof	EHit upon the idea FHit the jackpot
Jump Intr.& Tr.	PWe jumped naked in[to] the swimming pool! (Intr.)	Same	EMy heart start jumping because of his beautiful blue eyes	P In Milano Cantide tickets are bought downstairs in the Hall before jumping the steps which lead to the platforms. (Tr.)	Pjump the fence EJump to conclusions EJump from childhood to old age
Push Tr.	PPush sth./ smb.	PPush the button	EPush yourself	EPush smb. to do sth.	EPush their boundaries/their limits

	A2	B1	B2	C1	C2
Stand Intr. & Tr.	**P**I will stand at the front of my house. (Intr.)	**P**Can't stand sth./ smb. (Tr.)	**E**I was thinking about how stupid we were for letting an argument stand between us.	**F**Stand a chance	**F**Stand still
Throw Tr.	**P**Throw balls	**P**Same	**E**I've heard that you're going to throw a party for Anna.	**E**The more you throw yourself into learning English in an English-speaking country, the more interesting and fascinating you will feel.	**E**Throw more light on the matter

B1

	B1	B2	C1	C2
Blow Intr. & Tr.	**P**Wind blows. (Intr.) **P**Blow all candles (Tr.)	**E**By being made more attractive for younger families with children and shopkeepers you can blow some new life into our village. **E**I shouted 'I have a gun and if you make any move I will blow your brains'.	**F**Blow his own trumpet **F**Blown out of proportion	Same
Divide Tr.	**P**The class was divided in[to] two groups.	**P**The city is divided into two parts by the River Danube: Buda and Pest.	**E**Divide the barbarian way of life from a civilised one	**E**Opinions are divided. **E**My life was divided.
Face Tr.	**P**There is a desk [to] the right of the room which faces my bed.	**E**You wouldn't believe the problems I faced when I left your house.	**F**Face the music **F**Face extinction	**E**But I faced ignorance. **E**Finally I found out that his company had faced bankruptcy.
Fit Intr. & Tr.	**P**The desk has to be very small and has to fit into the corner. (Intr.)	**P**Fit the animals into the zoo. (Tr.)	**E**To fit consumers' needs Fits better with the company's expectations	**E**A lot of people did not fit the society.

	B1	B2	C1	C2
Grab Tr.	PI quickly hung up and grabbed clothes and my cell phone.	EGrab opportunity	EGrab your heart	EThe story grabbed me
Land Intr.	PWhen we landed, my suitcase was not there.	PAn innocent pigeon landed on his rifle's cannon. EHer father's palm landed on her left cheek.	EYour booking landed on my doormat	E [Piggy] land dead in the sea.
Pour Intr. & Tr.	PThe rain is pouring down. (Intr.) PThe look on his face stopped me cold, as if someone had just poured a freezing water bucket down my back. (Tr.)	He woke up and cleaned off the blood that poured from his injured eyebrow.	Sameø	EAnd all the memories poured back into my brain.
Spill Tr.	PSpill smb.'s coffee	PUnless we understand this, we'll cry over spilt milk.	*Everybody knows that this shouldn't have happened, but water is already spilled, and there is no way we can put this back to its original position.	EAs globalisation moves forward, markets are opened up and as rival firms spill into the countries competition gets fierce, which leads to mounting pressure on companies.
Stick Intr. & Tr.	PI stick posters of my favourite football team, Manchester United, on the wall. (Tr.)	PThe body of his boss's wife lay on the ground, a knife stuck in her heart.	EOur company's name will 'stick' in people's minds (Intr.)	EI cannot stand all those mothers who stick their children to a television's screen just as if it were a pacifier.
Tear Intr. & Tr.	Clothes tear (intr.)	EA terrible scream tore the night.	ETorn between their dreams and their real possibilities	Same

B2

	B2	C1	C2
Acquire Tr.	**P**I will be able to acquire more stamps for my collection. **E**I have already acquired experience in that field.	Same	**E**The first thing I acquired was honesty in everything. **E**People . . .who acquired high social positions/status
Capture Tr.	**P**Joe, the serial killer, was captured. **E**That should absolutely be captured on film	**E**Captured in my mind **E**Captured the audience	**E**She captured our hearts. **E**To capture Las Vegas spirit.
Drag Intr. & Tr.	**P**Another man approached the agent, both watching as officers dragged the man to a nearby car. (Tr.)	Same	**E**Time dragged on. (Intr.) **E**I dragged myself out of bed.
Melt Intr. & Tr.	**P** I put the coke out so that the iced parts would melt and went to the balcony. (Intr.) **P**Tall, blond and with eyes that could melt ice. (Tr.)	**E**The songs melted one into another	**E**All melted with tears of despair and impossible passion.
Ruin Tr.	**P**Our plans were ruined.	Same	Same
Rush Intr. & Tr.	**P**I rushed to Tom's house. (Intr.)	**P**Blood rushing through your veins.	**E**Questions rushing through my mind. **F**It has always been very busy but these days people seem to have a harder time facing the fact that not everything can be rushed. (Tr.)
Skip Tr.	**P**He skipped the meal.	**F**Skip the formalities **E**Skip the area code	**E**Her eyes skipped from one person to another
Spread Intr. & Tr.	**P**Smoke began to spread in the kitchen. (Intr.) **P** To see large birds that couldn't spread their wings (Tr.) **E**She travels all over the world to spread a bit of her culture. (Tr.)	Same	**F**Spread like wild fire
Swallow Tr.	**P**When Mrs McGillicuddy was upstairs, she swallowed a fish bone.	**E**Family factories are slowly being swallowed by big companies.	**F**There will be no choice but to swallow the pride. **E**Four CDs had swallowed all the money I had left. **E**I should have swallowed those words.
Upset Tr.	**P**This really upset me.	**E**Roving dogs upset the dustbins	**E**Upset her plans **E**Upset her routine life

C1

	C1	C2
Accumulate Tr.	P I accumulated information. E To relax after the stress accumulated in many jobs	Same
Boast Intr. & Tr.	P It boasted a lot of tastes for vegetarians. (Tr.) P My dad always boasts that he saw them when they came to Japan. (Intr.)	Same
House Tr.	E The activity will not be housed in the college.	Same
Opt Intr.	P You may opt to follow computer or business courses.	Same
Reassure Tr.	P I can reassure you that the effects on everyday life have not been as dramatic as you fear.	Same
Shape Tr.	E This strength shaped her image so much.	E His ultimate goal was to shape the girl for his own artistic and decadent pleasure.
Stain Tr.	E That may have stained the company's reputation.	E Stevens was so stained by all the trivialities of his life that he could not show his true self to Miss Kenton. The pillow was stained with something that looked like blood.
Quote Intr. & Tr.	E We would like to quote some facts.	Same
Urge Tr.	P I also urge you to improve the service at your hotel.	E Fatigue from 10-hour journey on a economy class urged her body to rest.
Zoom Intr.	E He zoomed up the status ladder.	None

C2

	C2
Drain Intr. & Tr.	E The colour seemed to have drained out of everything around me. (Intr.) E The constant temperature drains the energy from you. (Tr.)
Limp Intr.	P Most of them limped in their new shoes.
Pierce Tr.	P My tank was pierced. E The sound would pierce the stuffy, still air of her cramped apartment.
Raid Tr.	P Jack and the hunters raid the shelters at night.
Reap Tr.	E You will reap great rewards.
Saunter Intr.	P She sauntered down the street.
Smear Tr.	P The room was smeared with graffiti.
Squander Tr.	P I squandered my money. E I had already squandered my emotions.
Stagger Intr. & Tr.	P Fred staggered toward a telephone booth. (Intr.) E The news staggered the whole town. (Tr.)
Sway Intr. & Tr.	P The huge old tree was swaying in the wind. (Intr.) E I refused to be swayed by their arguments. (Tr.)

8.2 Verb particle combinations

Verb particle combinations are presented separately from single lexical items, for two reasons. They involve lexical units larger than a single word, first of all. And their semantics is regularly non-compositional (see Lohse, Hawkins and Wasow 2004 for detailed illustration of this). Thus, in *look the word up*, *look up* is a different entity from *look* and it needs to be listed and described quite separately from the latter. The particle *up* can be distinguished from the preposition *up* (as in *walk up the stairs*) by the permutability test: we can say both *look X up* and *look up X* but only *walk up the stairs* (not **walk the stairs up*). There are a number of subtypes of these verb+particles in English that can be distinguished by the tests presented in Lohse, Hawkins and Wasow (op. cit.), but the important points in this context are that that they are not single word items and their particles are not prepositions. Some prepositions do pattern like particles in that they define a semantically non-compositional unit with their verbs, but they are still prepositions by the permutation test. Consider *count on your uncle*. The combination *count on* is quite different in meaning from *count* alone, but *on* is still a preposition here (there is no **count your uncle on*). These verb preposition combinations in English are discussed in detail in Hawkins (2000, 2004), to which the reader is referred. Verb particle combinations can be either transitive, as in *look the word up* (*the word* being the direct object), or intransitive, as in *look up* without an object. There is no longer the possibility of a permutation in this latter case, in the absence of an object, and as a result the particle/preposition distinction becomes moot and *look up* can be analysed either as an (intransitive) verb particle combination, or as a verb preposition combination.

In what follows we have selected ten verb particle combinations for which we present both the first attested (transitive and/or intransitive) usage plus later extensions in verb meaning. The data in these grids are taken from the CLC. As for the single-word verbs we recorded the first occurrence of the phrasal verb as listed in the Wordlists for A2–B2 levels (checking these entries against passing scripts only, with the exception of A1 for which electronic data were lacking) and selected the C1 and C2 phrasal verb directly from the CLC. We then searched the corpus for the semantic progression of these phrasal verbs at subsequent levels. We observed a similar progression in lexical–semantic complexity from A2–C2 to that exhibited in the single-item grids. For example, *pour out* in its primary sense occurs at B2 while a metaphorical use comes in later at C2 (*tourists . . . pour out of the jumbo jet*). Interestingly, in many cases the transitive forms appear before the intransitive. Transitive phrasal arguments have an additional direct object argument, and we might expect all things being equal that they would appear later than their intransitive counterparts (by the principle of Maximise Structurally and Semantically Simple Properties, see Chapter 5.3). But in addition to structural complexity there are also considerations of semantic complexity and of frequency (see Maximise Frequently Occurring Properties in Chapter 5.2) that will affect the time course of lexical acquisition for these particle verbs. For example, *stick out* as an intransitive is much more frequent than its transitive counterpart and appears earlier. And the more primary meaning of *run away* in *run away from home* appears earlier than the more extended sense in *run away from a problem*.

Making distinctions of primary, extended and figurative meanings for these particle verbs is more difficult theoretically than it is for single-word verbs, and so we have decided not to risk controversial labelling assignments in the grids below. More detailed research in this area is in any case already underway within the EPP (see Capel and Martinez 2010), for the C levels as well as A and B levels.

Verb + Particles	A2	B1	B2	C1	C2
Blow up Intr. & Tr.			We blew up as many balloons as we could. (Tr.)	No new	Like thunder the quarrel blew up. (Intr.)
Fall apart Intr.			It looks like it is going to fall apart any day. All her dreams and wishes fell apart.	To begin with, we thought that the membership is falling apart.	People are falling apart.
Look up Intr. & Tr.		She gave me a dict-ionary to look up the words. (Tr.)	A lot of people look up to him as an idol. (Intr.)	No new	No new
Pour out Intr. & Tr.			No new		Those are the tourists, which pour out of the jumbo jet. The joy of living was pouring out of her.

Verb + Particles	A2	B1	B2	C1	C2
Put on Tr.	The girls go to buy a beautiful dress in Valencia, and cut their hair and put on some make up.	I drew a deep breath and tried to put on the light. I'm afraid of put[ting] too m[any] pounds on.	No new	The closest any of them ever got to fashion were their Sunday clothes, which they put on before going to Sunday mass and took off as soon as they got back home. We should look for a school with expanded individual lessons, where a lot of stress is put on grammar. I am relieved to find out that the local government has finally put on some projects that could put an end to this problem.	I was recently informed that the local radio station intents to put on a two-hour programme for young people. The dogs put on a show in the square.
Run away Intr.			At the age of fourteen, she ran away from home.	I try to run away from this new world.	However it's a problem we can't run away from.
Stick out Intr. & Tr.				Skimpy tops and skirts, funky-ripped jeans, zany platform-shoes or boy's knickers sticking out of their low-pulled trousers. (Intr.)	I wouldn't stick my neck out and say he wasn't trying to deceive me. (Tr.)

Verb + Particles	A2	B1	B2	C1	C2
Take off Intr.	It was bothering me and I took it off and left it on the kitchen table.	The plane took off at 12 and how big was my surprise when just an hour and half later, I discovered the rock mountains around the sea!	If you hire new ones your sales will probably take off.		Since the moment that computers took off, they became an issue which everybody (knowledgeable or not) would feel the necessity of making use of.
Walk away Intr.			They kissed deeply and walked away out of the platform.	Here were only four candidates left and only one of them would walk away with one million euro's hand cash.	Would she learn from it if she walked away now and started somewhere new, where they would not know what had happened?
Wrap up Tr.			It was wrapped up in paper with a red ribbon.		She is perfection in every sense: beauty, intelligence, charm and youth all wrapped up in one. He was totally wrapped up in his thoughts when he left the house.

9 Conclusions and future directions

The positive criterial features of the CEFR proficiency levels discussed in Chapters 7 and 8 have been presented vertically from level to level, with a particular emphasis on transitional features from one level to the next (see Chapter 1.4). In this chapter we begin with a summary of these features presented horizontally, so that the characteristics of each level can be brought together conveniently in one place (Section 9.1). We then discuss (in Section 9.2) the relationship between these grammatical and lexical features and the kinds of functional features summarised in the illustrative descriptors of the CEFR (see Chapter 1.1). In Section 9.3 we discuss practical applications of this research, illustrating some points that were made in the introductory chapter (Section 1.4) and in Section 9.4 we summarise its theoretical relevance in the light of the literature review of Chapter 4 and the principles of second language acquisition presented in Chapter 5. Section 9.5 looks ahead to future research and publications within the English Profile Programme.

9.1 Horizontal summary of criterial features

The following grammatical and lexical features have been presented as criterial for levels A2–C2 in Chapters 7 and 8. Relevant sections are given in parentheses.

9.1.1 Criterial features for A2

A Mean Length of Utterance figure of 7.9 (Section 7.3)

Simple intransitive clauses, NP-V (7.1.1)

Transitive clauses, NP-V-NP (7.1.2)

Ditransitive clauses, NP-V-NP-NP (7.1.7)

Verbs with a finite complement clause, NP-V-S, *I knew that you have a new house too.* (7.1.3)

Verbs with subject-controlled infinitival complements, NP-V-VPinfin, *I want to buy a coat* (7.1.4)

Direct WH-questions (7.1.5)

Pronoun plus infinitive, *something to eat* (7.1.6)

Postnominal modification with *-ed, famous paintings painted by* . . . (Section 7.1.8)

No Subject-to-Subject Raising verbs and adjectives (7.2.1)

No Subject-to-Object Raising verbs (unpassivised) (7.2.2)

No Subject-to-Object Raising verbs plus Passive (7.2.3)

No Tough Movement (7.2.4)

An [*of* [*of*]] double embedding of postnominal genitives, *the colours of the back of the mobile phone* (7.3)

Modals MAY, CAN and MIGHT in the Possibility (epistemic) sense (7.4)

Modal MUST in the Obligation (deontic) sense (7.4)

Modal SHOULD in the Advice (deontic) sense (7.4)

The following single-word lexical verbs are first attested at A2 (8.1):

> *break* (Tr.), *brush* (Tr.), *climb* (Tr.), *cut* (Tr.), *fall* (Intr.), *hit* (Tr.), *jump* (Intr.), *paint* (Tr.), *push* (Tr.), *stand* (Intr.), *throw* (Tr.), *walk* (Tr.), These A2 lexical verbs are all first attested in their Primary (P) senses (8.1)

The following verb–particle combinations are first attested at A2 (8.2): *put on* (Tr.), *take off* (Tr.)

9.1.2 Criterial features for B1

A higher Mean Length of Utterance figure of 10.8 at B1 compared with 7.9 at A2 (Section 7.3)

Verbs with object-controlled infinitival complements, *I ordered him to gather my men to the hall* (7.1.9)

Verbs with object-controlled *-ing* complements, *I saw a girl standing behind me* (7.1.10)

Postnominal modification with *-ing, I received your mail asking for the sales report* (7.1.8)

It Extraposition with finite clauses, *It's true that I don't need a ring to make me remember you* (7.1.11)

Verbs with a PP plus finite complement clause, NP-V-PP-S, *He said to me he would like to come back soon* (7.1.12)

Relative clauses formed on a genitive position, *painter whose pictures I like so much* (7.1.13)

Pseudocleft with WH as direct object, *what I saw was so amazing* (7.1.14)

Indirect WH-questions in finite clauses, *Guess where I have been* (7.1.15)

Indirect WH-questions in infinitival phrases, *I did not know where to look for it anymore* (7.1.16)

Complex auxiliaries WOULD RATHER and HAD BETTER (7.1.17)

Adverbial subordinate clauses with *-ing* that follow the clause to which they are attached, . . . *the Hotel Taj provides more facilities, including computers* . . . (7.1.18)

Subject-to-Subject Raising constructions with the verb *seem* and the adjective *supposed* (7.2.1)

Subject-to-Object Raising constructions (unpassivised) with the verbs *expect, like, want* (7.2.2)

No Subject-to-Object Raising constructions plus Passive (7.2.3)

Tough Movement with the adjective *easy* (7.2.4)

An [*of* [-*s*]] double embedding of an *-s* genitive within an *of* genitive, *the subject of my boss's talk* (7.3)

Modal MAY in the Permission (deontic) sense (7.4)

Modal MUST in the Necessity (epistemic) sense (7.4)

Modal SHOULD in the Probability (epistemic) sense (7.4)

The following single-word lexical verbs are first attested at B1 (8.1):

> *blow* (Tr. & Intr.), *divide* (Tr.), *face* (Tr.), *fit* (Intr.), *grab* (Tr.), *land* (Intr.), *pour* (Tr. & Intr.), *run* (Tr.), *spill* (Tr.), *stand* (Tr.), *stick* (Tr.), *tear* (Tr.)

These B1 lexical verbs are all first attested in their primary (P) senses (8.1)

The following verb–particle combinations are first attested at B1 (8.2): *look up* (Tr.), *take off* (Intr.)

9.1.3 Criterial features for B2

A higher Mean Length of Utterance figure of 14.2 at B2 compared with 10.8 at B1 (Section 7.3)

Adverbial subordinate clauses with *-ing* that precede the clause to which they are attached, *Talking about spare time, I think we could go to the Art Museum* (7.1.18)

It Extraposition with infinitival phrases, *it would be helpful to work in your group as well* (7.1.19)

Pseudocleft with WH as subject, *what fascinated me was that I was able to lie on the sea surface* (7.1.20)

Verbs with an NP plus finite complement clause, NP-V-NP-S, *I told him I loved his songs* (7.1.21)

Secondary predications, *go and paint the houses yellow and blue* (7.1.22)

Productive Subject-to-Subject Raising constructions with the verbs *appear, cease, fail, happen, prove, turn out*, and the adjectives *certain, likely, sure, unlikely* (7.2.1)

New Subject-to-Object Raising constructions (unpassivised) with the verbs *imagine, prefer* (7.2.2)

Subject-to-Object Raising constructions plus Passive with the verbs *expected, known, obliged, thought* (7.2.3)

New Tough Movement constructions with the adjectives *difficult, good, hard* (7.2.4)

An [[*of*] -*s*] double embedding of an *of* genitive within an -*s* genitive, *the United States of America's government* (7.3)

The following single-word lexical verbs are first attested at B2 (8.1):

> *acquire* (Tr.), *capture* (Tr.), *drag* (Tr.), *fit* (Tr.), *melt* (Tr. & Intr.), *ruin* (Tr.), *rush* (Intr.), *skip* (Tr.), *spread* (Tr. & Intr.), *swallow* (Tr.), *upset* (Tr.)

These B2 lexical verbs are all first attested in their primary (P) senses (8.1)

The following verb–particle combinations are first attested at B2 (8.2):

> *blow up* (Tr.), *fall apart* (Intr.), *pour out* (Tr. & Intr.), *run away* (Intr.), *walk away* (Intr.), *wrap up* (Tr.)

The following error types improve significantly from B1 to B2 (2.3):

> DD (Derivation of Determiner), IV (Incorrect Inflection of Verb)

9.1.4 Criterial features for C1

A higher Mean Length of Utterance figure of 17.3 at C1 compared with 14.2 at B2 (Section 7.3)

New Subject-to-Subject Raising constructions with the verb *chance* (7.2.1)

New Subject-to-Object Raising constructions (unpassivised) with the verbs *believe, find, suppose, take,* (7.2.2)

New Subject-to-Object Raising constructions plus Passive with the verbs *assumed, discovered, felt, found, proved* (7.2.3)

No new Tough Movement constructions (7.2.4)

An [[-*s*] -*s*] double embedding of an -*s* genitive within an -*s* genitive, *the bride's family's house* (7.3)

Modal MIGHT in the Permission (deontic) sense (7.4)

The following single-word lexical verbs are first attested at C1 (8.1):

> *accumulate* (Tr.), *boast* (Tr. & Intr.), *house* (Tr.), *opt* (Intr.), *quote* (Tr.)
> *reassure* (Tr.), *shape* (Tr.), *stain* (Tr.), *urge* (Tr.), *zoom* (Intr.),

The following error types improve significantly from B2 to C1 (2.3):

> AGN (Noun Agreement Error), DD (Derivation of Determiner), MQ (Missing Quantifier), MT (Missing Preposition)

9.1.5 Criterial features for C2

A higher Mean Length of Utterance figure of 19.0 at C2 compared with 17.3 at C1 (Section 7.3)

No new Subject-to-Subject Raising constructions (7.2.1)

New Subject-to-Object Raising constructions (unpassivised) with the verbs *declare*, *presume*, *remember* (7.2.2)

New Subject-to-Object Raising constructions plus Passive with the verb *presumed* (7.2.3)

New Tough Movement constructions with the adjective *tough* (7.2.4)

The following single-word lexical verbs are first attested at C2 (8.1):

> *drag* (intr.), *drain* (Tr. & Intr.), *limp* (Intr.), *pierce* (Tr.), *raid* (Tr.), *reap* (Tr.), *rush* (Tr.), *saunter* (Intr.), *smear* (Tr.), *squander* (Tr.), *stagger* (Tr. & Intr.), *sway* (Tr. & Intr.),

The following error types improve significantly from C1 to C2 (2.3):

> AGN (Noun Agreement Error), DD (Derivation of Determiner), CN (Noun Countability Error), RQ (Replace Quantifier), RY (Replace Adverb)

9.2 Form–function relations

We are aware of the fact that a checklist of criterial features, of the kind we have just summarised, is not the whole story in assessment, learning and teaching. It is just one part of profiling English as a second language. The grammatical and lexical means we are highlighting are used to perform a variety of functions, such as referring, requesting, and so on. These functions can be performed in a variety of ways (see also Green forthcoming 2012) and the ability to perform them has been an important indicator of proficiency, on which the whole CEFR is based (see Chapter 1.1). For example, when asking somebody to hold the door open, you can say just 'Hold the door' if your arsenal of linguistic means is limited, or 'I am so sorry to bother you but would you be so kind as to hold the door open for me please?' Moreover, it is not just the linguistic means that are necessary for an adequate performance of functions, but knowledge of social relationships and interactions that makes the use of language appropriate for the occasion. And then there is the question of the appropriateness of the response to the task outlined in an exam question, which means that a detailed report about lack of service in a hotel will not necessarily be adequate if the task is to write an official letter of complaint to the general manager of the hotel. All of this has to be incorporated into the process of assessment, and it has to be learned and taught. The collaborative research that constitutes the English Profile Programme aims to provide a model that includes all these aspects of second language command, linguistic, cognitive and social.

One of the remarkable and original contributions of van Ek and Trim's Threshold series (see Chapter 6) is that it contained both a detailed taxonomy of language functions (and general meanings or notions) as well as a detailed listing of grammatical and lexical properties of English that can be used to express them. A brief illustration is given in Table 9.1 for two of these functions taken from *Threshold 1990* p.39, 'requesting someone to do something' (intonation

Table 9.1 Illustrative language functions (van Ek and Trim *Threshold 1990*:39)

Requesting someone to do something
Please + VP imperative
Please sit down.
VP imperative + please
Stop talking please
Would/could you (please) + VPinf
Could you please close the door?
Would you be so kind as to + VPinf
Would you be so kind as to wait?
Kindly + VP imperative + (please)
Kindly make less noise please
Would you mind + VP gerund
Would you mind opening the window?
Can I have + NP + VP past
Can I have my shirt washed?

Suggesting a course of action (involving both speaker and addressee)
Let's + VPinf!
Let's go!
Shall we + VPinfin?
Shall we dance?
We could + VPinf
We could go for a walk.
What/How about + NP/VP gerund
How about walking home?
We might (perhaps) + VPinf
We might perhaps go by train.
Why not + VPinf?
Why not fly there?
Why don't we + VPinf?

symbols included in their original examples have been omitted here), and 'suggesting a course of action (involving both speaker and addressee)'.

This listing of function–form mappings is clearly very useful for learners. Important functions in everyday language use are identified and a number of their grammatical and lexical exponents are listed. As we pointed out in Chapter 1.2, one and the same function can be performed by many linguistic structures or single words, often with subtle nuances in meaning. Conversely, one and the same structure can perform different functions: **Can I have + NP + VPpast** is often not an indirect request, it can simply be a direct question about a possibility, as in *Can I have my article published in this journal?* It is important to draw attention to these mappings between forms and functions as van Ek and Trim do.

Green (forthcoming 2012) builds on this Threshold-level work by extending it to the C levels for the EPP. Van Ek and Trim did not write a volume for the C levels, and moreover the C levels are under-described in the CEFR scales. Green notes that adequate functional descriptors for the C levels are often lacking in the Council of Europe's 2001 document. He incorporates the 'criterial feature' concept developed here for grammatical and lexical exponents into a revised description of C-level functions, searching for criterial differences in functional competence between B2 and C1, and between C1 and C2. The criterial features in grammar and lexis that have been identified in the present volume (summarised in Section 9.1) now make possible a new set of form–function relations that link criterial features in the functions to criterial features in the exponents.

Even though these links are not one-to-one but many-to-many, as we have pointed out, it is still useful for learners to have them laid out clearly on the page, as van Ek and Trim do. A number of the criterial properties for B1 summarised in Section 9.1.2 above, for example, are among several linguistic forms and structures that make possible the expression of B1 functions such as 'Can describe experiences and events, dreams, hopes and ambitions and briefly give reasons and explanations for opinions and plans' (Council of Europe 2001, Table 1 Common Reference Levels: global scale, p.24, see Chapter 1.1 above). Hopes and ambitions are often expressed by Subject-to-Object Raising constructions (*I'd like you to phone me*, *I want you to say hi to everybody*, *I expect you to be a little bit surprised*, all of which are attested B1 examples, see Chapter 7.2.2). Verbs with object-controlled *-ing* complements describe experiences and events (*I saw a girl standing behind me*, *Maria saw him taking a taxi*, again attested B1 examples, see Chapter 7.1.10). So do Subject-to-Subject Raising constructions with *seem* (*They seem to be really interesting*, see Chapter 7.2.1) and *It* Extraposition structures (*It seems that . . ., It is true that . . .*, see Chapter 7.1.11). Adverbial subordinate clauses with *-ing* add descriptive details to events and experiences (*the Hotel Taj provides more facilities, including computers*, see Chapter 7.1.18). And a productive structure for giving reasons and explanations is the B1 construction with a verb plus PP plus finite complement clause (as in *He said to me he would like to come back soon*, *He explained to me that . . .*, *They admitted to the authorities that . . .*, and so on, see Chapter 7.1.12).

These are clear structural and lexical exponents that enable learners at B1 to express the functions defined for that level. At the same time, however, there are many grammatical and lexical details of learner English that cannot be linked to functional and notional details of the relevant levels in a straightforward way. Many of the new syntactic and morpho-syntactic patterns characteristic of B1 (Threshold, Section 9.1.2), rather than B2 (Vantage, Section 9.1.3), rather than C1 (Effective Operational Proficiency, Section 9.1.4) are not predictable on the basis of the new functions that have been defined for these levels. In other words, some of our grammatical and lexical features actually enable users to express the communicative functions that have been described for the level in question. But other grammatical and lexical properties are simply correlated with particular levels and are characteristic of sentences that express a variety of functions.

For example, postnominal modifiers with *-ed* are an A2 feature (*beautiful paintings painted by famous Iranian painters*), whereas those with *-ing* are B1 (*your mail asking for the sales report*). There is no obvious reason for this in terms of the expanding functional competence of learners at B1. They are both devices that contribute to richer referential descriptions of entities, but the later acquisition of the one compared with the other is not functionally motivated. It points instead to expanding knowledge of the syntax of the English Noun Phrase, and to the learning of new structural types at A2 and B1 that can be used to express a variety of meanings and functions. Similarly, doubly embedded [*of* [*of*]] genitives are A2 (*the colours of the back of the mobile phone*) whereas [*of* [*-s*]] genitives are B1 (*the subject of my boss's talk*). It is hard to think of any reason for this in terms of the communicative functions being learned at these levels. The different kinds of Extraposition structures, involving finite versus infinitival extraposed clauses, also highlight the need for a separate set of statements involving an expanding syntactic competence: *it* Extraposition with finite clauses is a B1 feature (*it's true that I don't need a ring . . .*), but with infinitivals it is B2 (*it would be helpful to work in your group*). Whatever the communicative functional correlates are for Pseudocleft constructions, it is hard to imagine that these functions could account for the syntactic difference between WH as a direct object of its clause, which is a B1 feature (*what I saw was so amazing*), and WH as subject, which is B2 (*what fascinated me was that I was able to lie on the surface*). Subject-to-Subject Raising structures are B2 (*The car has proved to be one of the most important inventions of our century*). Passivised Subject-to-Object Raising constructions like *the low cost of membership and entry was assumed to be an advantage* are C1.

There are clearly interesting syntactic patterns here, and one can imagine possible processing and complexity reasons for the later acquisition of the different genitives, for example (see Chapter 7.3), and for different types of raising structures (see Chapters 5.3 and 7.2). But communicative functional reasons for these kinds of differences are far from obvious. Remember how these functions were described in Table 1.1 in Chapter 1.1 above. Learners at B1 'can understand the main points of clear standard input on familiar matters regularly encountered in work, school, leisure, etc.', learners at B2 'can understand the main ideas of complex text on both concrete and abstract topics, including technical discussions in his/her field of specialisation', and learners at C1 'can understand a wide range of demanding, longer texts, and recognise implicit meaning'. The ALTE Can Do statements for listening and speaking skills at these levels include (for B1) 'CAN express opinions on abstract/cultural matters in a limited way or offer advice within a known area . . .', (for B2) 'CAN follow or give a talk on a familiar topic or keep up a conversation on a fairly wide range of topics', and (for C1) 'CAN contribute effectively to meetings and seminars within own area of work or keep up a casual conversation with a good degree of fluency, coping with abstract expressions' (Council of Europe 2001:251). The syntactic structures that are criterial for these levels contribute to the performance of language functions such as these, but they also have an autonomous reality that exists separately from them and that needs to be described in grammatical terms and explained in terms of learning and/or processing (see Chapter 5).

This partial autonomy can be seen particularly clearly with negative criterial features. Improvements in the error categories of the different levels will clearly make for more successful communication, and hence for the more successful performance and expression of all language functions that characterise each level. But there appears to be no clear linkage between forms and functions in most of the error types and their quantities and success rates in learning need to be defined separately for each level.

All of this underscores the importance of defining grammatical and lexical features of the CEFR levels as fully and accurately as possible, in addition to criterial differences in functional competence, and of adopting a multi-factor approach to both the description and the explanation of SLA as proposed in Chapter 5. The significance of grammar and lexis has recently been underscored by Khalifa and Weir (2009:118) who argue that 'on the whole it could be said that it is the lexical and grammatical resources rather than function which are more significant in determining level' and they see as a reason for this that 'it is the exponents used to express function that become more complex rather than the functions themselves'. We agree with this conclusion, though we have also argued that many grammatical features and error types are not in any clear alignment with any corresponding functions and have an independent reality in the learners' evolving syntax and morphosyntax. So it isn't just the grammatical and lexical exponents of the CEFR functions that are criterial for the different levels, it's the non-exponents and autonomous rules of the grammar as well. The general point made by Khalifa and Weir, that we need to return to an emphasis on grammar and lexis, is surely right, however, and supplying such an emphasis, as we do in this book, can 'lead to better and more comprehensive illustrative descriptors . . . In this way the CEFR will become the really useful tool that it was intended to be' (Milanovic 2009:5). It is to this practical usefulness that we now turn.

9.3 Practical applications

The research programme outlined and illustrated in this book is intended to be useful. Now that we have identified a range of criterial features we can elaborate on this and show how they can be put to use for teaching, learning and testing purposes.

Consider first teaching and learning and the preparation of teaching materials. The CLC gives us empirical evidence for developmental stages in the learning of constructions, words and word meanings in English. It gives us quantitative data on learner errors in syntax, morpho-syntax and lexical choice. Teaching materials and methods can now be calibrated to the criterial features of each level. The grammatical and lexical properties of English can be presented to learners in ways that are level-appropriate, and learners can be encouraged to focus on both positive and negative features of the target level(s), thereby optimising their chances of success.

In other words, we believe that the criterial feature approach to reference level descriptions exemplified in this book can make teaching and learning more efficient. Explicit exercises and grammar points can now target precisely those features that are criterial for the different levels, with the result that the teaching of grammar and of constructions with their lexical instantiations can be made appropriate for the level at which each student finds him- or herself. Written and spoken materials can now be selected that encourage implicit learning of the syntactic and morpho-syntactic structures and rules that are criterial for the different levels. Study guides and tips for learners can be written that incorporate the criterial features of each level and that help learners prepare for their respective exams.

We can also apply insights from the principles in Chapter 5, even for constructions and lexical items that have not yet been explicitly searched for in the CLC. Grammar and lexicon should, all things being equal, be introduced in a sequence that reflects their frequency in the input, as revealed through native speaker corpora like the BNC. In other words, relative frequency in the input can be used as a guide for teachers and textbook writers when making decisions about the order in which to introduce items to learners.

All of these practical benefits are made possible by the criterial feature approach and are already being implemented by Cambridge University Press and Cambridge Assessment in their publishing plans for the future.

For example, learners striving for **B1** can be introduced to Object Control structures that are first attested at this level (see Chapter 7.1.9) such as:

B1 *I ordered him to gather my men*

and to subordinate clauses with WH-movement, i.e. indirect questions in finite clauses (see Chapter 7.1.15):

B1 *Guess where I have been.*
I don't know how I could have done it.
I can't understand what she's saying.

and in infinitival phrases (see Chapter 7.1.16):

B1 *I did not know where to look for it anymore.*
I don't know what to do.
I didn't know what to buy for you.

Learners at B1 can be introduced to the lexical verbs that successful candidates in B1 exams know, e.g. *divide* (Tr.), *fit* (Intr.), *grab* (Tr.), *spill* (Tr.), *stick* (Tr.), *tear* (Tr.) and to the expanding meanings of verbs learned earlier (see Chapter 8.1). The verb *break* which appears for the first time at A2 is used in the extended sense of INTERRUPT at B1: *I think the most important aim of a holiday is to break your daily routine.*

Learners striving for **B2** can be introduced to the lexical verbs and meanings produced at this level (see Chapter 8.1) and to the constructions that are first attested then, such as secondary predications (see Section 7.1.22):

B2 *paint the houses yellow and blue*

Most Subject-to-Subject Raising constructions are B2:

B2 *The car has proved to be one of the most important inventions of our century.*

Teachers can introduce new lexical verbs and their extended meaning possibilities to learners preparing for **C1**, e.g. *accumulate* (Tr.), *boast* (Tr. & Intr.), *quote* (Tr.), *reassure* (Tr.), *shape* (Tr.), *stain* (Tr.). The verb *break* appears first in the idiomatic sense of *break the bank* at C1. Different raising structures characteristic of C1 need to be mastered at this level such as:

C1 *I believe her to be this country's best representative*

C1 *the low cost of membership and entry was assumed to be an advantage.*

Teachers wanting to help learners attain **C1** can focus on the many error types that appear to improve significantly from B2 to C1, e.g. AGN (Noun Agreement Error), DD (Derivation of Determiner), MT (Missing

Preposition), and MQ (Missing Quantifier), while learners striving for C2 can focus on the significant improvements from C1.

Explicit exercises and grammar points can now target these criterial features at the different levels, making the teaching of grammar more efficient. The selection of lexical verbs can also be calibrated to different levels in an appropriate way. Both grammar and lexicon can be introduced in a sequence that reflects their frequency in the input and their inherent complexity (see Chapter 5.2), as revealed through native speaking corpora and as reflected in the CLC. Written and spoken materials can also be selected that encourage implicit learning of these syntactic and morpho-syntactic properties and rules and by choosing samples of English from the CLC and other corpora that include them.

This research provides content that can also help to validate the scores that examiners of English provide. The assignment of a level and a grade to a sample of learner English currently relies on judgments that examiners make based on their experience and training during which they are exposed to sample scripts from the different levels. They have learned to assign scores with good inter-examiner agreement, but there is still a certain amount of intuition that they bring to the task, i.e. examiners may be implicitly rather than explicitly aware of what to look for in many cases. The empirically based research we have illustrated in this book provides support for the reality of the increasing proficiency in grammar and lexis at each higher level, in addition to the expanding functional competence, that is reflected in examiners' scores. We saw this already in Chapter 2.2 in the expanding Mean Length of Utterance figures that suggested an expansion in the range and complexity of constructions and lexical exponents that learners were mastering at each higher level. And we gave substance to this expansion in the criterial feature sets exemplified in Chapter 7. With these criterial features at hand, assessment can now become even more precise and more reliable.

Here is how we see this application working. An individual script, let us abbreviate it as S, by a candidate taking an exam at level X can be searched for the presence versus absence of criterial features derived from all passing scripts at X, and from those at the immediately lower level X-1 or at the immediately higher level X+1. Not all our criterial feature types will be equally useful for diagnosis. A number of negative properties, or error types, may not be usable since they are based on frequencies derived from all scripts, and an individual script may not have enough relevant instances to permit statistical comparison. Nor can any individual script be expected to show many of the positive properties derived from all scripts, because the individual script may again be too small and many positive properties will be absent.

What we can do, however, is to apply a partly deterministic, partly probabilistic process to assessment that is based on the identification of criterial features and the elimination of levels. For example, script S might contain several constructions and lexical items that are [B2, C1, C2] features, B2 being transitional. This establishes that S is at least B2. The script might contain no uniquely [C1, C2] features, however. These levels are provisionally eliminated, therefore, and B2 is supported probabilistically. S may even contain a unique B2 feature, such as a mean length of utterance (MLU) or other complexity indicator close to the aggregate for all B2 scripts. This strongly supports the diagnostic assignment of B2 to S.

Of course, as hundreds of criterial features become available for different levels, things will not be so straightforward. There may be, in a script, a limited set of [C1, C2] features co-existing with a B2 level of complexity and other [B2, C1, C2] features. Certain rules of resolution will be needed in such cases. Examiners have had to deal with transitional cases all along, of course. A criterial features approach now enables us to make explicit the practical difficulties they pose for examiners, and the features identified in our research can be used as the data for precise quantitative methods that can resolve some of the assessment problems exemplified here and justify the examining decisions made. They can also be used in the preparation of diagnostic grammar tests that assign students to their appropriate levels of instruction based on their command of English grammar. Yet a further practical application for assessment is in the area of improved examiner training.

We expect also that the theoretical work that underpins the present book will be useful for further research on negative criterial features and on applications within an assessment context (for example, diagnostic uses of assessment and examiner training), just as it is for the positive features that we have focused on in Part 2. Alexopoulou, Yannakoudakis and Briscoe (2011) have presented evidence from FCE data in the CLC which spans three CEFR levels (B1–C1) that the quantity of distinctive positive features for a CEFR level tends to increase from grades E to A, but they found no correlation between negative features (i.e. errors) and grades. In other words, 'attempts to produce more complex structures are rewarded even when errors persist' (ibid.). In the past the field of second language acquisition has been too preoccupied with error counts and with error analysis as a domain within which L2 learners' competence should be assessed. The fact that positive features 'carry more weight' in the marking of scripts than the quantity of errors is a welcome sign that the emphasis of examiners is now being placed more on what learners *can do* rather than on what they *cannot* do. The goal of the English Profile Programme and of research in this area should be to determine not the gross quantity of errors, but rather their predictive quality at each level. The principles we have outlined in Chapter 5 suggest that the quality of negative criterial features (errors) and their impact on assessment will depend significantly on features such as frequency, complexity and communicative effect (e.g. the extent to which they impede communication), in the same way that these principles have shaped the positive features of different CEFR levels and corresponding assessments, as shown here.

There are also practical benefits for publishing from the research programme we have described. New publishing materials can now be written, incorporating the criterial features of each level. Publishers can also develop market-specific ELT materials for different groups of learners. For example, learners whose first languages have no definite and indefinite articles (see Chapter 2.5) can be given English language materials that encourage explicit and implicit learning in this area. More generally, the learning stages, transfer effects and error types characteristic of Spanish learners of English can be reflected in textbooks and teaching materials designed specifically for them. The same holds for Chinese learners, and Japanese learners, and Russians. The current book has focused more on criterial features that are general and that hold regardless of the L1 rather than on L1-specific features, but further investigation of these latter is a major focus of English Profile research going forward (see Section 9.5 and Salamoura and Saville (2010:123) for the benefits of identifying both L1-independent and L1-specific criterial features per CEFR level).

9.4 Theoretical relevance

The criterial features we have extracted from the CLC are also of potential interest to theoreticians studying language acquisition. They can give us unique insights into the time course of second language acquisition, i.e. into the sequencing with which the thousands of properties that constitute knowledge of English are acquired by L2 learners. The clear progression from simpler to more complex structures and more complex words and word meanings provides a new set of data that can inform theories of simplicity and complexity. The progression from more to less frequent items sheds light on frequency effects, and on their relationship to simplicity and complexity, a major current issue in psycholinguistics (see Chapter 4.4). Earlier proficiency levels contain structures, words and word meanings that are easier to process, and so contribute data that are relevant to the precise relationship between learning and processing. In Chapter 5 we formulated a number of principles of these types that emerge from the CLC. The strength of an empirical and corpus approach is that we see patterns that current theories do not necessarily predict. We notice correlations across the syntax, the morpho-syntax, and the lexicon. The data suggest a set of interacting principles that we have formulated in Chapter 5. Some of our principles have already been proposed in other studies of first and second language acquisition (see Chapter 4 for the literature review). Our database and approach offer refinements and further details, and can reveal the competition between, and the relative strength of, the various factors. The different first languages of the learners in the CLC also enable us to address the role of transfer in SLA, one of the big and still unresolved issues in the field. We can examine how first languages of different types influence the various interlanguage stages between the L1 and L2 English.

Our principles can account for the relative sequencing of criterial features at the different proficiency levels. In particular we are now in a position to model the interacting forces that constrain or facilitate positive and negative transfer for given structures and given pairs of languages and to account for the similarities and differences between these two types of transfer. Positive transfer is constrained by complexity and infrequency in the input, and facilitated by simplicity and frequency (see Chapter 5.2 and 5.3). Negative transfer is permitted in order to achieve an expressive power and communicative efficiency in L2 comparable to that in L1 while minimising learning effort and/or processing effort (see Chapter 5.5). Conversely, the Communicative Blocking of Negative Transfer is expected when negative properties from L1 to L2 are filtered in proportion to communicative efficiency: the more an L1 property impedes efficient communication in L2, the less negative transfer there is. The negative transfer of head-final orders into L2 English by Japanese learners does not occur (see Chapter 4.3 for literature summary) and is blocked, we argue, because of its communicative inefficiency: speakers importing Japanese word orders into English would simply not be understood! But Spanish-style head-initial variants of English word order that do not impact efficient communication are negatively transferred (e.g. *I read yesterday the book*).

One needs a rich data set like the CLC in order get started with a multi-factor research project such as this. What is now needed is a computer simulation for SLA along the lines of Simon Kirby's (1999) simulation for first language acquisition that lays out explicitly all the possible pathways that interlanguages can take from a given L1 to a given L2, defining those that are more or less likely, and contrasting them with those that are impossible.

For corpus linguistics the CLC has provided both a challenge and a reward. The challenge from the outset has been how best to access relevant data about the CEFR levels. Initially this was done through lexical searches and manually introduced error codes. More recently Briscoe and Carroll's RASP parser has made possible the application of sophisticated automatic tagging and parsing techniques to learner data, thanks to joint work by Ted Briscoe and Paula Buttery. This is a novel development for corpus linguistics, but since much of the data is errorful, and hence not of the type on which RASP was trained, this complicated tagging and parsing. The solution lay in exploiting the error-coded half of the CLC, in effect using the normalised and corrected data for searches (see Chapter 3). Relative paucity of data has also necessitated the collection of new data in electronic form, which is currently in progress. Despite this the EPP has initiated a novel and original application of the RASP parser to learner data, and by tagging and parsing the British

National Corpus in the same way a systematic comparison can now be made between acquisition data at different levels and native speaking data for the same grammatical and lexical properties, as for example in the comparative data for verb co-occurrence frames in the CLC and the BNC (see Chapter 5.2).

The research project of this book has drawn on numerous other branches of the language sciences, including models of formal syntax, studies of the lexicon and lexical semantics, language typology and cross-linguistic variation, and others, in addition to psycholinguistics broadly construed and computational linguistics. Our findings are, we believe, of relevance to these fields in turn.

The present book has both practical and theoretical goals, therefore. It is a contribution to the applied areas that study the experiences of learners and teachers and examiners and that make proposals that are useful. It is also intended as a contribution to SLA, by providing empirical patterns and principles derived from them that can inform answers to theoretical questions. It is our belief that applications will only be successful if they rest on solid theoretical and empirical foundations. And conversely we believe that the experiences of practitioners, and the data that have been collected by practitioners in pursuit of practical goals are relevant for theories of learning and use, shedding light on scientific questions that have not yet been resolved.

9.5 Looking ahead

We have proposed an illustrative set of grammatical and lexical criterial features for the learning of English, summarised in Chapter 9.1, and some principles of learning in Chapter 5. We have stressed from the outset, however (see Chapter 1.4), that our principal goal in this book is to define an interdisciplinary research programme and to show, through these illustrative features and sample principles, how researchers from different theoretical and applied areas of the language sciences can work together to achieve both theoretical and practical goals, as we are currently doing within the English Profile Programme. Much remains to be done if we are to reach this programme's goal of providing theoretically significant and practically useful 'reference level descriptions' for English using the CLC and other learner corpora. In this final section we outline some of the areas of investigation that we think merit particular attention going forward and that will contribute most effectively to the EPP at this time. It is our hope that others will feel motivated to respond to the issues and challenges that this research programme has defined.

We have commented (in Chapter 3.5) on the need for more corpus data and for different kinds of data, from English learners around the world who exemplify different linguistic and demographic variables that we need to analyse and control for. The CLC is currently the largest learner corpus in existence by far, but the collection of new data is one of the highest priorities of the EPP for the future. And decisions about what types of data to collect and how to code and analyse them will be driven by research goals and hypotheses within the different strands of the project, as described in Saville and Hawkey (2010). For research on grammatical and lexical criterial features we see the following areas and methods as being most in need of attention at this point.

We need more criterial features of a grammatical nature going beyond the illustrative set given in Chapter 7.1. There are many more construction types of English that remain to be investigated and that are potentially criterial for one or another level. Our learning principles make predictions for their relative sequencing in acquisition, which need to be tested. Practical applications of this work require more information about the grammar of each CEFR level for syllabus design, for the preparation of teaching materials, and for assessment.

The investigation of raising constructions in Chapter 7.2 has highlighted the importance of looking at particular lexical 'triggers' for particular constructions and rules. Depending on the complexity of a structure (and raising is a complex operation by any grammatical measure) and on the frequency of a particular lexical instantiation, we find dramatically different first attestations in the CLC. Subject-to-Object Raising, for example, is first found at B1 with the more common raising verbs and then with new lexical triggers at each subsequent level all the way to C2. Such lexically specific grammatical features need to be investigated for a whole host of constructions. This will be of theoretical interest since it will enable us to test in a fine-tuned way whether the relative sequencing is in accordance with our predictions, for example in the sensitivity to frequency. It will also be practically useful since teachers and textbook writers will then know which particular verbs to introduce at different levels when they teach and develop exercises for English constructions.

The double embedding concept defined in Chapter 7.3 has, we believe, real potential for future expansion beyond the double genitive data that we gave there. The basic point is that individual structural types of English may be criterial for one of the earlier levels on their own, but in combination with one another they can give us criterial features for higher levels as well. Indeed a big part of the expanding mean length of utterance at higher levels (see Chapter 2.2) comes not just from the learning of more complex individual structures, but from more elaborate combinations of finite subordinate clauses within infinitival phrases, of relative clauses within genitives, and so on. Documenting these combinations and their criterial levels is, again, both theoretically interesting and practically useful for teaching and learning.

Perhaps the most important research goal for the future is to identify many more L1-specific criterial features (see Chapter 2.5), i.e. criterial properties of the levels that hold for particular L1s or types of L1s. The differences that we could point to in Chapter 2.5 between Missing Determiner error rates in languages with and without articles were striking. Indeed, we suspect, based on our investigation of the manual subcorpus (see Chapter 2.2), that differences between different L1s will be equally striking in a number of grammatical areas, as a result of transfer, either positive (see Chapter 5.1) or negative (Chapter 5.5). Several such grammatical areas need to be investigated systematically and the predictions need to be tested. Having a large set of L1-specific features will then make possible the practical applications summarised in Chapter 9.3 such as market-specific English language textbooks for Spanish, Chinese, Japanese learners, etc. The particular first languages chosen for concentration will depend on the expertise of investigators, of course, and on the availability of sufficient amounts of learner data. But we would like to stress how vital it is to include typologically diverse languages in this context, such as head-final Japanese and Korean, and the typologically mixed head-initial and head-final Chinese, in addition to the Romance languages or Greek, which are from a typological perspective very similar to (head-initial) English. In addition to this major typological difference between languages in head ordering (see Corbett et al 1993 for a discussion of heads and head ordering phenomena) there are considerable differences between languages with respect to individual properties such as definite and indefinite articles, and different selections of L1s should be made based on these contrasts with English. This range of typological diversity will then make it possible to test our predictions with respect to the transfer and non-transfer of L1 properties.

Moving from grammar and lexis and from language typology to techniques of linguistic analysis, this book has employed a mix of deductive, hypothesis-driven, and inductive, or data-driven, search techniques for criterial features. The result has been, we believe, a theoretically richer and practically more useful set of criterial features than could have been achieved by either method alone. What is needed going forward is a more sophisticated statistical analysis of both the positive features (Chapter 7) and the negative features (Chapter 2.3) than we have provided here. This could involve data analysis using item response theory, including differential item functioning, and there are other possible methods as well. As with all such analyses there are big theoretical questions that need to be addressed in addition to the mathematical calculation of statistical significance. When quantifying the frequencies of a particular error, for example, what exactly will count as a correct instance relative to which the errors are quantified? This is often not straightforward at all. What are the correct word orders relative to which a word order error is calculated? What are the correct subject–verb agreements relative to which errors are counted in a language like English which has minimal overt agreement and so many zero verb forms? For positive features, how many of the constructions in question, and of particular lexical instantiations, do we want to say need to be present at a level for it to be criterial? We have adopted the 10-to-1 rule for criterial differences between levels in this book (Chapter 2.6), counting a feature as criterial for the higher level if it exceeds this and for the lower level if it falls below it. But is this the right ratio? And how many instances of a construction, lexically specific or otherwise, need to be present at a level, relative to a certain sample size, for us to say that it is productive at that level and hence criterial? Having a larger and more diverse corpus will make it possible for these issues to be addressed in a more satisfactory manner than we could achieve at this preliminary stage.

Finally, we welcome future EPP research that extends and revises the principles of Chapter 5. These principles combine but may also compete, resulting in interlanguage variation, or in the delay of positive transfer when properties are complex, for example. The precise manner of their interaction needs to be investigated further (see also Hawkins 2010). There are undoubtedly other factors that need to be added to our principles, for example pedagogical factors (teaching materials and methods) and social factors (motivation, for example). Principles may need to be reformulated, and rules of interaction defined. We welcome all such developments, supported by learner data.

More generally, we welcome all constructive extensions of this criterial feature research programme as outlined in this book, and we look forward to seeing the many applications and improved efficiencies in practice that we believe will result from it.

For updates on the latest developments in the English Profile project, please visit the website (www.englishprofile.org).

References

Alexopoulou, D, Yannakoudakis, H and Briscoe, T (2011) *From features to grammars*, paper presented at 10ᵗʰ English Profile Seminar, Cambridge 10–11 February 2011.

Alexopoulou, T (2008) Building new corpora for English Profile, *Research Notes* 33, 15–19.

Andersen, E S (1992) Complexity and language acquisition: Influences on the development of morphological systems in children, in Hawkins, J A and Gell-Mann, M (Eds) *The Evolution of Human Languages,* Redwood City, CA: Addison-Wesley, 241–271.

Andersen, R W (1984) The one-to-one principle of interlanguage construction, *Language Learning* 34 (4), 77–95.

Anderson, D L (2005) *The acquisition of Tough Movement*, unpublished PhD dissertation, University of Cambridge.

Ariel, M (1999) Cognitive universals and linguistic conventions: the case of resumptive pronouns, *Studies in Language* 23 (2), 217–269.

Atkinson, D (2002) Toward a sociocognitive approach to second language acquisition, *The Modern Language Journal* 86 (4), 525–545.

Austin, J L (1962) *How to Do Things with Words*, Oxford: Clarendon Press.

Bachman, L F (1990) *Fundamental Considerations in Language Testing*, Oxford: Oxford University Press.

Baddely, A (1990) *Human Memory: Theory and Practice*, Hillsdale, NJ: Earlbaum.

Bates, E and MacWhinney, B (1981) Second language acquisition from a functionalist perspective: Pragmatic, semantic and perceptual strategies, in Winity, H (Ed.) *Native Language and Foreign Acquisition*, New York: Annals of the New York Academy of Sciences, 190–214.

Bates, E and MacWhinney, B (1982) Functionalist approaches to grammar, in Wanner, E and Gleitman, L R (Eds) *Language Acquisition: The State of the Art*, Cambridge: Cambridge University Press, 173–218.

Bates, E and MacWhinney, B (1987) Competition, variation and language learning, in MacWhinney, B (Ed.) *Mechanisms of Language Acquisition*, Hillsdale NJ: Erlbaum, 157–193.

Berwick, R (1985) *The Acquisition of Syntactic Knowledge*, Cambridge, MA: MIT Press.

Birdsong, D (1989) *Metalinguistic Performance and Interlanguage Competence*, New York: Springer.

Bley-Vroman, R (1989) The logical problem of second language learning, in Gass, S and Schachter, J (Eds) *Linguistic Perspectives on Second Language Acquisition*, Cambridge: Cambridge University Press, 41–68.

Bowerman, M (1985) What shapes children's grammars?, in Slobin, D I (Ed.) *The Crosslinguistic Study of Language Acquisition*, Hillsdale, N.J.: Lawrence Erlbaum, 1,257–1,319.

Bowerman, M (1988). The 'no negative evidence' problem: How do children avoid constructing an overly general grammar?, in Hawkins, J (Ed.), *Explaining language universals*, Oxford: Basil Blackwell, 73–101.

Briscoe, E, Carroll, J and Watson, R (2006) The second release of the RASP system, *Proceedings of the COLING/ACL 2006 Interactive Presentation Sessions*, Sydney, Australia.

Briscoe, E J (2000) *Dictionary and system subcategorisation code mappings*, unpublished manuscript, www.cl.cam.ac.uk/users/alk23/subcat/subcat.html, University of Cambridge Computer Laboratory.

Briscoe, E J and Carroll, J (1997) Automatic extraction of subcategorization from corpora, in *5th ACL Conference on Applied Natural Language Processing*, Washington DC, 365–363.

Brumfit, C (2001) *Individual Freedom in Language Teaching*, Oxford: Oxford University Press.

Burt, M K (1971) *From Deep to Surface Structure: An Introduction to Transformational Syntax*, New York: Harper and Row.

Buttery, P (2009) *RASP crib sheet*, unpublished manuscript, University of Cambridge.

Bybee, J L (2007) *Frequency of Use and the Organization of Language*, Oxford: Oxford University Press.

Callies, M (2008) Argument realization and information packaging in tough-movement constructions – A learner-corpus-based investigation, in Gabrys-Barker, D (Ed.) *Morphosyntactic Issues in Second Language Acquisition Studies*, Clevedon: Multilingual Matters, 29–46.

Capel, A (2010) Insights and issues arising from the English Profile Wordlists project, *Research Notes* 41, 2–7.

Capel, A and Martinez, R (2010) *EPP Wordlists: Validation and future developments*, paper presented to the EPP Seminar, Cambridge, February 2010.

Chomsky, N (1957) *Syntactic Structures*, The Hague: Mouton.

Chomsky, N (1965) *Aspects of the Theory of Syntax*, Cambridge, MA: MIT Press.

Clahsen, H (1984) The acquisition of German word order: A test case for cognitive approaches to L2 development, in Andersen, R W (Ed.) *Second Languages: A Cross-linguistic Perspective*, Rowley MA: Newbury House, 219–242.

Comrie, B (1989) *Language Universals and Linguistic Typology* (2nd edition), Chicago: University of Chicago Press.

Corbett, GG, McGlashan, S and Fraser, N (Eds) (1993) *Heads in Grammatical Theory*, Cambridge: Cambridge University Press.

Corder, S P (1981) *Error Analysis and Interlanguage*, Oxford: Oxford University Press.

Council of Europe (2001) *Common European Framework of Reference for Languages: Learning, Teaching, Assessment,* Cambridge: Cambridge University Press.

Croft, W (2003) *Typology and Universals* (2nd edition), Cambridge: Cambridge University Press.

Cross, J and Papp, S (2008) Creativity in the use of verb+noun combinations by Chinese learners of English, in Gilquin, G, Papp, S and Diez-Bedmar, M B (Eds) *Linking Up Contrastive and Learner Corpus Research*, Amsterdam: Rodopi, 57–81.

Dahl, Ö (2004) *The Growth and Maintenance of Linguistic Complexity*, Amsterdam: John Benjamins.

Davies, A (1991) *The Native Speaker in Applied Linguistics*, Edinburgh: Edinburgh University Press.

De Velle, S (2009) Certificating IELTS writing and speaking examiners, *Research Notes* 38, 26–29.

Diessel, H (2004) *The Acquisition of Complex Sentences*, Cambridge: Cambridge University Press.

Doughty, C and Long, M (2003) *The Handbook of Second Language Acquisition*, Oxford: Blackwell.

Dryer, Matthew S (1992) The Greenbergian word order correlations, *Language* 68, 81–109.

Eckman, F (1977) Markedness and the contrastive analysis hypothesis, *Language Learning* 27 (2), 315–330.

Eckman, F (1984) Universals, typologies, and interlanguage, in Rutherford, W (Ed.) *Language Universals and Second Language Acquisition*, Amsterdam: John Benjamins, 79–105.

Eckman, F, Moravcsik, E A and Wirth, J R (1989) Implicational universals and interrogative structures in the interlanguage of ESL learners, *Language Learning* 39 (2), 173–205.

Ellis, N (1998) Emergentism, connectionism and language learning, *Language Learning* 48 (4), 631–664.

Ellis, N and Larsen-Freeman, D (2009) *Language as a Complex Adaptive System*, Chichester: Wiley-Blackwell.

Ellis, R (1984) *Classroom Second Language Development*, Oxford: Pergamon.

Ellis, R (1985) Sources of variability in the interlanguage, *Applied Linguistics* 6 (2), 118–131.

Ellis, R (2003 [1994]) *The Study of Second Language Acquisition*, Oxford: Oxford University Press.

Eubank, L (1996) Negation in early German-English interlanguage: more valueless features in the L2 initial state, *Second Language Research* 12 (1), 73–106.

Farrell, P (2005) *Grammatical Relations*, Oxford: Oxford University Press.

Filipović, L and Vidaković, I (2010) Typology in the L2 classroom: Second language acquisition from a typological perspective, in Pütz, M and Sicola L (Eds) *Inside the Learner's Mind: Cognitive Processing in Second Language Acquisition*, Amsterdam: John Benjamins, 69–291.

Flynn, S (1996) A parameter-setting approach to second language acquisition, in Ritchie, W and Bhatia, T (Eds) *Handbook of Second Language Acquisition*, San Diego, CA: Academic Press, 121–158.

Frazier, L (1985) Syntactic complexity, in Dowty, D, Karttunen, D L and Zwicky, A (Eds) *Natural Language Parsing*, Cambridge: Cambridge University Press.

Gass, S (1987) The resolution of conflicts among competing systems: A bidirectional perspective, *Applied Psycholinguistics* 8 (4), 329–350.

Gass, S (1989) How do learners resolve linguistic conflicts?, in Gass, S and Schachter, J (Eds) *Linguistic Perspectives on Second Language Acquisition*, Cambridge: Cambridge University Press, 183–199.

Gass, S and Selinker, L (Eds) (1992) *Language Transfer in Language Learning*, Amsterdam: John Benjamins.

Gass, S and Selinker, L (2008 [1994]) *Second Language Acquisition: An Introductory Course*, London: Routledge.

Gell-Mann, M (1992) Complexity and complex adaptive systems, in Hawkins,

J A and Gell-Mann, M (Eds) *The Evolution of Human Languages*, Redwood City, CA: Addison-Wesley, 3–18.

Gibson, E (1998) Linguistic complexity: Locality of syntactic dependencies, *Cognition* 68 (1), 1–76.

Gilquin, G (2008) Combining contrastive and interlanguage analysis to apprehend transfer: Detection, explanation, evaluation, in Gilquin, G, Papp, S and Diez-Bedmar, M B (Eds) *Linking up Contrastive and Learner Corpus Research*, Amsterdam: Rodopi, 3–33.

Givón, T (1991) Markedness in grammar: Distributional, communicative and cognitive correlates of syntactic structure, *Studies in Language* 15 (2), 335–370.

Givón, T (1999) Generativity and variation: The notion "rule of grammar" revisited, in MacWhinney, B (Ed.) *The Emergence of Language*, Mahwah, NJ: Laurence Erlbaum Associates.

Givón, T (2001) *Syntax. An Introduction, Vol.2*, Amsterdam: John Benjamins.

Goldberg, A E (2006) *Constructions at Work. The Nature of Generalization in Language*, Oxford: Oxford University Press.

Gram, L and Buttery, P (2009) *A tutorial introduction to iLexIR Search*, unpublished manuscript, University of Cambridge.

Green, A B (forthcoming 2012) *Language Functions Revisited: Theoretical and Empirical Bases For Language Construct Definition Across the Ability Range*, Cambridge: UCLES/Cambridge University Press.

Greenberg, J H (1963) Some universals of grammar with particular reference to the order of meaningful elements, in Greenberg, J H (Ed.) *Universals of Language*, Cambridge, Mass.: MIT Press, 73–113.

Greenberg, J H (1966) *Language Universals, with Special Reference to Feature Hierarchies*, The Hague: Mouton.

Gregg, K R (2003) SLA theory: construction and assessment, in Doughty, C and Long, M (Eds) *Handbook of Second Language Acquisition*, Malden, MA: Blackwell.

Gregg, K R (2010) Shallow draughts: Larsen-Freeman and Cameron on complexity, *Second Language Research* 26 (4), 549–560.

Hakansson, G, Pienemann, M and Sayehli, S (2002) Transfer and typological proximity in the context of second language processing, *Second Language Research* 18 (3), 250–273.

Haspelmath, M (2002) *Morphology*, London: Arnold.

Haspelmath, M (2006) Against markedness (and what to replace it with), *Journal of Linguistics* 42 (1), 25–70.

Haspelmath, M (2006) *Parametric Versus Functional Explanations of Syntactic Universals*, unpublished manuscript, Leipzig, Max Planck Institute for Evolutionary Anthropology.

Hawkey, R and Barker, F (2004) Developing a common scale for the assessment of writing, *Assessing Writing* (9) 2, 122–159.

Hawkins, E W (1981) *Modern Languages in the Curriculum*, Cambridge: Cambridge University Press.

Hawkins, J A (1978) *Definiteness and Indefiniteness: A Study in Reference and Grammaticality Prediction*, New Jersey: Humanities Press New Jersey, and London: Croom Helm.

Hawkins, J A (1983) *Word Order Universals*, New York: Academic Press.

Hawkins, J A (1986) *A Comparative Typology of English and German: Unifying the Contrasts*, Austin: University of Texas Press, and London: Routledge.

Hawkins, J A (1987) Implicational universals as predictors of language acquisition, *Linguistics* 25, 453–473.

Hawkins, J A (1990) A parsing theory of word order universals, *Linguistic Inquiry* 21 (2), 223–261.

Hawkins, J A (1991) On (in)definite articles: Implicatures and (un)grammaticality prediction, *Journal of Linguistics* 27 (2), 405–442.

Hawkins, J A (1994) *A Performance Theory of Order and Constituency*, Cambridge: Cambridge University Press.

Hawkins, J A (1999) Processing complexity and filler-gap dependencies across grammars, *Language* 75 (2), 244–285.

Hawkins, J A (2000) The relative order of prepositional phrases in English, *Language Variations and Change* 11, 231–266.

Hawkins, J A (2004) *Efficiency and Complexity in Grammars*, Oxford: Oxford University Press.

Hawkins, J A (2007) Acquisition of relative clauses in relation to language universals, *Studies in Second Language Acquisition* 29 (2), 337–344.

Hawkins, J A (2009) An efficiency theory of complexity and related phenomena, in Gil, D, Sampson, G and Trudgill, P (Eds) *Complexity as an Evolving Variable*, Oxford: Oxford University Press, 252–268.

Hawkins, J A (2010) *Competing motivations in grammar, performance and learning: common principles and patterns in three areas of language*, language talk given at the Conference on Competing Motivations, Max Planck Institute for Evolutionary Anthropology, Leipzig, Germany, 23–25 November 2010.

Hawkins, J A and Buttery, P (2009) Using learner language from corpora to profile levels of proficiency: Insights from the English Profile Programme, in Taylor, L and Weir, C J (Eds) *Language Testing Matters: Investigating the Wider Social and Educational Impact of Assessment*, Cambridge: Cambridge University Press, 158–175.

Hawkins, J A and Buttery, P (2010) Criterial features in learner corpora: Theory and illustrations, *English Profile Journal* 1 (1), e5.

Hawkins, J A and Gell-Mann, M (Eds) (1992) *The Evolution of Human Languages*, Menlo Park, CA: Addison-Wesley.

Hoekstra, T and Kooij, J (1988) The innateness hypothesis, in Hawkins, J A (Ed.) *Explaining Language Universals*, Oxford: Basil Blackwell.

Huddleston, R and Pullum, G (Eds) (2002) *The Cambridge Grammar of the English Language*, Cambridge: Cambridge University Press.

Hulstijn, J and Marchena, E (1989) Avoidance: Grammatical or semantic causes?, *Studies in Second Language Acquisition* 11, 241–255.

Hyltenstam, K (1984) The use of typological markedness conditions as predictors in second language acquisition: The case of pronominal copies in relative clauses, in Andersen, R W (Ed.) *Second Languages: A Cross-linguistic Perspective*, Rowley, Mass.: Newbury House, 39–58.

Jakobson, R (1968) *Child Language, Aphasia and Phonological Universals*, The Hague: Mouton.

Jenkins, J (2009) *English in the world: A reality check*, plenary talk at English Language and Literature Studies: Image, Identity and Reality Conference, Belgrade, 4–6 December 2009.

Jespersen, O (1909–49) *A Modern English Grammar on Historical Principles*, Copenhagen: Munksgaard.

Jones, N (2000) Background to the validation of the ALTE 'Can-do' project and the revised Common European Framework, *Research Notes* 2, 11–13.

Jones, N (2001) The ALTE Can Do Project and the role of measurement in constructing a proficiency framework, *Research Notes* 5, 5–8.

Jones, N (2002) Relating the ALTE Framework to the Common European Framework of Reference, in Alderson, J C (Ed.) *Case Studies on the Use of the Common European Framework of Reference*, Strasbourg: Council of Europe Publishing, 167–183.

Kawaguchi, S (1999) The acquisition of syntax and nominal ellipsis in JSL discourse, in Robinson, P (Ed.) *Representation and Process: Proceedings of the Third Pacific Second Language Research Forum* vol 1, Tokyo: Pacific Second Language Research Forum, 85–93.

Kawaguchi, S (2002) Grammatical development in learners of Japanese as a second language, in di Biase, B (Ed.) *Developing a Second Language*, Melbourne: Language Australia.

Keenan, E L and Comrie, B (1977) Noun phrase accessibility and Universal Grammar, *Linguistic Inquiry* 8 (1), 63–99.

Keenan, E L (1979) On surface form and logical form, *Studies in the Linguistic Sciences* 8 (2).

Kellerman, E (1978) Giving learners a break: Native language intuitions as a source of prediction about transferability, *Working Papers on Bilingualism* 15, 59–92.

Kellerman, E (1983) Now you see it, now you don't, in Gass, S and Selinker, L (Eds) *Language Transfer in Language Learning*, Rowley, MA: Newbury House, 112–134.

Kellerman, E (1985) If at first you do succeed . . . , in Gass, S and Madden, C (Eds) *Input in Second Language Acquisition*, Cambridge, MA: Newbury House, 345–353.

Khalifa, H and Weir, C (2009) *Examining Reading: Research and Practice in Assessing Second Language Reading,* Studies in Language Testing volume 29, Cambridge: UCLES/Cambridge University Press.

Kirby, S (1999) *Function, Selection and Innateness,* Oxford: Oxford University Press.

Korhonen, A, Krymolowski, Y and Briscoe, E J (2006) A large subcategorization lexicon for natural language processing applications, *Proceedings of LREC, 2006.*

Krashen, S (1982) *Principles and Practice in Second Language Acquisition*, Oxford: Pergamon.

Lado, R (1957) *Linguistics Across Cultures: Applied Linguistics for Language Teachers,* Ann Arbor, Michigan: University of Michigan.

Larsen-Freeman, D (1997) Chaos/Complexity science and second language acquisition, *Applied Linguistics* 18 (2), 141–165.

Larsen-Freeman, D and Cameron, L (2008) *Complex Systems in Applied Linguistics*, Oxford: Oxford University Press.

Lehrer, A and Kittay, E F (Eds) (1992) *Frames, Fields and Contrasts*, Hillsdale, NJ: Lawrence Erlbaum Associates.

Levinson, S C (2000) *Presumptive Meanings*, Cambridge, MA: MIT Press.

Lindblom, B and Maddieson, I (1988) Phonetic universals in consonant systems, in Hyman, L M and Li, C N (Eds) *Language, Speech and Mind: Studies in Honour of Victoria A. Fromkin*, London: Routledge.

Lindblom, B, MacNeilage, P and Studdert-Kennedy, M (1984) Self-organizing processes and the explanation of phonological universals, in Butterworth, B, Comrie, B and Dahl, Ö (Eds) *Explanations for Language Universals*, New York: Mouton.

Lohse, B, Hawkins, J and Wasow, T (2004) Processing domains in English verb-particle constructions, *Language* 80 (2), 238–261.

McCarthy, M (2010) Spoken fluency revisited, *English Profile Journal* 1 (1), retrieved from http://journals.cambridge.org/action/displayJournal?jid=EPJ

McDonald, J and Heilenman, K (1991) Determinants of cue strength in adult first and second language speakers of French, *Applied Psycholinguistics* 12 (3), 313–348.

McLaughlin, B (1987) *Theories of Second Language Learning*, London: Edward Arnold.

McLaughlin, B (1990) Restructuring, *Applied Linguistics* 11 (2), 113–128.

McWhorter, J (2001) The world's simplest grammars are creole grammars, *Linguistic Typology* 5 (2–3), 125–166.

MacWhinney, B (1987) The competition model, in MacWhinney, B (Ed.) *Mechanisms of Language Acquisition*, Hillsdale NJ: Erlbaum, 249–308.

MacWhinney, B (1992) Transfer and competition in second language learning, in Harris, R (Ed.) *Cognitive Processing in Bilinguals*, London: Elsevier.

MacWhinney, B (2005) A unified model of language acquisition, in Kroll, J F and de Groot, A M B (Eds) *Handbook of Bilingualism: Psycholinguistic Approaches*, Oxford: Oxford University Press, 49–67.

Maddieson, I (2005) Lateral consonants, in Haspelmath, M, Dryer, M S, Gil, D and Comrie, B (Eds) *The World Atlas of Language Structures*, Oxford: Oxford University Press, 38–42.

Mair, C (1987) Tough-movement in present-day British English: A corpus-based study, *Studia Linguistica* 41 (1), 59–71.

Mair, C (1990) *Infinitival Complement Clauses in English: A Study of Syntax in Discourse*, Cambridge: Cambridge University Press.

Mellow, J D (2008) The emergence of complex syntax: A longitudinal case study of the ESL development of dependency resolution, *Lingua* 118 (4), 499–521.

Milanovic, M (2009) Cambridge ESOL and the CEFR, *Research Notes* 37, 2–5.

Miller, G A and Chomsky, N (1963) Finitary models of language users, in Luce, R D, Bush, R and Galanter, E (Eds) *Handbook of Mathematical Psychology*, Vol. 2, New York: Wiley, 419–492.

Moravcsik, E (2006) *An Introduction to Syntax: Fundamentals of Syntactic Analysis*, London: Continuum.

Müller-Gotama, F (1994) *Grammatical Relations: A Cross-linguistic Perspective on their Syntax and Semantics*, Berlin: de Gruyter.

Myers-Scotton, C (2006) *Multiple Voices: An Introduction to Bilingualism*, Malden, MA: Blackwell Publishers.

Newmeyer, F (1998) *Language Form and Language Function*, Cambridge, MA: MIT Press.

O'Grady, W (2003) The radical middle: Nativism without Universal Grammar, in Doughty, C and Long, M (Eds) *Handbook of Second Language Acquisition*, Malden, MA: Blackwell, 43–62.

O'Grady, W (2005) *Syntactic Carpentry: An Emergentist Approach to Syntax*, Mahwah, NJ: Lawrence Erlbaum Associates.

O'Grady, W (2008) The emergentist program, *Lingua* 118 (4), 447–464.

Odlin, T (1989) *Language Transfer*, New York: Cambridge University Press.

Odlin, T (1990) Word order transfer, metalinguistic awareness and constraints on foreign language learning, in VanPatten, B and Lee, J (Eds) *Second Language*

Acquisition – Foreign Language Learning, Clevedon, Avon: Multilingual Matters, 95–117.

Odlin, T and Alonso-Vázquez, C (2006) Meanings in search of the perfect form: A look at interlanguage verb phrases, *Rivista di Psicolinguistica Applicata* 6, 53–63.

Petch-Tyson, S (1998) Writer/reader visibility in EFL written discourse, in Granger, S (Ed.) *Learner English on Computer*, New York: Addison-Wesley Longman, 107–118.

Pienemann, M (1998) *Language Processing and Second Language Development: Processability Theory*, Amsterdam: John Benjamins.

Pienemann, M (2003) Language processing capacity, in Doughty, C and Long, M H (Eds) *Handbook of Second Language Acquisition Theory and Research*, Oxford: Blackwell, 679–714.

Pienemann, M (2005) Processing constraints on L1 transfer, in Kroll, J F and de Groot, A M B (Eds) *Handbook of Bilingualism: Psycholinguistic Approaches*, Oxford: Oxford University Press, 128–153.

Platzak, C (1996) The initial hypothesis of syntax, in Clahsen, H (Ed.) *Generative Perspectives on Language Acquisition*, Amsterdam: John Benjamins, 369–414.

Postal, P (1974) *On Raising*, Cambridge, Mass.: MIT Press.

Preiss, J, Briscoe, E J and Korhonen, A (2007) A system for large-scale acquisition of verbal, nominal and adjectival subcategorization frames from corpora, *Proceedings of the 45th Annual Meeting of the Association of Computational Linguistics, Prage, June 2007*, Association for Computational Linguistics, 912–919. (Available at www.aclweb.org/anthology/P/PO7/PO7-1115)

Preston, D (1989) *Sociolinguistics and Second Language Acquisition*, Oxford: Blackwell.

Primus, B (1999) *Cases and Thematic Roles: Ergative, Accusative and Active.* Tübingen: Niemeyer.

Profilo della lingua italiana. I livelli del QCER A1, A2, B1, B2. Publisher: La Nuova Italia.

Profile deutsch (2005) Manual / Manuel & CD-ROM, Langenscheidt.

Purpura, J E (1999) *Learner Strategy Use and Performance on Language Test: A Structural Equation Modelling Approach*, Studies in Language Testing volume 8, Cambridge: Cambridge University Press.

Quirk, R (1957) Relative clauses in educated spoken English, *English Studies* 38, 97–109.

Quirk, R, Greenbaum, S, Leech, G and Svartvik, J (1985) *A Comprehensive Grammar of the English Language*, London: Longman.

Rimmer, W (2006) Measuring grammatical complexity: The Gordian knot, *Language Testing* 23 (4), 497–519.

Roland, D and Jurafsky, D (1998) How verb subcategorization frequencies are affected by corpus choice, *Proceedings of the 17th International Conference on Computational Linguistics vol. 2*, 1,122–1,128.

Roland, D, Jurafsky, D, Menn, L, Gahl, S, Elder, E and Riddoch, C (2000) Verb subcategorization frequency differences between business news and balanced corpora: The role of verb sense, *Proceedings of the Workshop on Comparing Corpora vol. 9*, 28–34.

Rutherford, W (1983) Language typology and language transfer, in Gass, S and Selinker, L (Eds) *Language Transfer in Language Learning*, Rowley MA: Newbury House, 358–370.

Salamoura, A and Saville, N (2009) Criterial features across the CEFR levels: Evidence from the English Profile Programme, *Research Notes* 37, 34–40. (Available online at: www.CambridgeESOL.org/rs_notes/rs_nts37.pdf)

Salamoura, A and Saville, N (2010) Exemplifying the CEFR: Criterial features of written learner English from the English Profile Programme, in Bartning, I, Maisa, M and Vedder, I (Eds) *Communicative proficiency and linguistic development: Intersections between SLA and language testing research*, Eurosla Monographs Series (1), 101–132. (Available at: http://eurosla.org/monographs/EM01/101-132Salamoura_Saville.pdf)

Saville, N and Hawkey, R (2010) The English Profile Programme- the first three years, *English Profile Journal* 1 (1), retrieved from http://journals.cambridge.org/action/displayJournal?jid=EPJ

Schachter, J (1974) An error in error analysis, *Language Learning* 27 (2), 205–214.

Schachter, J (1988) Second language acquisition and its relationship to Universal Grammar, *Applied Linguistics* 9 (3), 219–235.

Schwartz, B and Sprouse, R (1996) L2 cognitive states and the full transfer/full access model, *Second Language Research* 12 (1), 40–72.

Schwartz, B and Sprouse, R (2000) When syntactic theories evolve: Consequences for L2 acquisition research, in Archibald, J (Ed.) *Second Language Acquisition and Linguistic Theory*, Oxford: Basil Blackwell, 156–186.

Searle, J R (1969) *Speech Acts*, Cambridge: Cambridge University Press.

Searle, J R (1975) Indirect speech acts, in Cole, P and Morgan, J L (Eds) *Speech Acts, Syntax and Semantics Vol.3*, New York: Academic Press, 59–82.

Seliger, H (1989) Semantic transfer constraints on the production of English passive by Hebrew-English bilinguals, in Dechert, H and Raupach, M (Eds) *Transfer in Language Production*, Norwood NJ: Ablex, 21–33.

Selinker, L (1972) Interlanguage, *International Review of Applied Linguistics* 10 (1–4), 209–231.

Slobin, D I (1973) Cognitive prerequisites for the development of grammar, in Ferguson, C A and Slobin, D I (Eds) *Studies of Child Language Development*, New York: Holt, Rinehart and Winston, 175–208.

Slobin, D I (1977) Language in childhood and in history, in Macnamara, J (Ed.) *Language Learning and Thought: Perspectives in Neurolinguistics and Psycholinguistics*, Maryland: University of Maryland Press, 185–214.

Slobin, D I (1985) Crosslinguistic evidence for the language-making capacity, in Slobin, D I (Ed.) *The Crosslinguistic Study of Language Acquisition Vol 2*, Hillsdale NJ: Erlbaum, 1,157–1,256.

Strömqvist, S (1998) From child speech to literary art – On language development and descriptions of motion, in Ragnarsdóttir, H and Strömqvist, S (Eds) *Learning to Talk about Time and Space (Proceedings from the Third NELAS Conference)*, Reykjavík and Göteborg: Kompendiet, 203–234.

Tarone, E (1983) On the variability of interlanguage systems, *Applied Linguistics* 4 (2), 143–163.

Taylor, L and Jones, N (2006) Cambridge ESOL exams and the Common European Framework of Reference (CEFR), *Research Notes* 24, 2–5.

Taylor, L and Galaczi, E D (2011) Scoring validity, in Taylor, L (Ed.) *Examining Speaking: Research and Practice in Assessing Second Language Speaking*, Studies in Language Testing volume 30, Cambridge: UCLES/Cambridge University Press, 171–233.

Tomasello, M (2000) Do young children have adult syntactic competence?, *Cognition* 74 (3), 209–253.

Tomasello, Michael (2002) The emergence of grammar in early child language, in Givón, T and Malle, B F (Eds) *The Evolution of Language out of Pre-language*, Oregon:University of Oregon, 309–328.

Tomasello, M (2003) *Constructing a Language: A Usage-Based Theory of Language Acquisition*, Cambridge MA: Harvard University Press.

Trévise, A (1986) Is it transferrable, topicalization?, in Kellerman, K and Sharwood Smith, M (Eds) *Crosslinguistic influence in Second Language Acquisition*, New York: Pergamon, 186–206.

Trim, J L M (2007) *Background to the Threshold series*, presentation to the English Profile Seminar, Cambridge, February 2007. (Available at www. englishprofile.org)

Trim, J L M (2009) *Breakthrough*. (Available at www.englishprofile.org)

Vainikka, M and Young-Scholten, M (1994) Direct access to X′-theory: Evidence from Korean and Turkish adults learning German, in Hoekstra, T and Schwartz, B (Eds) *Language Acquisition Studies in Generative Grammar*, Amsterdam: John Benjamins, 265–316.

Vainikka, M and Young-Scholten, M (1996a) Gradual development of L2 phrase structure, *Second Language Research* 12 (1), 7–39.

Vainikka, M and Young-Scholten, M (1996b) The early stages of adult L2 syntax: Additional evidence from Romance speakers, *Second Language Research* 12 (2), 140–176.

Van Ek, J A and Trim, J L M (1991a) *Threshold 1990*, Cambridge: Council of Europe/Cambridge University Press.

Van Ek, J A and Trim, J L M (1991b) *Waystage 1990*, Cambridge: Council of Europe/Cambridge University Press.

Van Ek, J A and Trim, J L M (2001) *Vantage*, Cambridge: Council of Europe/ Cambridge University Press.

VanPatten, B (1996) *Input Processing and Grammar Instruction*, Norwood, NJ: Ablex.

Wasow, T (2002) *Postverbal Behavior*, Stanford: CSLI Publications.

Whaley, L J (1997) *Introduction to Typology: The Unity and Diversity of Language*, Thousand Oaks, California: Sage Publications.

White, L (1987) Markedness and second language acquisition: The question of transfer, *Studies in Second Language Acquisition* 9 (3), 261–286.

White, L (1989) *Universal Grammar and Second Language Acquisition*, Amsterdam: John Benjamins.

White, L (2003) *Second Language Acquisition and Universal Grammar*, Cambridge: Cambridge University Press.

Williams, C (2006) *The Cambridge Learner Corpus for researchers on the English Profile Project*, unpublished manuscript, RCEAL, University of Cambridge.

Williams, C (2007) *A preliminary study into verbal subcategorisation frame usage in the CLC*, unpublished manuscript, RCEAL, University of Cambridge.

Zobl, H (1980) The formal and developmental selectivity of L1 influence on L2 acquisition, *Language Learning* 30 (1), 43–57.

Zumbo, B D (2007) Three generations of differential item functioning (DIF) analyses: Considering where it has been, where it is now, and where it is going, *Language Assessment Quarterly* 4 (2), 223–233.

Author Index

Lexical Index

Language Index

Subject Index